THE NEW
IMMIGRATION

THE NEW IMMIGRATION

IMPLICATIONS FOR POVERTY AND PUBLIC ASSISTANCE UTILIZATION

Leif Jensen

STUDIES IN SOCIAL WELFARE
POLICIES AND PROGRAMS,
NUMBER 10

GREENWOOD PRESS
New York · Westport, Connecticut · London

Library of Congress Cataloging-in-Publication Data

Jensen, Leif
    The new immigration: implications for poverty and public
assistance utilization / Leif Jensen.
        p.   cm. — (Studies in social welfare policies and programs,
    ISSN 8755-5360 ; no. 10)
      Bibliography: p.
      Includes index.
      ISBN 0-313-26455-4 (lib. bdg.: alk. paper)
      1. Social work with immigrants—United States.   2. Social work
    with minorities—United States.   3. United States—Emigration and
    immigration—Social aspects.   4. Poor—United States.   I. Title.
    II. Series.
    HV4010.J46   1989
    362.8'4'00973—dc19   88-25096

British Library Cataloguing in Publication Data is available.

Library of Congress Catalog Card Number: 88-25096
ISBN: 0-313-26455-4
ISSN: 8755-5360

First published in 1989

Greenwood Press, Inc.
88 Post Road West, Westport, Connecticut 06881

Printed in the United States of America

The paper used in this book complies with the
Permanent Paper Standard issued by the National
Information Standards Organization (Z39.48-1984).

10   9   8   7   6   5   4   3   2   1

Copyright Acknowledgment

The author and publisher are grateful to the following for granting the use of
material:

Excerpts from Leif Jensen, "Poverty and Immigration in the United States:
1960–1980" in Gary Sandefur and Marta Tienda (eds.), *Divided Opportunities:
Minorities, Poverty and Social Policy,* New York: Plenum Publishing Corp., 1988.

For Kirsten, Reidar and Britta

Contents

Tables

Preface

Lofty sentiments notwithstanding, the United States has consistently sought to exclude impoverished immigrants on the grounds that many become dependent on social welfare institutions. The period from 1960 through 1980 saw a resurgence of concern. This was in response to a dramatic rise in immigration and increases in both the percent of immigrants arriving from less-developed countries and those arriving to be reunited with kin. Despite the historic and current centrality of this issue, relatively little research has explored immigrant poverty and use of social welfare benefits. In this volume, I speak to these issues by analyzing data from the 1960, 1970 and 1980 U.S. Censuses.

This book would not have been written without advice and support from many people and institutions. First of all, I thank my wife Kirsten. Without her love, friendship and encouragement, who knows where I'd be—certainly not writing this preface. This project came at the expense of time spent with my son Reidar and daughter Britta who deserved better, but who will always be a source of tremendous pride, wonder and comic relief. Dagny Jensen, Roy and Louise Esiason and Elsie White also gave strong support—each in their own fashion—during recent years.

This research was conceived and carried out at the University of Wisconsin in Madison. The guidance, inspiration and insight of Marta Tienda were invaluable during every phase of the project. Few professors are as devoted to their students, and I am eternally grateful for having been one of hers. Larry Bumpass, Gary Sandefur, Karl Taeuber and W. Lee Hansen all commented on an earlier version, resulting in a much improved volume. I also thank Frank Goza, Bob Jenkins, Doug Wissoker and Roger Wojtkiewicz who critiqued my work and made this a more enjoyable experience. I benefited greatly from the technical and clerical expertise of Franklin W. Monfort, Cheryl Knobeloch, Susan Walsh, Gary Heisserer, Diane Duesterhoeft and Sara Rudolph. As always, I take the blame for any errors that remain in this volume.

I am also indebted to a number of institutions. I was well supported by the Center for Demography and Ecology (CDE) at the University of Wisconsin via an NICHD training grant in demography (HD-07014). A grant to CDE from NICHD (HD-05876) provided computational support. Further institutional support was provided by a DHHS research grant (40A83) awarded to the Institute for Research on Poverty (Marta Tienda and Gary Sandefur, coprincipal investigators). Finally, the University of Wisconsin, Department of Rural Sociology provided office space and clerical support— not to mention comradery.

THE NEW
IMMIGRATION

1

Introduction

The issue of immigration to the United States has reemerged in recent years and is currently the subject of considerable public scrutiny, conjecture and debate. Echoing the past, the clamor has been in response to another great wave of newcomers—a new immigration.

In large part, the roots of this new immigration can be traced to the 1965 amendments to the Immigration and Nationality Act of 1952. The 1965 legislation altered preexisting immigration policy in three ways. First, it raised the overall ceiling so that many more people could immigrate legally. Second, it gave priority to those entering to rejoin kin over those entering on the merits of their job skills. Third, and most important, it dismantled a quota system that had formerly discriminated against those from non-northern and western European countries and replaced it with a much more equitable worldwide distribution of visas (Bouvier and Gardner 1986).

These changes caused both a substantial increase in the flow of immigration to the United States and a sudden shift among newcomers toward Third World countries of origin. Table 1.1 documents the steady increase in immigration since the 1950s. It also shows a decline in the absolute and relative number of arrivals from Europe and a corresponding increase in immigration from Latin America and Asia. While only 28% of all immigrants were from either Asia or Latin America during the 1950s, during the early 1980s over 80% were from these regions.

Several concerns over the new immigration have been voiced (Cafferty, et al. 1983; Glazer 1985; Briggs and Tienda 1985; Fallows 1983). While they are all interrelated to some degree, these concerns can be loosely dichotomized into a set addressing cultural repercussions and another focusing on economic impacts (Bouvier and Gardner 1986). The overarching economic

Table 1.1
Flow and Region of Origin Composition of Immigrants to the United States: 1951–1984

| Region of Origin | Year of Arrival | | | |
| | 1951-1960 | | 1961-1970 | |
	N	%	N	%
Europe	1326[a]	53.0	1123	33.8
Asia	153	6.1	428	12.9
Latin America	619	24.7	1303	39.3
Africa	14	0.6	29	0.9
Other[b]	391	15.6	435	13.1
Total Specified	2503	100.0	3318	100.0
Total Not Specified	12		4	
Total	2515		3322	
	1971-1980		1981-1984	
Europe	800	17.9	263	11.5
Asia	1588	35.5	1103	48.2
Latin America	1813	40.5	803	35.1
Africa	81	1.8	58	2.5
Other[b]	195	4.4	60	2.6
Total Specified	4477	100.1[c]	2287	99.9[c]
Total Not Specified	16		7	
Total	4493		2294	

Source: Immigration and Naturalization Service (1984).

[a] In thousands
[b] Includes Canada
[c] Does not sum to 100 due to rounding error

concern is whether the new immigrants are a net economic benefit or detriment to the receiving nation. This issue is, in turn, composed of several particular questions. Do immigrants displace natives in the labor force? Do immigrants lower the wage rate of natives? Do immigrants take more from public coffers via their use of social services than they contribute via taxes and expansion of the economy? Are we admitting too many immigrants who are chronically poor and dependent on the largess of the state? Far from just an area of academic interest, these questions have been debated in Congress and by the general public. Many fear that the new immigration has had generally negative economic effects and that the new immigrants are disproportionately poor and dependent on welfare programs.[1] It is the latter question that I explore in this volume.

In July of 1986, coinciding with the 100th anniversary of the Statue of Liberty, a *New York Times*/CBS News survey queried a representative sample of the U.S. population about their attitudes toward immigrants and immigration. This survey confirms widespread agreement with the assumptions that immigrants tend to be poor and welfare dependent. For example, the survey asked "What's the first thing that comes to mind when you hear the word immigrant?" Out of the myriad possible responses many cited "poor" and "welfare" as the first thing that came to mind. In fact, these were the most frequent answers among those who gave a specific problem as their response. On another question, almost half (47%) of the respondents felt that *most* new immigrants wind up on welfare.[2] On balance, Americans felt that recent immigrants offer more problems than contributions, and it is not surprising that a plurality wanted immigration reduced.

Worries about the cultural and economic impact of the new immigration are also evident in the titles of recent books on the topic. These include, *Clamor at the Gates: The New American Immigration* (Glazer 1985), *The Tarnished Door: The New Immigrants and the Transformation of America* (Crewdson 1983), *The Unavoidable Issue: U.S. Immigration Policy in the 1980s* (Papademetriou and Miller 1983) and *The Immigration Time Bomb: The Fragmenting of America*[3] (Lamm and Imhoff 1985).[4]

Unfortunately, empirical exploration into the economic impact of the new immigration has lagged far behind popular concern. Certain assertions, such as "the most recent arrivals are particularly likely to be poor and dependent on social welfare programs," have little hard evidence to support or refute them. This lack of evidence has prolonged and intensified the heated debate over the new immigration. Much of this debate, Michael Teitelbaum (1986, p. 161) explains, "has spilled from the pens or mouths of committed advocates and, thus, has partaken of their penchant for exaggerated and selective use of evidence." Accordingly, in this volume, I thoroughly explore the nature of poverty and public assistance utilization among immigrants to the United States over the period 1960–1980.[5] In so doing, I answer the following questions. Has there been an increase in the level of poverty and degree of public assistance utilization among immigrants to the United States over the past 20 years? How do these levels compare to those for the native born? How are these levels patterned across key race and nativity groups? How do individual and family characteristics behave along with nativity in affecting the propensity of families to be poor or to receive public assistance?

OVERVIEW OF CHAPTERS

Theoretically, there are reasons to suspect that immigrants, particularly recent arrivals, tend to be poor and dependent on social services. Assimilation theory predicts initial periods of hardship for immigrants, but posits upward economic mobility with time spent in the United States. This and other theoretical issues that bear on nativity differentials in poverty and welfare use will be presented in chapter 2.

These ideas regarding the socioeconomic status of immigrants did not evolve in a vacuum, but were largely developed in light of the experiences of earlier waves of immigrants to the United States. Accordingly, chapter 2 reviews U.S. immigration history, with a particular emphasis on aspects that are relevant to poverty and public assistance receipt. This discussion contextualizes the new immigration and forms the conceptual infrastructure for the ensuing analyses. The chapter concludes with a more elaborate statement of the problem and a summary of extant empirical work on this topic.

My interest in a relatively small proportion of the population, namely immigrants, both before and after the onset of the new immigration, imposes considerable constraints on the choice of data for analysis. I analyzed Public Use Sample (PUS) Data from the 1960, 1970 and 1980 U.S. Censuses of Population and Housing. The reasons for doing so are detailed in chapter 3. This chapter covers methodological issues including data, measurement and estimation techniques.

The next four chapters present the results of the empirical analysis. The first two focus on poverty while the subsequent two consider public assistance utilization. Chapter 4 provides tables describing the levels of poverty in the years 1959, 1969 and 1979. Conditional poverty rates are provided for key race and nativity groups. While these results are informative by themselves, they also establish baseline information for the multivariate analyses that follow.

Chapter 5 builds the conceptual background for a multivariate model of poverty at the family level. These models are then estimated via logistic regression. The first models presented are simple, in that few independent variables are used to estimate the probability that a family is poor. These simple models provide more rigorous confirmation of conclusions drawn from the descriptive analyses of poverty (chapter 4). I then estimate more complex models of poverty that account for individual- and family-level characteristics. In all of these multivariate analyses, the principal intent is to establish the net effect of immigrant status on the propensity to be poor.

The next two chapters explore public assistance utilization.[6] Again, I establish the gross and net effect of nativity on the receipt of public assistance benefits. Is it true that immigrants, particularly recent arrivals, have a penchant for welfare as many Americans believe? Have there been significant changes over time in the propensity of immigrants in general, and recent immigrants in particular, to receive welfare benefits? The next two chapters provide thorough answers to these and other related contentions.

Chapter 6 establishes baseline information on the use of public assistance by nativity and race groups. Among other things, these descriptive tables document whether, in the aggregate, immigrants use welfare to a greater degree than natives. I then introduce and estimate multivariate logistic regression models of public assistance receipt. These establish the place of nativity as one among several individual- and family-level predictors of welfare receipt.

Because the mere propensity to receive public assistance is only one aspect of the welfare burden imposed by a particular group, I also examine the absolute amount of public assistance received. In chapter 7, I use ordinary least squares (OLS) regression on the subsample of welfare recipients to estimate total family public assistance receipt. Again, in addition to immigrant status, other individual and family variables are used as predictors.

Chapter 8 synthesizes key findings of the empirical analysis. In so doing, I draw conclusions regarding both the popular concerns and theoretical issues surrounding the pervasiveness of poverty and public assistance receipt among the new immigrants. I now turn to the historical context and theoretical underpinnings regarding poverty, welfare dependence and immigration.

NOTES

1. The terms welfare and public assistance are used interchangeably throughout this book. They refer to a number of income-conditioned, cash assistance programs including Aid to Families with Dependent Children (AFDC), general assistance and Supplemental Security Income (SSI). The latter includes Old-Age Assistance, Aid to the Blind and Aid to the Permanently and Totally Disabled (Levitan 1985).

2. One respondent noted that "the welfare rolls are filled with the names of immigrants who have little education. With the economy now, immigrants are a greater drain than a help" (Pear 1986).

3. The alarmism of *The Immigration Time Bomb* (Lamm and Imhoff 1985) is reminiscent of the population explosion pieces of the 1960s, such as Paul Ehrlich's (1968) *The Population Bomb*. It presents a rather one-sided treatment of the immigration debate (Gardner 1986).

4. Fewer works bear titles that cast the new immigration in a less negative light, but examples would be: *Still the Golden Door: The Third World Comes to America* (Reimers 1985) and *Latin Journey: Cuban and Mexican Immigrants in the United States* (Portes and Bach 1985).

5. This period includes immigrants who arrived before the 1965 immigration legislation—before the new immigration—as well as those who arrived after it was well underway.

6. Because receipt of public assistance cannot be uniquely determined with the 1960 PUS, these chapters examine welfare receipt in 1969 and 1979 only.

2

The New Immigration, the Same Old Questions: Historical and Theoretical Context

Broadly viewed, this volume is about immigrant-native differentials in poverty and transfer program participation during the period 1960–1980. The goal of the present chapter is to contextualize this research topic in the stream of U.S. immigration history and in theories of migration and assimilation. First, I chronicle U.S. immigration history paying special attention to poverty, pauperism and relevant immigration legislation. This is followed by a review of theories of migration and assimilation. I then offer a statement of the problem and conclude with a review of existing empirical work on this topic.

A BRIEF HISTORY OF IMMIGRATION TO THE UNITED STATES

A well-worn but by no means hackneyed phrase is that the United States is a "nation of immigrants." In *The Uprooted,* Oscar Handlin (1951, p. 3) opens, "Once I thought to write a history of the immigrants in America. Then I discovered that the immigrants *were* American history." Throughout the years, immigration to the United States has been punctuated by massive waves of newcomers. Frequently, three such waves are identified. Together with two eras of comparatively light immigration, I discuss five periods in U.S. immigration history. These are the colonial period to 1820, 1820–1900 (the first wave), 1860–1930 (the second wave), 1930–1965 and 1965 to the present (the third wave).[1]

Colonial Period to 1820

From the 1600s until about 1820 the North American continent began to be populated by the peoples of northern and western Europe.[2] Immigrants to the New World were arriving primarily from England. Proportionately fewer immigrants hailed from Ireland, Germany, France and Scandinavia. For several reasons, compared to the absolute number of immigrants who would arrive later, the flow during the pre-1820 period was not great (Easterlin, et al. 1980). Transoceanic travel was meager and hazardous. Life in the colonies was comparatively harsh and there were relatively few employment opportunities outside of agriculture.

Like U.S. immigration history in general, flows during this time were halting; immigration ebbed during the revolutionary war and the War of 1812. It has been estimated that between 1630 and 1790 cumulative immigration was "well under 1 million" (Easterlin, et al. 1980) and that between the revolutionary war and 1819, a quarter of a million people managed to survive the voyage to the United States (Bouvier and Gardner 1986).

Not all newcomers during this period were welcomed by the growing European-origin population. Protests against certain types of immigrants arose in response to two perceived problems—one cultural, the other economic. First, there were outcries against some immigrants on the grounds that they were culturally different from the native, Puritan stock and thus compromised the preeminence of the white Anglo-Saxon Protestant value system. Groups such as the Irish, who differed with respect to religion, and the Germans, who differed by language, were treated with derision and distrust (Jones 1960). The cultural threat was heightened when immigrants formed ethnic communities in which their culture and language could thrive. When Germans concentrated in such an enclave in Pennsylvania, colony-wide distrust prompted the establishment of "charity schools," which sought to promote English and otherwise "anglicize" the Germans (Jones 1960).

Of greater relevance to the present research, immigrant poverty and pauperism[3] were the second source of protest against certain immigrants. Fears that an appreciable number of immigrants were poor were not unfounded. First, many arrived as indentured servants. The only way they could emigrate from Europe was to exchange four to seven years of labor for their passage across the Atlantic. They worked as agricultural laborers, common laborers or household servants. Because they were largely unskilled, once their period of servitude expired, their impoverishment continued (Jones 1960). Second, a number of European countries (particularly England and Germany) purged their own relief rolls by actively facilitating the emigration of their poor (Stephenson 1926). Richmond Mayo-Smith (1890, pp. 169-170) wrote that

in small and poor communities the burden of supporting those unable to work has always been severely felt. By emigration there seemed to be a way of escaping it. The poor, with a little financial aid, might be sent on a journey from which they would never return. . . . The poor themselves were often anxious to go, being deluded by false and exaggerated reports of the chances for success. . . . It was easy to accede to these desires and by a small advance of money at the present moment to escape the future support of the paupers.

Faced with the prospect of providing for waves of impoverished immigrants, most colonies did not respond passively. Rather, they enacted policies designed both to curtail the immigration of the poor and to lessen the burden caused by those paupers who did arrive. Typically, head taxes were levied on ship captains for each immigrant deemed likely to become a public charge. The revenue raised was used to defray the cost of municipal welfare programs (Hansen 1940). Another tactic was to hold ship captains or domestic sponsors liable in the event that one of their immigrants became a public charge. Despite these efforts, there is evidence that some impoverished immigrants were entering surreptitiously. To evade their liability, ship captains landed immigrants in smaller ports at night (Hansen 1940).

These two sources of protest, cultural distrust and poverty, are witnessed repeatedly throughout U.S. immigration history. They are also interrelated in many respects. For example, it was in part a response to their poverty that certain groups (e.g., the Germans and Scotch-Irish) formed ethnic enclaves (Jones 1960). This enabled coethnics to share resources and provide mutual support. As noted previously, these enclaves incited considerable cultural tension. Moreover, poverty made it difficult for inhabitants to exit these enclaves, and their impoverished condition and alien ways made them the object of considerable public scorn.

1820–1900: The First Wave

The first great wave of immigration to the United States began in the 1820s (see Table 2.1). Immigration to the United States was 143,000, 599,000, 1,717,000 and 2,598,000 during the four decades beginning in 1820, respectively. As impressive as the rate of increase in immigration was the immigration rate (the number of immigrants relative to population size). For example, between 1845 and 1854, when over 3 million immigrants arrived, the total U.S. population averaged 20 million. Like the waves of immigrants that arrived prior to the 1820s, the first-wave arrivals were mostly from northern and western Europe—particularly the British Isles, Germany and Scandinavia.[4]

Five sets of factors can be identified to explain the emergence and stability of the first wave (Jones 1960). First, owing to the industrial revolution, capital to labor ratios were soaring in Europe; machines were replacing people, especially in agriculture (Davis 1974). This transition imposed great pressures to emigrate. Second, the demographic transition was underway in Europe. The doubling of the European population between 1750 and 1850

Table 2.1
Flow and Region of Origin Composition of Immigrants to the United States: 1821–1980

Decade	North-western Europe	South-eastern Europe	Latin America	Asia	Other	Total Specified	Not Specified	TOTAL
1821-1830	95.6[a] 86.7[b]	3.2 2.9	9.3 8.4	0.0 0.0	2.2 2.0	110.4 100.0[c]	33.0	143.4
1831-1840	489.7 92.6	5.9 1.1	19.8 3.7	0.0 0.0	13.7 2.6	529.1 100.0	69.9	599.0
1841-1850	1592.1 95.9	5.4 0.3	20.7 1.2	0.0 0.0	41.6 2.5	1659.8 99.9	53.1	1717.0
1851-1860	2431.3 94.6	21.2 0.8	15.4 0.6	41.5 1.6	59.4 2.3	2568.8 99.9	29.2	2598.0
1861-1870	2039.4 88.8	25.7 1.1	12.7 0.6	64.8 2.8	154.4 6.7	2297.0 100.0	18.0	2315.0
1871-1880	2143.3 76.2	128.6 4.6	20.4 0.7	124.2 4.4	394.7 14.0	2811.2 99.9	0.8	2812.0
1881-1890	4132.3 78.8	603.1 11.5	33.6 0.6	69.9 1.3	407.3 7.8	5246.2 100.0	0.8	5247.0

Period														
1891-1900	2236.2	60.8	1319.2	35.9	35.6	1.0	74.8	2.0	8.1	0.2	3673.9	99.9	14.1	3688.0
1901-1910	4055.3	46.3	4000.7	45.7	182.6	2.1	323.5	3.7	199.4	2.3	8761.5	100.1	33.5	8795.0
1911-1920	1451.8	25.3	2870.0	50.0	401.5	7.0	247.2	4.3	764.4	13.3	5734.9	99.9	1.1	5736.0
1921-1930	1332.8	32.4	1130.3	27.5	592.2	14.4	112.1	2.7	939.8	22.9	4107.2	99.9	0.2	4107.0
1931-1940	204.2	38.7	143.3	27.1	51.5	9.8	16.1	3.0	112.9	21.4	528.0	100.0	0.0	528.0
1941-1950	516.4	49.9	104.7	10.1	183.1	17.7	32.4	3.1	198.3	19.2	1034.9	100.0	0.1	1035.0
1951-1960	998.6	39.9	327.2	13.1	619.0	24.7	153.2	6.1	404.5	16.2	2502.5	100.0	12.5	2515.0
1961-1970	608.4	18.3	515.1	15.5	1303.1	39.3	427.6	12.9	463.9	14.0	3318.1	100.0	3.9	3322.0
1971-1980	299.7	6.7	500.7	11.2	1812.6	40.5	1588.2	35.5	275.9	6.2	4477.1	100.0	15.9	4493.0

a Gross immigration in thousands.
b Percent of Gross Immigration from this region.
c Base excludes immigrants with origin "not specified." May not sum to 100.0 due to rounding error.

rendered the scarcity of jobs and land more severe and heightened pressures to emigrate (Stephenson 1926). Third, due to technological improvements in shipping, transoceanic voyages were becoming safer and less costly (Mayo-Smith 1890). Fourth, U.S. industry actively recruited immigrant labor by advertising high-wage jobs (Portes and Bach 1985). Finally, with improvements in communication technology and postal services, stories of a better life in the United States traveled back to Europe, thereby increasing the momentum of emigration (Mayo-Smith 1890).

In addition to these causes of the first wave, certain countries experienced extenuating population pressures. Ireland, for example, suffered through several consecutive years of potato crop failure (1845–1849). The resulting scarcity of food and means of subsistence pushed many toward the United States (Mayo-Smith 1890). Most of these Irish immigrants were quite poor upon arrival. Moreover, as Marcus Hansen (1940, p. 108) writes, "Even when employment was obtained, the Irishman remitted such a large percentage of his small wage to his native land that poverty and squalor seemed to be his perpetual state."[5]

Because most arrivals in the first wave differed insignificantly from the native Puritan stock, many had little difficulty blending into the host society in time. As shall be discussed below, such rapid assimilation usually entails some measure of economic prosperity. One might assume, therefore, that the level of poverty among first-wave arrivals was inconsiderable and of no concern to the native population. There are several reasons to doubt this assumption. First, while abating, indentured servitude continued to be one mode of entry into U.S. society. Second, because many arrivals were displaced agricultural workers with few alternative occupational skills, they were relegated to marginal agrarian occupations in the United States. Frequently arriving with little wealth, emigrants had limited opportunities to buy their own parcels of land. Many settled in eastern seaboard cities. This was particularly true of the Irish whose limited farming experience further restricted their opportunities. Third, the cheaper voyages allowed poorer people and families to emigrate voluntarily. After paying their fares, many arrived with little and were "immobilized by their poverty" (Jones 1960, p. 118). The poorest arrivals were forced to settle in cities. Finally, some European countries continued to encourage and facilitate the emigration of the poor (e.g., Sweden as late as 1840). That there was an appreciable degree of poverty among the first wave is revealed in the following quote (Jones 1960, p. 133).

Immigrant poverty was reflected in the fact that, wherever they congregated, the foreign-born constituted a large proportion of those dependent upon state and municipal assistance. Between 1845 and 1860 between one-half and two-thirds of Boston's paupers consisted of immigrants, and in New York City in 1860 no fewer than 86 per cent of those on relief were of foreign birth.

1860-1930: The Second Wave

Beginning in about 1860, immigration from southern and eastern Europe began to increase. This surge constitutes the second great wave of immigration to the United States and was not to end until 1930. Table 2.1 shows that in relative terms, immigration from northwestern Europe began to trail off, while the share from southeastern Europe showed a sharp increase. From 1860 until 1920, the percent of all immigrants hailing from southeastern Europe was, for each decade respectively, 1, 5, 12, 36, 46 and 50%. Thus, an important feature of the second wave was a shift in the country-of-origin composition of immigrants.

The second wave occurred for a number reasons. First, transoceanic travel became even more efficient. Second, southeastern Europe lagged behind northwestern Europe in industrial development. Thus, many of the factors that caused the first wave of immigration, such as the population pressures caused by the demographic transition and the development of transportation and communication infrastructures, occurred later in southeastern Europe. Third, as this region became more industrialized, emigrants' labor force skills became more transferable. Finally, the labor recruitment that had attracted so many Irish spread to southeastern Europe (Jones 1960).

These immigrants differed in marked ways from the first wave. First, their darker complexion and non-Protestant religions (most were either Catholic or Jewish) made it more difficult to blend into the predominantly Anglo-Saxon society. Also, the second wave differed from the first with respect to the conditions extant in the United States at the time of their arrival. For the later arrivals, the northeast was more industrialized and offered ample opportunities for nonagricultural employment. Agricultural pursuits involving ownership of land were becoming more limited. Consequently, immigrants of the second wave began to settle in urban areas in unprecedented numbers. Frequently they congregated in ethnic enclaves near their places of work. Because most of these new immigrants had little wealth upon arrival and because they tended to have poorly paying jobs, the appearance of these ethnic enclaves reflected the destitution of those residing in them.

In part, the miserable outward appearance of these ghettos was not due to the degree of poverty among immigrants, but to the fact that cities were ill-prepared to house the deluge of newcomers (Handlin 1951). Impromptu units were made available and older houses and apartments were vacated and split into multiple units. Nonetheless, there was a growing perception that the United States was admitting far too many impoverished immigrants. That many were appalled at the living conditions in these ethnic ghettos and that they attributed this to the current nature of immigration is revealed by the following passage from the *Yale Review* by Rita Simon (1985, p. 102).

Ignorant, unskilled, inert, accustomed to the beastliest conditions, with little social aspirations, with none of the desire for air and light and room, for decent dress and home comfort, which our native people possess and which our earlier immigrants so speedily acquired, the presence of hundreds of thousands of these laborers constitutes a menace to the rate of wages and the American standard of living. . . . Taking whatever they can get in the way of wages, living like swine, crowded into filthy tenement houses, piecing over garbage barrels, the arrival on our shores of such masses of degraded peasantry bring the greatest danger that American labor has ever known.

More generally, the assertion that second-wave immigrants were inferior to previous arrivals resulting in problems of poverty is evident in the following two excerpts from the popular press of the day (quoted in Simon 1985, pp. 98, 107).

The character of our immigration has also changed—instead of the best class of people, we are now getting the refuse of Europe—outcasts from Italy, brutalized Poles and Hungarians, the offscourings of the world (*Philadelphia Enquirer,* Nov. 29, 1890).

The swelling tide of immigrants from Southern Europe and the Orient who can neither read nor write their own language and not even speak ours, who bring with them only money enough to stave off starvation but a few days, is a startling national menace that cannot be disregarded with safety (*New York Herald,* Nov. 10, 1900).

The question of whether the "quality" of immigrants had declined with the second wave found its way into the scholarly press as well. For example, Paul Douglas (1919), in a piece titled "Is the New Immigration More Unskilled Than the Old?," took issue with previous empirical work and concluded the second wave was *not* more unskilled than the first. Moreover, Douglas (1919, p. 403) accused his colleagues of bias by closing that "it is the custom of each generation to view the immigrants of its day as inferior to the stock that once came over [sic]. Some of this prejudice against the newer races has not been wholly absent from some of the writings upon American immigration problems."

Despite the poverty, prejudice and discrimination faced by second-wave immigrants, there is ample evidence suggesting that they enjoyed significant upward economic mobility, both within and between generations (Handlin 1941; Warner and Srole 1945; Briggs 1978). An important treatise on this topic is Stanley Lieberson's *A Piece of the Pie* (1980). While Lieberson was primarily interested in comparing the progress of the southern, central and eastern European immigrants (the second wave) to that of native-born blacks, his imaginative use of existing data showed that the second wave made considerable economic gains. Lieberson (1980, pp. 1–2) writes that

these new European groups piled up in the slums of the great urban centers of the East and Midwest. . . . They were largely unskilled, minimally educated, poor, relegated to undesirable jobs and residences, and life was harsh. The descendants of these [southeastern] European groups have done relatively well in the United States. By all accounts, their education, occupations, and incomes are presently close to—or even in excess of—white Americans from the earlier Northwestern European sources. . . . [I]t is clear that the new Europeans have "made it" to a degree far in excess of that which would have been expected or predicted at the time of their arrival here.

The disdain among many natives toward second-wave immigrants was caused by perceived negative social and economic consequences—including the admission of many poor and indigent immigrants. In part, this disdain was manifest in the doctrine of "nativism," which called for more restricted immigration. The Know-Nothings, a nativist political party, called for the deportation of all foreign paupers (Stephenson 1926). As is still the case today, negative stereotypes of new immigrants persisted owing to the lack of hard evidence to support or refute them. With little evidence to dispel the alarmist claims of the nativists, this movement gained considerable popular strength around the turn of the century.

While immigrants from southeastern Europe predominated during the second wave (1860–1930), China and Japan were the source of a small but important stream. These Asian immigrants settled mostly in San Francisco. Because they were so vastly different from the European stock, they were the object of virulent racism (Jones 1960). Anti-Chinese sentiment resulted in the first *federal* immigration legislation, the Chinese Exclusion Act of 1882, which was a major victory for the nativists. This act quickly halted Chinese immigration.

The Chinese Exclusion Act was the first in a series of increasingly restrictive federal immigration reforms. For present purposes, it is noteworthy that in 1891, Congress acted to restrict entry of various "classes" of persons, most notably paupers. Persons deemed likely to become public charges were turned away at ports of entry and steamship companies were required to return all unacceptable immigrants. To further deter the immigration of the poor and to help fund the social services for those who managed to enter, the head tax on each arrival steadily increased between 1882 and 1907 (Jones 1960). Also, those who became public charges (paupers) within a year of entry were subject to deportation (Easterlin, et al. 1980). In 1910, about 24,000 would-be immigrants were turned away, most (70%) on the grounds that they were "potential charity cases" (Easterlin, et al. 1980).

Fears of immigrant pauperism were not unfounded. George Stephenson (1926, p. 144) reports the findings of a congressional investigation in Pittsburgh that revealed that "over five hundred immigrant paupers and insane had arrived at that city within a period of six months, many of the paupers . . . wearing clothes that bore the branded name of the workhouse of which they had been inmates in Ireland." Scholarly writings of the day offer empirical support for the high degree of poverty and indigence among second-wave arrivals. Mayo-Smith (1890, p. 158), for example, reviewed state-level data from New York and Massachusetts and concluded that "it is in the statistics of pauperism and poor relief that we find the most accentuated indication of the presence of the immigrants. Many of them are almost entirely without resources. When they fail to get work their scanty savings are quickly exhausted and they are obliged to apply to public or private charity." Whether the incidence of poverty actually was greater among the second wave than the first is not known, but this was the perception at the time.

Other restrictionist legislation included the Immigration Act of 1917, which institutionalized literacy as a criterion for entry. Historians view this act—which demanded that in order to enter, adult immigrants be able to read and write in some language (not necessarily English)—as an attempt to curtail immigration from southeastern Europe in a more subtle, but still racist way (Stephenson 1926; Jones 1960). It met with great opposition from business leaders and resident immigrant groups and was vetoed a number of times before finally passing. Mayo-Smith (1890, p. 161) wrote that "illiteracy in the United States is vastly increased by immigration. It could hardly be otherwise. The immigrants are from the lower classes, where illiteracy is always most prevalent." It seems reasonable that the literacy requirement was partly intended to curb the immigration of those destined for the bottom of the socioeconomic ladder. To that end also, this act doubled the head tax on each entrant. Finally, the 1917 act extended the prohibition of Chinese immigration to most other Asian countries (Jones 1960).

The swelling clamor for a more restrictive immigration policy, one that would restrict the massive influx of impoverished southeastern Europeans, resulted in the Immigration and Nationality Acts of 1921 and 1924. These acts curtailed immigration from all but northwestern European countries by means of the National Origin Quota System. This system set annual per country immigration quotas at 2% of the country-of-origin distribution of the 1890 U.S. population. Because the United States was still predominantly composed of people of northwestern European descent in 1890, the Quota System greatly favored this region as a source of future immigration.

The country-of-origin composition of immigrants changed accordingly (see Table 2.1). Whereas between 1907 and 1914, 21% of average annual U.S. immigration was from northwestern Europe (with most of the remaining 79% hailing from elsewhere in Europe), under the 1924 act, 87% were from northwestern Europe (Easterlin, et al. 1980). Moreover, because the pressures that led to northwestern European emigration had abated by 1930, the absolute volume of immigration declined sharply. Thus ended the second great wave of immigration to the United States.

1930–1965

During the first three decades of the twentieth century, net immigration to the United States averaged 4 million per decade. Between 1931 and 1940 there was net emigration on the order of 85,000. The volume of immigration slowly increased thereafter, but never approached the peak years of the early 1900s. Moreover, the origin composition continued to reflect the Quota System.

Concern over poverty and indigence among immigrants during this interim period naturally subsided. However, amid the severe oversupply of labor during the depression (a period when there was net emigration), there was some concern over the influx of unskilled immigrants. Some felt that such newcomers would further depress wages for unskilled labor and would overburden strained social welfare services. Accordingly, in 1930, President Herbert Hoover redoubled efforts to exclude those likely to become public charges (Easterlin, et al. 1980). Maldwyn Jones (1960, p. 280) states that "this policy of administrative restriction . . . insured the exclusion of all but the most prosperous European immigrants."

During the 1940s, immigration policy was liberalized somewhat in response to a severe labor shortage caused by World War II. The Chinese Exclusion Act was repealed in 1943 and the War Brides Act (1946) and Displaced Persons Acts (1948, 1950) helped resettle war brides and refugees (Simon 1985). Also, to satisfy the great demand for labor, the United States actively recruited seasonal Mexican agricultural labor under the Bracero Program (Samora, et al. 1971). To be sure, Mexican immigration to the southwest United States reached appreciable numbers by 1910 (Jones 1960), but this flow ebbed during the 1920s and 1930s. The Bracero Program established networks that increased total Mexican immigration during the 1940s and 1950s. There is ample evidence that most of these immigrants were unskilled and a great many were poor. Jones (1960, p. 292) notes that "they were fated . . . to suffer the penalities attached to color . . . their concentration in the Southwest, an acutely race-conscious section, condemned them to a distinct status as a lower caste, nearly always suffering discrimination in employment and social life, and segregation in housing and education."

Another important piece of legislation of the 1930–1965 period was the Immigration and Nationality Act of 1952. This legislation established a preference system that gave priority to those would-be immigrants with valuable occupational skills and secondary preference to those wishing to be reunited with kin (see Table 2.2). However, this act is more noteworthy because, despite vehement opposition by President Harry Truman and the 1952 Presidential Commission on Immigration and Naturalization, it did *not* abolish the National Origin Quota System. Truman vetoed the act principally because of the blatant racism of the Quota System it left intact. To quote from President Truman's veto message (Presidential Commission on Immigration and Naturalization 1953, pp. 277–278),

The greatest vice of the present quota system, however, is that it discriminates, deliberately and intentionally, against many of the peoples of the world. . . . The idea

Table 2.2
A Comparison of the 1952 and 1965 Immigration Preference Systems

Preference	Preferences Under Immigration and Nationality Act of 1952[a]
First	Highly skilled immigrants whose services are urgently needed in the United States and the spouses and children of such immigrants (50%).
Second	Parents of U.S. citizens over age 21 and unmarried adult children of U.S. citizens (30%).
Third	Spouses and unmarried adult children of permanent resident aliens (30%).
Fourth	Brothers, sisters and married children of U.S. citizens and accompanying spouses and children (50% of numbers not required for first three preferences).
Nonpreference	Applicants not entitled to one of the above preferences. (50% of numbers not required for first three preferences, plus any not required for fourth preference).

Preferences Under the 1965 Amendments to the Immigration and Nationality Act of 1952[b]

18

Preference

First   Unmarried adult children of U.S. citizens (20%).

Second   Spouses and unmarried adult children of permanent resident aliens (20%).

Third   Members of the professions and scientists and artists of exceptional ability (10%, requires labor certification).

Fourth   Married children of U.S. citizens (10%).

Fifth   Brothers and sisters of U.S. citizens over age 21 (24%).

Sixth   Skilled and unskilled workers in occupations for which labor is in short supply in the United States (10%, requires labor certification).

Seventh   Refugees from communist countries or communist-dominated countries or the general area of the Middle East (6%).

Nonpreference Applicants not entitled to one of the above preferences. (Any numbers not required for preference applicants).

Source: Bouvier and Gardner (1986, Table 2).

a Exempt from numerical quotas: Spouses and unmarried minor children of U.S. citizens.

b Exempt from numerical quotas: Spouses, unmarried minor children and parents of U.S.

behind this discrimination policy was, to put it baldly, that Americans with English and Irish names were better people and better citizens than Americans with Italian or Greek or Polish names. . . . Such a concept is utterly unworthy of our traditions and our ideals. It violates the great political doctrine . . . that "all men are created equal." . . . The basis of this quota system was false and unworthy in 1924. It is even worse now.

Despite this opposition, over two-thirds of the Eighty-second Congress voted to override Truman's veto, thereby retaining the discriminatory Quota System. Apparently, Congress felt that the Quota System was the best way to "preserve the sociological and cultural balance of the population" (Glazer 1985, p. 5–6). While restrictionism began to ebb in the late 1940s, public opinion polls were roughly consistent with congressional sentiment. That is, in 1953, 39% of the respondents to a national poll felt the United States was admitting too many immigrants, while only 13% felt it was not admitting enough (Simon 1985).

1965–1987: The Third Wave

The third great wave of immigration to the United States, those arriving after 1965, are the focus of this study. The 1965 amendments to the Immigration and Nationality Act of 1952 were an important cause of the third wave. This legislation had several important effects on immigration. First, as noted in chapter 1, the increased limits and more even distribution of visas brought on a surge in immigration (see Table 1.1). To be sure, this increase began before 1965 (reflecting, in part, the influx of Hungarian and Cuban refugees). However, immigration continued to increase after 1965 primarily because of the 1965 legislation. Second, the country-of-origin composition shifted such that flows from Asian and Latin American countries came to predominate. I now discuss this legislation and the third wave in more detail.

The civil rights movement of the 1960s raised national consciousness regarding racial prejudice and institutional discrimination, and reaffirmed the nation's fundamental tenet that all persons are created equal. The restrictionism and ethnocentrism that allowed the National Origin Quota System to be retained in 1952 dissolved in the political milieu of the 1960s. An immigration policy that systematically favored northwestern European immigrants stood in direct opposition to the ethic of equality of opportunity.

It was in this historical context that the 1965 amendments to the Immigration and Nationality Act were passed. The legislation dismantled the Quota System, which was phased out over a 31-month period. The Quota System was replaced with a far more equitable worldwide distribution of visas. Rather than basing quotas on the nationality distribution of the 1890 U.S. Census, the new legislation established a 20,000 annual per country limit for the Eastern Hemisphere,[6] with the total not to exceed 170,000 yearly. In addition, it placed an annual limit of 120,000 on Western Hemisphere immigration. Originally, the latter slots were available on a first come, first serve basis, but the same 20,000 per country limit was extended to Western Hemisphere immigration in 1976.

The 1965 legislation also reprioritized the preference categories (first established in 1952) by giving greatest preference to those wishing to be reunited with immediate family (see Table 2.2). Moreover, these first-preference immigrants were not counted toward a country's quota limit and could enter in unlimited numbers.[7] Those immigrating on the merits of their occupational skills were given relatively lower priority (third and sixth preference). At first, this preference system was applicable to Eastern Hemisphere immigration only. Mexicans, for example, could not take advantage of the family reunification provisions. The preference system was extended to *all* immigrants in 1976 (Easterlin, et al. 1980). Thus, the 1965 legislation increased immigration by raising the overall ceiling and by greatly increasing the visas available in countries where the demand to emigrate to the United States was high. The latter also caused the shift toward Asian and Latin American countries that has characterized the third wave.

Another important aspect of the third wave, not directly related to the 1965 legislation, is the sizable refugee flow of recent decades. From 1960 to 1980, roughly a half of a million Cubans immigrated to the United States, most of whom entered as refugees (Immigration and Naturalization Service 1984). The 1970s also witnessed sizable refugee flows from Indochina, particularly after the fall of Saigon in 1975 (Gardner, et al. 1985). Up to 1980, about a quarter of a million Indo-Chinese entered the United States as refugees (Department of Health and Human Services 1983).

The parallels between this wave and the second wave are noteworthy. Disequilibriums in employment opportunities, improved transportation and the diffusion of information about the United States contributed to both waves. In both cases, there was a noticeable shift toward relatively less-developed countries of origin.[8] During the early 1900s, this shift raised concern over the economic impact of immigrants. Many questioned whether the new southeastern Europeans were displacing native labor, driving down wages and adding to a growing and burdensome mass of unemployable persons. These and other related concerns ultimately led to more restrictive immigration legislation. Interestingly, the current shift toward *today's* Third World countries has raised these same old questions (Cafferty, et al. 1983; Glazer 1985). Again, two of these questions, relating to the level of poverty and degree of social program utilization among the third wave, are explored fully in this volume.

The assertion that the 1965 legislation increased the level of poverty and indigence among immigrants is plausible for at least two reasons. First, the emphasis on family reunification over labor force skills as a basis for admission increases the likelihood that immigrants will have negligible labor market skills or skills that are incongruent with the U.S. economy. While there is reason to doubt the degree of this incongruity (Borjas and Tienda 1987), it has caused some concern among policy analysts. Second, the shift toward sending countries with less-advanced economies might compromise the transferability of immigrant job skills. Because the European countries siphoned off their destitute to the United States, many wonder whether U.S. immigration is a safety valve for Third World countries coping with massive unemployment (Portes and Bach 1985).

Because the third wave has taken place in an era of more thorough and rigorous social scientific data gathering, relatively more is known about the sociodemographic characteristics of these newest immigrants compared to previous waves. Much of this research literature has highlighted the importance of the country-of-origin transition and family reunification provisions on the characteristics of the third wave (Keely 1971, 1975; Cafferty, et al. 1983; Wong 1985). This literature documents an overall bifurcation in the educational and occupational distribution of immigrants. That is, compared to pre-1965 arrivals, the third wave is disproportionately represented by well-educated and poorly educated people (Wong 1985) and those with professional and unskilled occupations (Keely 1971, 1975, 1980; Tienda, et al. 1984). Systematic differences between regions of origin account for part of these aggregate trends. Asian immigrants made shrewd use of the occupational preference categories and the flow of Asian professionals increased accordingly (Gardner, et al. 1985). On the other hand, Europeans of the new immigration were showing a deterioration in job skills (Keely 1971). Much less is known about the level of poverty and public assistance dependency among the third wave—a void this research seeks to fill.

By way of summary of this historical overview, I emphasize the following points. First, throughout the years, the United States has had ambivalent, if not outright contradictory immigration policies. In one respect, the nation has been a fair-weather friend. During periods of labor shortage, as during the later 1900s or World War II, the nation actively recruited labor. During periods of low demand for labor, especially for unskilled labor, the clamor for immigration restriction increased.[9] Thus, while unskilled immigrants are more than welcome when they are needed, in difficult times they are eschewed.

Second, despite the lofty sentiments expressed in "give me your tired, your poor . . . " and the fact that the nation takes pride in being a refuge for the world's poor, impoverished immigrants have generally not been welcome. It is somewhat ironic that the poor is one group the nation has persistently tried to exclude. Impoverished immigrants whose labor is easily exploited and who are unlikely to become dependent on the state or private charities stand as exceptions. That we have been less concerned about the poor per se than about paupers, points to the importance of comparing trends in the level of poverty and public assistance utilization among the new immigrants.

Third, this review of U.S. immigration history underscores the difficulty of disentangling the cultural-racial and economic protests against immigration. Much of the outcry against the second wave was based ostensibly on economic grounds—that the southeastern Europeans were of poorer quality. Yet some assert that the opposition was largely grounded in notions of Nordic racial supremacy. Jones (1960, p. 255) writes that "the notion that the 'new' immigrants [were] different from and inferior to the old, arose not from popular antipathies but from the theorizing of a handful of race-conscious New England intellectuals." Assertions of deteriorating immigrant quality flourished in an era when social scientists lacked the resources or wherewithal to compile the data necessary to refute them.

This brief history has served to contextualize the present research problem in the stream of U.S. immigration history, in part, by drawing some of the parallels between past waves of U.S. immigration and the current one. On a more theoretical level, several insights can be drawn from theories of assimilation and migration that bear on the topic at hand. I now turn to these issues.

THEORIES OF ASSIMILATION AND MIGRATION

This section discusses theoretical issues surrounding two key social phenomena: assimilation and migration. For each, specific attention is given to the implications of these processes for poverty and welfare receipt among immigrants. In the context of these theoretical issues, I consider the impact of the 1965 legislative reforms on immigrant poverty and public assistance utilization.

Assimilation

Sociological theorizing and research on poverty and pauperism among immigrants is scant. However, the broader issue of socioeconomic mobility among immigrants has received attention. Much of this work hinges on the fundamental sociological concept of assimilation. Arguably, the cumulative life histories of the waves of immigrants to the United States have served as the primary empirical referent for theories of assimilation.

Assimilation has been defined in many ways. Milton Gordon (1964) synthesized many early definitions and proposed that assimilation was a multifarious process involving distinct dimensions or "stages." These included (in the context of immigration) acculturation, or the adoption of the host society's language, religion or other cultural characteristics; structural assimilation or interaction with host members in primary relationships; and the dissolution of prejudice and discrimination against the immigrant group. Gordon felt that once structural assimilation was attained, the remaining types of assimilation would be achieved in short order. Assimilation brings upward economic mobility.

In addressing the experience of immigrants, some scholars have assumed that assimilation is a unilinear process that both reflects and causes upward economic mobility. In introducing the third volume of their Yankee City series, W. Lloyd Warner and Leo Srole (1945, p. 2) write,

> This book tells part of the magnificent history of the adjustment of the ethnic groups to American life. . . . Each group enters the city at the bottom of the social heap . . . and through the several generations makes its desperate climb upward. The early arrivals, having had more time, have climbed farther up the ladder than the ethnic groups that followed them. It seems likely that oncoming generations of new ethnics will go through the same metamorphosis and climb to the same heights that generations of earlier groups have achieved.

This suggests that while poverty among immigrants is possible, perhaps even probable, at first, it is temporary not chronic—lasting only until assimilation begins.

This view was adopted by Segalman and Basu (1981) in their typology of the poor. Their "transitional poor," whose bout with poverty is brief, temporary and unrepeated, is made up primarily of immigrants. Once "cultural, language, and other assimilative adjustments" are achieved, they become "adequately self-sufficient themselves or are able to provide their children with a 'head start' on the road to socioeconomic upward movement" (Segalman and Basu 1981, p. 45).

This somewhat romanticized view of the upward mobility of immigrants is based on the experience of European immigrants of the late 1800s and early 1900s—the first and second waves. Warner and Srole (1945) and Handlin (1941), for example, found the Irish exemplary. A closer reading of both these works, however, reveals that assimilation and its attendant upward economic mobility are by no means assured. The process can be retarded in direct proportion to the dissimilarity between the immigrant and the dominant groups in the host society. That native blacks have failed to become fully assimilated provides stark testimony about the persisting significance of race (Glazer and Moynihan 1970). In addition, Warner and Srole (1945) saw the "time for assimilation" for southern and eastern Europeans as being moderate, Hispanics as slow and Asians as slow to very slow.

Repulsed by their squalid living conditions and affected by the nativism of the day, many social scientists of the early 1900s doubted the ability of even the southeastern Europeans to assimilate. For example, Fuller (1939, p. 46), asserts that "the very low standards of living, the high illiteracy, the prevalence of physical and mental disease, the competition with native labor which characterize the new immigrant types make their assimilation into American institutions a very difficult matter." Similar, though more blatantly racist opinions are expressed by Robert Hunter ([1904] 1965).

Most scholars would agree with Pierre van den Berghe (1978, p. 101) that immigrants to the United States have experienced "fairly rapid accultura-tion" but that "assimilation, especially of nonwhite immigrants, has often lagged behind their acculturation." This suggests that while nonwhites have adopted the majority's language and other cultural characteristics, racial markers have blocked their inclusion in those mainstream institutions that bring higher socioeconomic status. Clearly this has grave implications for the post–1965 immigrants, so many of whom are people of color. Spe-cifically, if retarded assimilation of nonwhite immigrants persists today, we would expect greater and more persistent poverty among the post–1965 im-migrant cohorts. On the other hand, if they are incompletely assimilated, they might not be as cognizant of public assistance programs or have the wherewithal to apply for them. In view of their economic disadvantages, im-migrants, especially recent arrivals, might have lower than expected rates of welfare utilization.

Migration

Basic theories of migration also bear on the question of poverty among immigrants. It is convenient to distinguish between equilibrium, structural and network perspectives of migration. These are discussed in turn.

The equilibrium approach focuses on the migration of labor (Ravenstein 1885, 1889; Todaro 1969; Lee 1966). Such theories lean toward the optimis-tic picture painted by Warner and Srole (1945) regarding the upward mobility of migrants. They assume that the decision to migrate is affected by perceived disequilibriums in the spatial distribution of societal resources. People move to places where opportunities are better. While initial periods of hardship are sometimes anticipated, they are endured in hopes of greater rewards in the future (Todaro 1969). Thus, while poverty may be a concern for some recent migrants, it should be temporary or "transitional" (Segal-man and Basu 1981).

This generalization underlies Barry Chiswick's (1979, 1980) benchmark work on immigrant earnings. He found that after an initial period of relatively low income, the rise in earnings with age (the age-earnings profile) is far steeper than that of natives. He predicts that in 15 years, on average, immigrant earnings actually surpass those of natives.

Chiswick (1979, 1980) explains that this "universal pattern" is due in large measure to the positive self-selection of immigrants. He theorizes that migrants, compared to those who remain in the homeland, have "greater ability and work motivation" (Chiswick 1980, p. 48) and that they recognize that this will yield great returns to migration.

Interestingly, there is evidence (Borjas 1985) suggesting Chiswick's (1979) conclusion that immigrants have much steeper age-earnings profiles than natives is an artifact of the deterioration in the background characteristics of immigrants. That is, because Chiswick used synchronic cross-sectional data, he compared earnings across synthetic immigrant cohorts. The sharp rise in earnings for immigrants he observed captures not only aging and assimilation effects, but also differences in human capital across cohorts. If the background characteristics of successive immigrant cohorts were deteriorating over time, then the earnings advantage of previous immigrants over later arrivals would appear artificially high. George Borjas (1985) has shown with repeated cross-sectional data that this in fact lies behind Chiswick's result.

Borjas's (1985) work has two important implications regarding poverty, welfare participation and immigration. First, the deterioration in background characteristics for recent entrants suggests a greater prevalence of poverty and dependence among them. Second, by refuting Chiswick's optimistic prediction of a steep age-earnings profile, the temporary nature of poverty among recent immigrants cannot be safely assumed.

The structural approach to migration stresses the contextual importance of the evolving world economic order. Adopting a world systems view of development (Wallerstein 1974; Portes 1978), migration results from the incorporation of the Third World into a global division of labor. One important aspect of First World penetration has been the rationalization of Third World agriculture and industry. The resulting imbalances in capital to labor ratios have created widespread employment pressures and great potential for emigration (Portes 1978; Bach 1983).

Alejandro Portes (1978) and Portes and Robert Bach (1985) have situated the recent trends in Mexican emigration to the United States in this broader structural context. Local elites find emigration valuable to release the oversupply of labor, especially because the costs and risks of emigration largely are borne by the emigrants and their families. Developed areas find such immigration beneficial as a source of cheap labor.[10]

While the equilibrium approach emphasizes those factors that pull migrants to places of destination, the structural approach emphasizes factors that push migrants from places of origin. A number of writers have noted that migrants who are responding more to push factors will be less selective (Findley 1977; Lee 1969) and less apt to succeed economically. If by increasing quotas for less-developed countries the 1965 immigration reform increased the proportion of immigrants who are being pushed more than pulled, we would expect greater poverty rates for recent immigrant cohorts. This argument also suggests that refugees, who represent an extreme case of migration due to push factors, will be more prone to poverty. The U.S. military involvement in Indochina induced vast refugee flows during the mid-1970s, many of whom settled in the United States. This is an additional reason to suspect greater poverty and welfare use among post-1965 immigrant cohorts.

Portes (1981) criticized the equilibrium model of labor migration as oversimplified. He disaggregates the generic labor migrant into three types based on mode of incorporation into the U.S. economy. Assuming a segmented labor market approach (Doeringer and Piore 1971), Portes differentiates between immigrants who gain access to the primary labor market, those who become employed in the secondary labor market and those who find work in ethnic economic enclaves (Wilson and Portes 1980; Wilson and Martin 1982).

Focusing on the primary-secondary dichotomy for now, access to the primary market depends on background human capital characteristics. Highly skilled and well-educated immigrants stand a much better chance of gaining primary employment. In part, this channeling is institutionalized because many such entrants (third and sixth preference categories) must prove that their skills are needed in the United States to gain admission. Except perhaps for an initial period of adjustment, poverty for primary labor migrants is of little concern. Those less well endowed with human capital stand a great chance, in Portes's view, of having to accept employment in peripheral industries. For them, economic hardship is a constant concern. Some have worried that low-skilled immigrants are currently contributing to a "perpetual underclass" (Bouvier and Gardner 1986). This is simply an alternative expression of the fear that too many new immigrants are poor and welfare dependent.

There are three reasons to suspect an increase in marginal employment and poverty among recent immigrants. All three reasons stem from the change in country-of-origin composition of immigrants since 1965. The first is the greater proportion from Third World countries, which suggests a greater relative number being lured by and recruited for the most marginal occupations. The second reason is the lower skill levels of recent cohorts (Keely 1975). The third reason—assuming racial discrimination blocks access to the primary labor market—is the increased proportion of nonwhites among recent immigrant cohorts.

Kenneth Wilson and Portes (1980) and Portes and Bach (1985) have documented the role of ethnic economic enclaves in facilitating the incorporation of immigrants into the U.S. economy. The Cuban enclave in Miami is the best example. The enclave is ethnically closed and highly vertically integrated. New Cuban immigrants start at the bottom, performing mostly menial jobs for coethnic employers. However, they are encouraged to save money with which they can invest in their own ethnic enterprise in time. This entrepreneurial activity engenders upward economic mobility. Thus, while new immigrants might begin with a marginal job, unlike the secondary labor market, upward movement *is* possible. The implication of this for poverty among immigrants is self-evident—incorporation into the enclave offers a unique protection against poverty.

The equilibrium approach to migration has been criticized for overemphasizing the importance of economic factors (Findley 1977). While the size and characteristics of migration streams are no doubt affected by economic push and pull factors in places of origin and destination, some have proposed the importance of "intervening opportunities" (Stouffer 1940) or "intervening obstacles" (Lee 1969). An important intervening factor in the migration process is the social network that evolves between immigrants in the host country and their family and friends in the country of origin (Findley 1977).[11] Portes and Bach (1985, p. 10) note that

> networks . . . are crucial in regulating migrant flows, ensuring the early survival of migrants, finding jobs, and maintaining up-to-date information on economic conditions in the home countries. Labor migration can thus be conceptualized as a process of network building, which depends on and, in turn, reinforces social relationships across space. The microstructures thus created not only permit the survival of migrants, but also constitute a significant undercurrent often running counter to dominant economic trends.

Networks have contradictory implications for both poverty and welfare utilization among immigrants. By reducing the cost of migrating, networks could promote the immigration of those with fewer resources or those who are less economically motivated, thereby increasing the prevalence of poverty and dependence among immigrants. On the other hand, the opposite might occur if previous immigrants help the newcomers find employment and housing and provide an informal source of economic support as an alternative to public assistance (Sassen-Koob 1979).

SUMMARY AND SYNTHESIS

Against the backdrop of the theoretical and historical issues just outlined, I now set forth a more thorough statement of the problem at hand. Since the mid-1960s, the United States has experienced its third wave of immigration. This new immigration has been characterized by an increase in (1) the flow of arrivals, (2) the proportion from less-developed countries and (3) the percent nonwhite. Like the second wave, this new immigration has rekindled a number of debates regarding the economic impact of immigration. Many complain that, to an unacceptable degree, the new immigration is composed of poor and destitute arrivals who wind up on the welfare rolls. These assertions have flourished and have been used as arguments to curtail future immigration, yet, they have received scant attention in the research literature.

The research problem pursued here is to document and explain immigrant-native differentials in public assistance utilization and poverty during the period 1960–1980. In light of the above theoretical discussion and description of the third wave, there are several reasons to suspect that there will be significant differences in the level of poverty and welfare use both between immigrants and natives and between immigrant year-of-arrival cohorts.

I adopt two fundamental elements of assimilation theory in approaching this subject. First, economic position tends to improve with time spent in the host society and, second, assimilation is retarded in direct proportion to the sociocultural differences between the host society and the group being assimilated. Recent immigrants are expected to show higher risks of poverty, compared to both natives and other immigrants, reflecting the difficult and broad socioeconomic adjustments they face. However, there are reasons to suspect that the level of poverty among recent arrivals has increased as the new immigration has proceeded. The shift toward Third World countries of origin and the de-emphasis of job skills as a basis for admission suggest that the new immigrants may have less transferable occupational skills. This would compromise their employability and increase prospects of poverty. Also, because an increasing percentage of new arrivals are people of color (Asians and Hispanics), prejudice and discrimination may cause the new arrivals to start from a disadvantaged economic position. Moreover, because the pace of assimilation is affected by the sociocultural divergence between immigrants and the host society (Warner and Srole 1945; Gordon 1964), the decline in poverty rates among the newest arrivals may be less steep. Cafferty, et al. (1983, p. 79) write that "the pertinent question is not whether the new immigrants are poor. Many immigrants have been poor. The question is whether there is any realistic possibility that they will emerge from poverty." This highlights the importance of comparing poverty rates across real and synthetic immigrant cohorts.

While push-pull analyses have been belittled in the literature (Portes 1978), I assume that those who migrate in response to the pull of economic opportunity are selective, both in terms of background characteristics and daring (Chiswick 1980; Fallows 1983). Conversely, those who respond to push factors should be particularly prone to poverty and transfer program utilization (Lee 1969). There are two reasons why the new immigrants may be less responsive to economic pull factors. First, refugees have accounted for a small but appreciable part of new immigrants—particularly among Asians. Specifically, Indo-Chinese refugees can be expected to have high poverty rates. Moreover, because these refugees have been granted relaxed eligibility for certain transfer programs, they are expected to have higher rates of public assistance receipt. Second, by emphasizing family reunification, the United States may be attracting immigrants who are less economically select. However, it should be noted that first and second preference arrivals may be migrating in response to employment opportunities to the same degree as labor migrants (Tienda 1983).

A final reason why poverty may be on the increase among new arrivals stems from the structural-historical perspective of Portes (1978). First World economic penetration into less-developed countries has increased pressures to emigrate. These émigrés are being pushed by a lack of employment in their native countries and pulled by the promise of marginal employment in the United States and elsewhere. Given the great wage disparities, their decision is economically rational, despite the fact that they might be poor by U.S. standards. It is also important to consider the mode of incorporation into the U.S. economy (Portes 1981). I assume that many immigrants, particularly recent immigrants, find employment in low-paying, dead-end jobs. This raises the prospect of widespread increases in poverty and social program participation among immigrants.

Many of these points also have relevance for the level of public assistance use among the new immigrants. That poverty rates among the more recent arrivals may have increased suggests similar increases in the level of dependence on transfer programs. However, this link can not be casually assumed. First, generally unassimilated new arrivals may be unfamiliar with the social programs available or, if they are familiar with the programs, may not have the wherewithal to apply for them. Second, it has been shown that many immigrants turn to informal sources of financial assistance, such as family and friends, in times of economic crisis (Moore 1971; Tienda 1980; Kritz and Gurak 1984).[12]

Even some scholars who concede that immigrants have no outright penchant for welfare utilization, still regard them as more likely to receive public assistance income. For example, Cafferty, et al. (1983, p. 21) assert the following.

Although, in general, immigrants do not migrate to the U.S. for the explicit purpose of receiving income transfers, and although recent immigrants may not be eligible for some transfers, this does not mean that transfers have no effect on the size and composition of the immigrant population in the United States. The knowledge that transfer payments are available if an immigrant is not successful reduces some of the risk of immigration, particularly for those whose economic prospects in the U.S. are less certain. The transfers also affect reemigration decisions. . . . With the availability of public income transfers, reemigration is less likely to occur.[13]

REVIEW OF EXISTING EMPIRICAL LITERATURE

The lack of evidence on poverty and welfare utilization among the new immigrants is one justification for this study. Despite the historical policy concern over poverty among immigrants and the more recent speculation that post-1965 immigrant cohorts may have higher poverty rates than witnessed among earlier cohorts, the interplay between poverty and immigration has received scant attention in the social science literature. Much of what has been done focuses on the internal migration of the poor (Bacon 1971, 1973). One prominent debate in this literature is whether the poor (and blacks in particular) migrate to places where welfare benefits are higher, net of other economic opportunities (Premus and Weinstein 1977; Cebula 1977). However, the question of poverty among U.S. immigrants, particularly the recent arrivals, has been ignored by scholars.

Consistent with abiding concerns, most related research addresses immigrant use of social services, as opposed to immigrant poverty per se. Even here, "little is known about the use of government services by immigrants" (Council of Economic Advisors 1986, p. 372).

Some studies have approached the issue broadly and have addressed the use of a wide range of social services by immigrants in relation to their contributions via sales and income taxes. Such studies speak to the net economic impact of immigrants. Estimates vary.

Using data from the 1976 Survey of Income and Education (SIE), Julian Simon (1980) estimated immigrant use of social security, unemployment compensation, public assistance and food stamps as well as education. These costs to U.S. society are offset by the taxes immigrants pay, which Simon estimates based on immigrants' income. Simon concludes that immigrants pay more into public coffers than they use, chiefly because of their underutilization of social security. While immigrants come to use social security as they age, they do so after paying into the system most of their productive lives. Moreover, Simon reasons, many leave behind offspring who themselves pay into the system.

Julian Simon is a well-known advocate of immigration (Simon 1981), so it is not surprising his results would support the claim that immigration is a good investment for natives. However, his 1980 study could be criticized for possibly understating the "immigrant burden" on two counts. First, he assumed that immigrant earnings, and thus the taxes they contribute, rise faster than they may in reality.[14] Second, Simon neglected to include certain public services, most notably medical care, in his estimation.[15]

Studies that cull a more exhaustive list of immigrant costs, to the neglect of some of their contributions, portray a different image. One Immigration and Naturalization Service (INS) study focused on the net economic cost of undocumented immigration (Immigration and Naturalization Service 1983).[16] In addition to the costs cited by Simon (1980), the INS considered police services and job displacement. Despite the fact that undocumented immigrants are even less likely to receive transfers than legal immigrants (Council of Economic Advisors 1986), the INS estimated that undocumented immigrants cost U.S. taxpayers twice as much as they contribute. While I do not doubt the scientific intentions of either Simon or the INS, it is noteworthy that both draw conclusions that square with their political convictions.[17]

Other studies have a more restricted focus, looking specifically at immigrant-native differentials in the use of transfer programs. Francine Blau (1984), for example, assumed that the probability of transfer income receipt was a function of individual, household and locational characteristics. She found that families headed by immigrants were less likely than otherwise comparable native families to receive public assistance income.

In an analysis that further dispelled the myth of immigrant dependency, Marta Tienda and Leif Jensen (1986) extended Blau's (1984) work in a number of ways. By using a larger data set—the Public Use Microdata A-Sample of the 1980 U.S. Census—they were able to perform separate analyses for whites, blacks, Hispanics and Asians. Tienda and Jensen (1986) also monitored the effects of family structure in a more comprehensive manner. Finally, they included several contextual variables in their analysis characterizing the area of residence. Tienda and Jensen (1986), in this more elaborate work, upheld Blau's (1984) overall conclusion: with few exceptions, immigrants are *less* likely to receive public assistance than otherwise comparable natives.

To summarize, the few studies that *do* address the relative propensity of immigrants to receive income-conditioned transfer payments suggest the following. Far from having a penchant for cash assistance, immigrants are less likely than natives to receive transfers, other things being equal. Even in the aggregate, immigrant utilization differs little from that of natives (Blau 1984; Simon 1984; Tienda and Jensen 1986). Popular concern over the burden of immigrants on social welfare coffers would appear to be misplaced. At the very least, these studies reject the common assertion that "most immigrants wind up on welfare."

A problem endemic to all of the above studies—whether regarding the broader issue of the total burden of immigrants or specifically the relative propensity of immigrants to receive transfers—is that they are restricted in one sense or another. As the Council of Economic Advisors (CEA) concluded (1986, p. 372), "Most available studies examine disparate immigrant groups in various time periods, often focusing on immigrants living in particular locations in the country." This makes it difficult to generalize about the national impact of immigration. This study examines all immigrants residing in all parts of the United States in 1970 and 1980.[18] As such, it has considerable breadth and provides a unique contribution to this empirical literature.

JUSTIFICATIONS FOR THE STUDY

In addition to the dearth of studies on this topic, this research derives justification from both its practical and theoretical ramifications. Taking these in order, it should be evident by now that a critical justification is its policy relevance. The lack of understanding of the nature and level of poverty and welfare utilization among the new immigrants has widened the parameters around debates over immigration policy—perhaps yielding undue credence to radical positions. The assertions that the new immigrants are poor and welfare prone, which have widespread popular adherence, have been used to promote more restrictive immigration policies.[19] This study speaks to the popular conventional wisdoms and informs the debates over the effects of past legislation and the need for further policy adjustments. Moreover, the pejorative nature of these assertions impose an unfair burden on the new immigrants who are already struggling to "make it" in the United States.

This study has relevance also for future immigration policy. As the rate of natural increase continues to decline slowly in the United States, immigration will become a more important component of total population growth (Bouvier and Gardner 1986). In addition, if the family reunification provisions continue in their present form, immigration from this source will increase substantially in the years to come (Jasso and Rosenzweig 1986).

The Immigration Reform and Control Act of 1986 addresses the problem of undocumented immigration and leaves *legal* immigration policy intact. The third wave is, therefore, not over. Thus, not only will this study help evaluate the 1965 immigration legislation, it will allow us to anticipate the level and nature of poverty and welfare use among future immigrants.

Finally, to the extent that future refugee flows to the United States are likely, it will be important to document poverty and transfer utilization among Indo-Chinese refugees in this analysis. This should provide insight into the uniquenesses of refugees as an immigrant group and should help inform future refugee policies.

In addition to these more practical matters, this study also contributes to our understanding of migration and assimilation as socioeconomic processes. First, out of the three principal components of the demographic equation—fertility, mortality and migration—the latter is the least thoroughly understood (Bouvier, et al. 1979). Because it is likely that migration will continue to become a more important aspect of total population change, contributions to our understanding of this phenomenon are needed. Moreover, an appreciable amount of international migration will likely be from Third to First World countries (Teitelbaum 1986). If governments are to prepare for these changes and formulate informed policies to deal with immigration, more will have to be learned about the special difficulties in adaptation and economic disadvantages that Third World immigrants face in advanced economies.

Second, despite the abiding interest in poverty and pauperism among immigrants throughout U.S. history, it has been the focus of very little research. The historical overview pointed out that second-wave arrivals were eschewed in part because of the perception that many were poor and indigent. There is ample evidence that many were poor initially, but we do not know (1) whether they were more destitute than first-wave arrivals with similar amounts of U.S. experience or (2) whether the degree of hardship of the second wave was any more enduring than that of the first wave. The public simply assumed second-wave immigrants were more chronically poor. While that period is outside the scope of this analysis, this volume represents an initial foray into the matter of poverty and indigence among immigrants, at least in the current era.

Third, this research is justified to the extent that it provides additional insights into the process of assimilation. To be sure, economic adjustment is a well-studied dimension of assimilation. However, the ascendance out of poverty and a decreased use of public assistance are important yet neglected measures of assimilation. In addition, I will establish the effects of other important indicators of assimilation—such as employment and occupational status—on poverty and welfare receipt.

Fourth, the multivariate analyses of public assistance utilization highlight differences between immigrants and natives in strategies used to cope with economic hardship. Immigration policymakers will benefit from knowing whether immigrants respond differently to poverty.

Notes

1. That two of these categories overlap is explained below.

2. I do not consider the slave trade as a source of immigration in this chronology. This immigration was involuntary and bears little resemblance to the current situation.

3. The terms poverty and pauperism do not connote the same thing in the immigration literature. Pauperism, which was a greater cause of the outcry against immigration, entails dependence on the state or private charity for economic support. Thus, a person in poverty is not necessarily a pauper.

4. In Table 2.1, northwestern Europe includes the following countries: Austria, Belgium, Denmark, Finland, France, Germany, Ireland, Luxembourg, the Netherlands, Norway, Sweden, Switzerland and the United Kingdom. All other European countries are defined as southeastern Europe.

5. There is some evidence that England and Scotland promoted the emigration of the Irish poor to the United States to deflect them from their own countries (Stephenson 1926).

6. In this case, the Western Hemisphere refers to North and South America and the Caribbean while the Eastern Hemisphere comprises all other countries.

7. More suspicious observers have suggested that the family reunification provisions were a subtle attempt to retain the effects of the Quota System (Briggs 1985). Clearly, reunification gives preference to relatives of groups who are already well represented in the population.

8. It is plausible that in the mind of the average American of the turn of the century, countries such as Italy and Yugoslavia seemed as economically backward as many Latin American and Asian countries are perceived to be today.

9. Some would say this ambivalence reflects good judgment. Vernon Briggs (1985), for example, would like to build greater flexibility into immigration policy such that ceilings could be raised or lowered in accordance with labor market conditions.

10. This pattern is particularly salient for illegal immigration to the United States because the vulnerability of these individuals may inhibit their wage-bargaining position.

11. The development of such immigrant networks is part and parcel of the process of "chain migration" in which successive immigrants enter, prompted and supported by their countrypersons who preceded them.

12. This may represent an unanticipated advantage of the family reunification provisions.

13. Questions of sample selection bias due to selective emigration are covered in chapter 3.

14. Simon (1980) made the same mistake as Chiswick (1979) by deducing a rise in earnings from monochronic cross-sectional data on income by duration of residence in the United States. As noted previously, this sharp rise may be an artifact of a decline in the human capital of immigrants (Borjas 1985).

15. Of course, one could compile a similar list of immigrant contributions omitted, such as the positive effect of an increased aggregate demand for goods and services.

16. While undocumented immigrants are not the focus of this study, this particular example is enlightening.

17. This is an unfortunate, and sometimes distasteful, aspect of the immigration debate. Because flimsy and misleading evidence *has* been used in the past, when one side points to a study that supports its view, the protagonists simply discount the study as slanted. These mutual suspicions have no doubt prolonged debate over the facts about immigration.

18. Recall that, because the 1960 PUS did not include total welfare income, the analysis of public assistance receipt is restricted to 1969 and 1979.

19. For example, a bill designed to curtail undocumented immigration (the Immigration Reform and Control Act of 1986) provided amnesty—and ultimately legal status—to many undocumented immigrants who could prove they continuously resided in the United States since January 1981. Many faulted this amnesty provision on the grounds that it would foster a rush on public assistance programs once legal status was attained. Underlying this is the assumption that immigrants are welfare prone, a position that is unsupported by what little literature exists on this topic.

3

Research Methodology

This chapter details the research methodology used in this analysis. I introduce the data, define a number of key variables, explain the statistical techniques employed and address possible sources of bias.

DATA

In general terms the research task is to determine the nature of poverty and social program participation among immigrants to the United States for the period 1960–1980. I am particularly interested in examining specific immigrant year-of-arrival cohorts (in part to establish trends among the most recent immigrants). As such, this research task imposes two considerable constraints on the choice of data. First, because immigrants in general, and recent arrivals in particular, represent a rather small proportion of the U.S. population, the data set analyzed had to be large enough to afford adequate coverage of these subpopulations. Second, because I examine poverty and welfare utilization across time, the data required a high degree of intertemporal comparability. The only data that fit these twin needs of size and comparability were the Public Use Sample (PUS) data of the 1960, 1970 and 1980 U.S. Censuses.

The Public Use Samples are large stratified samples of housing units enumerated in the U.S. Census. The samples contain sociodemographic information on housing units (the household record) and each person residing within them (the individual records). Specifically, I draw from the 1% PUS of the 1960 Census, the 1% State PUS of the 1970 Census (5% questionnaire) and the A-Sample of the Public Use Microdata Samples of the 1980 Census.

From these samples, special household-level data files were constructed; one each for 1960, 1970 and 1980.[1] These files, herein referred to as the "family files," are parallel in structure. Each record contains data on the household head, the head's spouse (if present), variables drawn verbatim from the household record of the PUS and, finally, other household characteristics that were computed from all the individual records in the household.

The PUS was chosen as the primary data source because its size permits reliable analyses of small subpopulations. However, this size greatly taxes computing resources. Thus, data for the family files were drawn from the PUSs using a stratified sampling strategy. The samples were stratified with respect to nativity and race. As many as possible, but no more than 10,000 households were sought among the following groups: foreign Asian, foreign Hispanic, foreign black, other foreign, native Asian, native Hispanic, native black and other native. Thus, rare immigrant groups, such as blacks, were all selected from the PUS, while only a small percentage of native-born whites were sampled. In the descriptive tables presented in later chapters, the data are weighted accordingly. To ensure reliable tests of statistical significance, the multivariate analyses are unweighted.

The unit of analysis used throughout this study is the family, which is defined as persons residing in the same household who are related by blood, marriage or adoption. Nonfamily households (persons living alone or households in which the head is unrelated to all other individuals) and persons living in group quarters are excluded. In all, I analyze 39,061, 42,515 and 48,267 families in 1960, 1970 and 1980, respectively.

The importance of the family, loosely defined, for understanding immigrant adaptation experiences has been established elsewhere (McLaughlin 1973; Tienda 1980; Perez 1986), yet it is often neglected in the research literature (Perez 1986). The family was chosen as the unit of analysis also because public assistance income, one of two key dependent variables, is largely intended for use by impoverished families. Family characteristics— such as number of children and headship configuration—determines need and eligibility for most welfare programs. Being the primary economic coping unit in U.S. society, alternative structures can affect the family's ability to commit workers to the labor market, thus reducing poverty and welfare need. That the family is an appropriate unit of analysis for studying poverty is evidenced by the census definition of poverty itself. Among persons living in families, poverty status is determined not by the relationship between their personal income and the poverty line, but between their total family income and that family's poverty line. The Census Bureau assumes that, for people living in families, poverty is conditioned on family characteristics and that it is endured by the entire family. Other writers who have examined immigrant-native differentials in welfare utilization have likewise used this unit of analysis (Blau 1984; Simon 1984; Tienda and Jensen 1986). Restricting the analysis to families excludes fewer households than one might expect. Calculations on the family files reveal that single-person immigrant households comprise only 21.4, 17.9 and 22.4% of all recent immigrant households in 1960, 1970 and 1980, respectively.

VARIABLE DEFINITIONS

This section defines four key variables used throughout this study. These include the two basic dependent variables—public assistance utilization and poverty—and two crucial independent variables—nativity and race.

Dependent Variables

Public Assistance Utilization. Public assistance refers to income derived from Aid to Families with Dependent Children (AFDC), general assistance and Supplemental Security Income (SSI). The latter includes Old-Age Assistance, Aid to the Blind and Aid to the Permanently and Totally Disabled. Taken together, public assistance is frequently termed "welfare" (Levitan 1985).

As a dependent variable, public assistance utilization is defined in two ways. First, in order to determine differential propensities to utilize these transfer programs, a binomial variable is specified for all families. This variable takes the value of 1 if any member of the family received any public assistance income in the year prior to the census and 0 otherwise. Another important dimension of welfare utilization is the total dollar amount received. Thus, the second form public assistance utilization takes is as a continuous variable indicating total public assistance receipt in the year prior to the census. For reasons that will become clear in chapter 7, this variable is determined only for those who received a positive amount of welfare income.

Poverty. The second dependent variable analyzed is poverty. The definition and measurement of poverty is a problematic and often contentious issue (Orshansky, et al. 1978). In this analysis, I use both an absolute and a relative measure of poverty. Absolute poverty is the most widely used in government documents and research publications. This definition places the poverty threshold at the annual income needed to maintain a minimally acceptable standard of living. Families are defined as poor if their post-transfer annual income is less than the absolute poverty threshold. Over time, the threshold can be adjusted up or down according to changes in the cost of living.

The absolute poverty lines used in this analysis were developed using the ground-breaking methodology of Benjamin Rowntree (1941).[2] Based on nutritional data gathered on U.S. prison inmates, Rowntree devised a low-cost food plan providing a subsistence-level caloric intake. Using the income levels needed to purchase this low-cost food plan, Rowntree was among the first to specify absolute poverty thresholds.

More rigorous and current data on minimum nutritional requirements were obtained in a 1955 household food-consumption survey sponsored by the U.S. Department of Agriculture. These data were used by the Council of Economic Advisors (CEA) to develop a new absolute poverty line. Because studies of spending patterns showed that low-income families spent about one-third of their income on food, the CEA placed the official poverty level at thrice the annual cost of the minimum food plan (about $3,000 for a typical family in 1963).

Mollie Orshansky of the Social Security Administration, who developed the official poverty lines used—with only minor modifications—since the 1960s, greatly improved on the CEA measure by taking account of unique needs related to size of family, age and sex of head, farm status and number of children (Orshansky 1965). Thus, for example, poverty thresholds for farm families and smaller families were lower, because it was assumed they could get along on less. It is this set of 124 poverty lines, first developed in 1963, that is used here. To take account of inflation, these thresholds are adjusted using the Consumer Price Index (CPI). Families whose annual incomes in the year before the census were below their appropriate poverty threshold are defined as poor and coded 1. Otherwise, families at or above poverty are coded 0.

These and other absolute poverty lines have come under sharp criticism over the years (Schiller 1980; Fuchs 1967). For one thing, being based on scientifically gathered nutrition data, the absolute thresholds are ostensibly objective. This objectivity is specious, however, because the factor by which the food plan must be multiplied to determine the allotment for clothing, shelter, transportation and other necessities is arbitrary. Ultimately, absolute poverty thresholds are based on a subjective decision about the minimum acceptable standard of living.

Second, the level of existence possible with an income at or slightly above the poverty line is austere to say the least. The Department of Agriculture's "economy" food plan, on which the thresholds are based, was meant for short-term emergencies (Rein 1976). It is nutritionally inadequate in the long run.

Some assert that once food is paid for, the remaining money cannot adequately provide other necessities of life—let alone entertainment and recreation (Schiller 1980; Blumberg 1980; Rein 1976). Because the standard of living of those who are just above poverty is one of significant destitution, many scholars feel that the official absolute thresholds understate the true amount of poverty in the United States (Kerbo 1983).[3]

To obtain a more complete picture of differentials in poverty, an additional definition is employed: relative poverty. Whereas absolute poverty relates income to a minimum standard, relative poverty relates income to average income in the population. The former reflects whether people do not have enough to get by, the latter, whether people have much less than average. Thus, the extent of relative poverty is considerably determined by a society's level of inequality. If real incomes increase steadily over time, while the income distribution (i.e., level of inequality) remains constant, then absolute poverty will decrease while relative poverty remains constant. In other words, the poor may be better off with respect to what they can buy, but they are no better off compared to what the well-to-do can now afford. Christine Ross, et al. (1987) demonstrate that this in fact typifies U.S. trends in poverty between 1949 and 1979. They found that absolute poverty declined from 41 to 13% over the period, while relative poverty declined from 24 to only 20%.

The measure of relative poverty used here is the same as that developed by Ross, et al. (1987). By their measure, a household is defined as poor if its total income is less the 44% of the median nonnegative household income of whites.[4] While 50% of the median is often proposed (Fuchs 1967), Ross, et al. chose 44% to be consistent with Robert Plotnick and Felicity Skidmore (1975).[5] Each measure of poverty has advantages and disadvantages. On one hand, relative poverty speaks to some of the deleterious effects of poverty resulting from feelings of deprivation with respect to the average.[6] On the other hand, tied to the level of inequality in society, a relative measure of poverty fails to capture changes in the material existence of the poor. While the absolute measure ignores these issues of inequality, it yields more meaningful cross-time comparisons by documenting the percent of people who fall short of the constant minimum standard of living. Accordingly, in the multivariate analyses of poverty to follow, I use the absolute measure.

Independent Variables

Nativity. The key independent construct in this analysis is nativity. As used here, nativity describes a person or family with respect to place of birth (foreign- versus native-born) and year of immigration (for the foreign-born). There are alternative ways to identify immigrant families. A conservative definition would require that all family members be foreign-born while a liberal definition might stipulate that only one immigrant need be present. In the ensuing analyses I define an immigrant family as one in which the head of the household is foreign-born. A family's year of immigration is likewise that of the foreign-born head's. This definition falls between the two extremes above. It also yields some parsimony, as it obviates the problem of assigning year of arrival in families with more than one foreign-born member. In a similar study, Julian Simon (1984) likewise defined family immigrant status by the nativity characteristics of the head.

Puerto Ricans posed some noteworthy dilemmas in this regard. Because the United States exercises a degree of sovereignty and jurisdiction over the

Commonwealth of Puerto Rico, those born in the island are legally regarded as native U.S. citizens (Nelson and Tienda 1985). However, in many respects island-born Puerto Ricans resemble immigrants. Puerto Ricans on the island are physically and often culturally distant from mainstream U.S. society, and the causes and consequences of their migration to the mainland resemble those of other immigrant streams. Some writers have chosen to regard island-born Puerto Ricans as natives, not immigrants (Cafferty, et al. 1983). Still others have faced this dilemma by ignoring Puerto Ricans altogether (Simon 1984; Blau 1984). However, because Puerto Ricans have been shown to have high levels of poverty and welfare receipt (Tienda and Angel 1982; Tienda 1984; Tienda and Jensen 1988; Bean and Tienda 1986), they are critical to the focus of this research and their omission could distort the findings. Moreover, because they so resemble other immigrant streams, I have chosen to define Puerto Ricans who were born outside the fifty United States as immigrants, with the understanding that this is technically imprecise. The empirical results on Puerto Ricans provided below should be interpreted in this light. Finally, because Puerto Ricans are considered U.S. citizens, those born in the island were not asked year of immigration in the census. Still, I was able to define recent Puerto Rican "immigrants" as those who did not reside in one of the fifty States five years prior to the census.

Because "year of immigration" was not ascertained in the 1960 PUS, analyses that necessitate a more refined treatment of immigrant cohorts are restricted to 1970 and 1980. However, because the 1960 census does provide residence in 1955, I define recent immigrants in 1960 as the foreign-born who resided outside the United States in 1955.

Race. The description of the new immigrants in chapter 2 pointed out important differences in the immigration experiences of major race and ethnic groups. Previous analyses of immigrant-native differentials in economic well-being and transfer income receipt have erred by not disaggregating immigrants by race or region of origin (Simon 1984). Others have failed to disaggregate enough. Francine Blau (1984), for example, differentiated between whites, blacks, Hispanics and others in her multivariate models, but failed to provide descriptive data that was similarly stratified. At a minimum, it is crucial to distinguish between the following four groups of immigrants: whites, blacks, Hispanics and Asians. To capture some of the remaining heterogeneity within these groups, I disaggregate both Hispanics and Asians into three ethnic components. Hispanics are subdivided into Mexican, Puerto Rican and Other Hispanic. Asians are subdivided into Japanese, Chinese and Other Asian.[7] Like nativity, a family's race-ethnicity is determined by that of the head of the family household. While groups such as non-Hispanic whites and Hispanics, or Chinese and Japanese differ less by racial than ethnic characteristics, for convenience, throughout this volume I refer to this variable as "race."

STRATEGIES OF DATA ANALYSIS

To study immigrant-native differentials in poverty and public assistance utilization, I pursue the following research strategy. The analyses of poverty and welfare use are pursued separately, but they unfold in parallel fashion. Both begin with descriptive tabulations that speak to important questions regarding immigrant-native differentials in poverty and public assistance utilization and how these differentials are patterned across key race groups and year-of-arrival cohorts. Of paramount importance in these tables is year of observation, for it is this dimension that will yield initial insights into the changes brought on by the new immigration. Year of arrival also is important as it allows me to discern trends in poverty and welfare use for real and synthetic immigrant cohorts.

Once these baseline observations are fully established, I turn to a multivariate strategy to explore the determinants of the propensity of a family to be poor or to receive welfare income.[8] These models determine the relative effects of a host of individual and family characteristics. The primary concern in these multivariate analyses is the net effect of nativity on poverty and welfare utilization.

In addition to the effect of nativity, another critical element in these multivariate analyses is provided by year of observation. This enables me to establish whether a given group, recent immigrants, for example, has become *more* likely to be poor or to receive welfare in the years since the 1965 immigration reform. In the multivariate analyses, I incorporate year of observation in the following manner. When the 1960, 1970 and 1980 family files are concatenated into one "stacked" data file, year of observation becomes an independent variable. Interacted with nativity, period interactions establish whether there has been a statistically significant change over time in the effect of nativity on families' poverty risks or welfare receipt.

The estimation procedure employed in these multivariate analyses is logit regression. Unlike Ordinary Least Squares (OLS), logit analysis yields unbiased and efficient estimates of binomial dependent variables (Hanushek and Jackson 1977). Transformed logit coefficients (Petersen 1985) reflect the effect of a unit change in the predictors on the probability that a family will be poor or will receive welfare. The models are estimated via maximum likelihood techniques using the GLIM System (Baker and Nelder 1978). In chapter 8, OLS regression is used on the subsample of welfare recipients to estimate total family public assistance receipt.

THREE POTENTIAL BIASES

Three possible sources of bias should be acknowledged. These are (1) the presence of undocumented immigrants in the data, (2) improved census coverage of minority populations in 1980 and (3) sample selection due to return migration. I address these in order.

The U.S. Census Bureau (Warren and Passel 1983) has estimated that over 2 million undocumented aliens were counted in the 1980 Census. Any resulting bias will be largely restricted to the Mexican-origin population. Census Bureau estimates suggest that about half of the undocumented immigrants counted in the 1980 census are Mexican and that two-thirds of the Mexicans enumerated in the census who claimed they arrived between 1975 and 1980 may have been in this country illegally. The likely direction of this bias is to overstate the amount of poverty and understate the degree of public assistance utilization among *legal* recent Mexican immigrants. This is because, compared to their legal counterparts, undocumented immigrants are known to have more marginal occupations (Cafferty, et al. 1983) and because their welfare use is known to be low (Council of Economic Advisors 1986).

An obvious corrective measure would be to exclude all undocumented immigrants from the analysis. Unfortunately, it is impossible to differentiate between documented and undocumented immigrants because no such question was included in the census (it is unlikely such an item would be valid anyway, due to high nonresponse or response error). Hence, no corrective measures are taken. Rather, I pay careful attention to this potential source of bias when interpreting my results for Hispanics in general and Mexicans in particular.

There are two reasons why the presence of undocumented Mexicans is so great on the 1980 Census. First, undocumented flows were known to increase substantially during the 1970s (Bean, et al. 1986). Second, compared to previous censuses, in 1980 the Census Bureau achieved much better coverage of minority populations (U.S. Bureau of the Census 1982). This constitutes a second potential source of bias in this analysis.

A subpopulation that has historically been undercounted in the U.S. Census is the poor (Hauser 1981). The poor are more transient and more likely to live in residences that can be overlooked by census enumerators. Today, the problem of homelessness has obvious implications for census coverage. That a greater percent of minority groups are poor helps explain why they are undercounted to a greater degree than nonminorities. The problem of undercounting is worse for some minorities than for others. Taking the worst case, in the 1980 Census, black men aged 20–24 were undercounted by 19% (U.S. Bureau of the Census 1982). The coverage of minorities improved between 1970 and 1980. This suggests a similar improvement in the coverage of the poor that could overstate, to some degree, the change in poverty over time. However, to the extent that families (the unit of analysis here) are undercounted less than single individuals, undercounting is less problematic for this study.

A third potential source of bias is sample selection through emigration.

Not all who immigrate to the United States remain here. Historically, emigration rates (the percent of a cohort of immigrants who ultimately emigrate during their lifetime) have been estimated to be one-third (Jasso and Rosenzweig 1982). This emigration rate was also found to apply to the 1960s (Warren and Peck 1980). Guillermina Jasso and Mark Rosenzweig (1982) estimated an emigration rate for the 1971 immigrant cohort to be closer to 50% (greater for Hispanics than Asians). Just as immigration is a selective process (Chiswick 1979), so too is emigration. To the extent that the returnees are disproportionately represented by those who have been economically unsuccessful in the United States, the immigrants who remain behind will appear unusually better off by comparison. Here again, I have not attempted to correct for this problem, but call attention to this potential source of bias when inferring assimilation from real and synthetic immigrant cohort comparisons. This sample selection is less problematic for the baseline and multivariate analyses of poverty and welfare utilization. In the former, I am interested in establishing actual aggregate rates and am unconcerned about the effects of unmeasured predictors. In the latter, I control for some of the factors—such as education and employment—known to affect emigration decisions.

NOTES

1. The family files were developed in conjunction with the Department of Health and Human Services research project titled "Research on the Labor Market and Program Participation of Hispanics, Immigrants and Southeast Asian Refugees," professors Marta Tienda and Gary Sandefur coprincipal investigators.

2. The foregoing discussion draws from Martin Rein (1976) and Bradley Schiller (1980, pp. 7–22).

3. It is interesting to note that survey data show that nonpoor Americans feel a poverty-level income is quite adequate to provide a family with the minimum necessities of life (Schiller 1980, p. 21).

4. To tie their relative poverty thresholds to the extant distribution of income, Ross, et al. (1987) calculated a "median welfare ratio"—the ratio of median household income to the average absolute poverty line. This was computed on households with nonnegative income, whose head was employed. A household was defined as poor if the ratio of its income to its absolute poverty line was less than 44% of the median welfare ratio.

5. In the analyses to follow, the values of 44% of the median welfare ratio are 0.931, 1.25 and 1.37 in 1959, 1969 and 1979, respectively.

6. At a theoretical level, relative deprivation has been linked to frustration, alienation and aggression (Simpson and Yinger 1985).

7. I would agree that a further subdivision of Other Hispanic (e.g., Cuban, Central American, etc.) and Other Asian (Korean, Vietnamese, etc.) might well be illuminating. However, data constraints rendered this alternative impossible.

8. The conceptual background for the specific models estimated is introduced in the chapters in which they appear.

4

Poverty among Immigrants: Descriptive Results

Public concern over poverty among immigrants has been voiced periodically throughout the entire history of American immigration. As noted in chapter 2, the exclusion of impoverished newcomers is one of the oldest and long-lasting goals of U.S. immigration policy. Since the advent of the most recent new immigration, concern over immigrant poverty has once again surfaced in popular media and in congressional debates. Despite the historical and current centrality of this issue, surprisingly little research has studied poverty per se among immigrants to the United States. In this chapter, I present an initial foray into this topic.

To recapitulate, in chapter 2 I proposed several reasons why immigrant poverty may have increased as a result of the 1965 amendments to the Immigration and Nationality Act. For example, the 1965 legislation prompted a shift toward Third World countries of origin, resulting in immigrant cohorts with a greater concentration of racial minorities and immigrants with less transferable occupational skills. Or, the greater priority placed on family reunification over labor market skills as criteria of entry may have brought to our shores less-skilled and less economically motivated immigrants.

It makes little sense to explore these issues, however, until baseline trends are established. The basic question guiding this chapter is: Has there been an increase in poverty among immigrants over the past 20 years? By providing descriptive information on trends in the level of poverty among immigrant and native families in 1959, 1969 and 1979, I answer this and other simple, yet critical, questions.

The chapter opens with a series of tables describing absolute poverty. Absolute poverty occurs when a family lacks the income needed to afford a minimum standard of living.[1] Conditional absolute poverty rates are computed for native and immigrant families. Because of the substantive importance of trends among the most recent arrivals, immigrant families are disaggregated into years since immigration categories: whether the head arrived 0–5, 6–10, 11–20 or over 20 years before the census. I will compare poverty rates among these arrival cohorts and present trends within them over time. To capture compositional changes, the poverty rates are then presented separately for four key race groups: whites, blacks, Hispanics and Asians. A family's race is determined by that of its head.[2] The first section concludes with a closer examination of trends among the most recent immigrants—those arriving five or fewer years before the 1960, 1970 and 1980 Censuses.

The next section establishes patterns of *relative* poverty across these race and nativity categories. Relative poverty is tied to the level of income inequality in society and reflects the degree to which families have much less than average family income. In this section, I document whether immigrant families in general, and recent arrivals in particular, are disproportionately likely to be poor in this relative sense when compared to native families.

Earnings comprise the majority of total income among U.S. families, and employment is a crucial factor keeping many of them from being poor (Tienda and Jensen 1988). To establish the degree to which this is true among immigrant versus native families, the final analytic section of this chapter presents "one-earner" poverty rates, that is, the poverty rates that would obtain if the earnings of those other than the head were excluded from family income. I establish the ameliorative impact of multiple earners by comparing these hypothetical poverty rates to the actual absolute poverty rates.

BASELINE TRENDS IN ABSOLUTE POVERTY

Table 4.1 documents basic trends in poverty for the period 1959–1979. This table provides absolute poverty rates for native and immigrant families and disaggregates the latter into years-since-immigration categories. The first row of this table shows a downward trend in poverty rates among all families. Most of this decline took place between 1959 and 1969, when the rates declined from 18.0 to 10.6%. This improvement is well known and has been reported elsewhere (Plotnick and Skidmore 1975; Kerbo 1983, p. 298; O'Hare 1985). The progress against poverty during the 1960s has been attributed to a number of factors, particularly the expansion of cash assistance programs (Blumberg 1980)[3] and a relatively strong economy (O'Hare 1985). Poverty rates continued to improve slowly during the 1970s, as evidenced by the decline to 9.3% by 1979.

The next two rows of Table 4.1 contain poverty rates for native and immigrant families, separately. First, native families exhibit the same mono-

Table 4.1
Absolute Poverty Rate for Families by Immigration Cohort and Year

Head's Nativity and Years Since Immigration	1959	1969	1979
All Families[a]	18.0	10.6	9.3
All Natives[a]	18.2	10.4	8.9
All Immigrants[a]	15.6	12.9	14.0
0-5 Years[a]	16.8	17.1	27.7
Over 5 Years[a]	15.6	12.4	11.7
0-5 Years		15.9	26.7
6-10 Years		11.1	15.0
11-20 Years		8.2	11.8
Over 20 Years		11.5	7.0

Source: U.S. Bureau of the Census. 1960, 1970 and 1980 Public Use Samples. Table first published in Jensen (1988).

[a]Includes Puerto Ricans.

tonic decline observed for all families. In 1959, 1969 and 1979, the poverty rates for natives were, respectively, 18.2, 10.4 and 8.9%. Immigrant families show a decline in poverty between 1959 (15.6%) and 1969 (12.9%), but a slight increase by 1979 (14.0%). Overall, immigrant families did not share in the progress against poverty nearly to the extent that native families did.

Within-year differences between immigrants and natives show that poverty among immigrant families was below that of natives in 1959 only (15.6 versus 18.2%). Sometime during the 1960s, this differential reversed itself. The poverty rate for immigrant families exceeded that of natives by 24% (2.5 percentage points) in 1969, and 57% (5.1 percentage points) in 1979.

In view of the history of immigration to the United States during this century, these results are intuitively reasonable. That immigrant poverty was comparatively low in 1959 is consistent with the historical record, which shows that these immigrants were largely white and relatively successful (Lieberson 1980). Moreover, the preference system established in 1952 almost ensured that only the most highly skilled were allowed to immigrate. That immigrant poverty surpassed that of natives during the 1960s could be explained by the following. As the new immigration proceeded and the flow of immigration increased, the stock of foreign-born heads of families quickly became younger, more nonwhite and less economically selective. These heads would have had less time to adjust and may have been faced with additional barriers due to race. While I address these possibilities to some extent in the analyses below, a more rigorous treatment awaits the multivariate analyses in chapter 5.

Thus far I have established that the decline in poverty among immigrant families during the 1960s was considerably slower than that for natives. While poverty among the latter continued to decline by 1979, immigrant poverty increased. Some insight into these observations can be obtained by comparing across years-since-immigration categories (the last six rows of Table 4.1). The steady and dramatic *increase* in absolute poverty among recent immigrant families (those with heads who arrived five or fewer years before the census) is noteworthy. Their poverty rates rose from 16.8 to 17.1 to 27.7% over the period. This increase certainly contributed to the rise in poverty among immigrant families overall between 1969 and 1979. However, the most recent immigrants are not solely responsible for the increase among all immigrants. Two other duration groups—those who immigrated 6–10 and 11–20 years before the census—had higher poverty rates in 1979 compared to 1969.

To summarize, poverty among immigrant families increased over the 1970s, a period when poverty among native families declined. Most of this increase was due to greater poverty among those immigrants who arrived after the 1965 immigration reforms. This would seem to support allegations that the United States has experienced an increasing prevalence of impoverished newcomers, particularly in recent years.

Table 4.1 also contains evidence of economic assimilation. I assume that a declining poverty rate among immigrants is a reasonable indicator of this process. Reading vertically, in both 1969 and 1979, those families who had been in the United States for 11–20 years had lower poverty rates than those here 6–10 years. The latter group, in turn, had lower rates than recent immigrant families—those here 0–5 years.[4] In chapter 3, I cautioned that declining poverty rates between these synthetic immigrant cohorts might not be an indicator of assimilation, but an artifact of selective emigration, aging or declining immigrant skills. The latter effect can be controlled by examining real immigrant cohorts. Only one such comparison exists in Table 4.1. In 1969, the poverty rate for those here 0–10 years (averaging the 0–5 and 6–10 year immigrants) was roughly 13.5%. By 1979 this same cohort had ten years to adjust and their poverty rate was 11.8% (the 11–20 year group). Thus, there is evidence of a decline in poverty for this real immigrant cohort.

Disaggregating Table 4.1 by race (reported in Table 4.2) documents how the above patterns of poverty among families differ for four major racial groups—whites, blacks, Asians and Hispanics.[5] That the immigration experiences of these groups differ in many respects provides alternative expectations for trends in poverty. Modern day white immigrants have traditionally entered on the merits of their job skills, though there is evidence that they increasingly took advantage of the family reunification provisions of the 1965 immigration legislation, perhaps resulting in aggregate deterioration of their background characteristics (Keely 1975). Thus, while I expect poverty among white immigrant families to be comparatively low, there may be evidence of a secular increase in their poverty rates. Hispanic immigrants (Mexicans and Puerto Ricans in particular) have typically endured more tenuous economic circumstances because of their more marginal employment (Bentley 1981). Comparatively high poverty rates are expected for Hispanics in general and Hispanic immigrants in particular. Asians, who have taken advantage of the occupational preference categories, have enjoyed some measure of economic success (Cafferty, et al. 1983). I expect Asian poverty rates to be low. However, Asian immigrants may show some increase over time due to the influx of Indo-Chinese refugees during the late 1970s. Black immigrants, while few in number, have likewise entered with marketable employment skills (Keely 1975). However, like Hispanics, black immigrants also face the manifold disadvantages associated with color (Tienda and Jensen 1988). Although black immigrant poverty should be far less than that of natives, it will unlikely be as low as that among white and Asian immigrant families.

The top row of Table 4.2 highlights the economic disadvantages of color. Black and Hispanic families, the largest American minority groups, had far greater poverty rates in each year than white or Asian families. Blacks were the most destitute. Nearly half of all black families were poor in 1959, as compared to only 14% of Asian families. Not far behind were Hispanic families, whose poverty rate was 35% in 1959.

Table 4.1 documented a continuous decline in poverty among families across the three censuses. Viewed separately by race, Table 4.2 shows that the same decline occurred among all but Asian families. Poverty among the latter increased from 8.8 to 10.4% between 1969 and 1979. The extent to which this is due to increasing poverty among Asian immigrants is discussed below.

Looking next at all immigrant families (without regard to years since immigration) the third row of Table 4.2 reveals a decline in poverty between 1959 and 1969 for all four racial groups. However, a similar decrease between 1969 and 1979 occurs only for white immigrant families—the rates for the other three groups either remained the same (Hispanics) or increased (blacks and Asians). Thus, whereas poverty for the population as a whole continued to decline slowly during the 1970s, this decline was *not* enjoyed among minority immigrants.

In regard to the trends in gross differences *between* immigrant and native

Table 4.2
Absolute Poverty Rates for Families by Immigration Cohort, Year and Race

Head's Nativity and Years Since Immigration	White			Black			Hispanic			Asian		
	1959	1969	1979	1959	1969	1979	1959	1969	1979	1959	1969	1979
All Families[a]	14.5	8.0	6.4	48.1	30.1	25.9	34.9	21.8	21.6	13.8	8.8	10.4
All Natives[a]	14.7	8.0	6.3	48.4	30.3	26.2	35.9	20.3	19.5	7.9	5.9	5.1
All Immigrants[a]	12.7	9.3	7.1	17.7	15.2	18.7	33.7	23.7	23.7	21.4	12.2	12.6
0-5 Years[a]	7.6	10.7	23.7	12.5	13.5	27.2	35.6	24.8	32.5	35.7	17.7	26.1
Over 5 Years[a]	13.0	9.2	5.5	18.1	15.9	17.0	33.4	23.4	22.2	20.0	10.5	5.2
0-5 Years	--	10.7	23.7	--	13.5	27.2	--	22.7	30.0	--	17.7	26.1
6-10 Years	--	9.5	6.8	--	8.0	16.2	--	13.1	23.3	--	13.5	5.7
11-20 Years	--	4.7	6.3	--	7.1	13.2	--	20.8	18.4	--	11.2	5.0
Over 20 Years	--	10.4	5.2	--	15.8	23.4	--	24.1	14.0	--	9.3	4.9

Source: U.S. Bureau of the Census. 1960, 1970 and 1980 Public Use Samples. Table first published in Jensen (1988).

[a] Includes Puerto Ricans.

families (comparing the second and third rows of Table 4.2), three patterns emerge. First, among white and Hispanic families, there are no glaring differences between immigrant and native poverty rates. For both, natives had higher poverty in 1959, while immigrants were slightly more likely to be poor in 1969 and 1979. Second, as expected, among black families, natives were much worse off in all three years. However, because the rates for black immigrants remained about the same, while those for black natives steadily declined, the immigrant advantage declined over time. Third, Asian immigrant families display much greater absolute poverty than their native counterparts, though this disparity was particularly great in 1959. "Major public concerns with the 'new immigrants' have been centered almost exclusively on Hispanics" (Cafferty, et al. 1983, p. 100). However, I have shown that, compared to Hispanics, the extent to which immigrant poverty exceeded that of natives was far greater among Asians—the other major racial component of the new immigration.

Table 4.1 revealed that poverty rates among recent immigrants—those arriving less than five years before the census—increased considerably between 1959 and 1979. Table 4.2 shows that this monotonic increase occurred for recent white immigrants—whose poverty rates increased from 7.6 to 10.7 to 23.7% during the period—and recent black immigrants—whose corresponding rates were 12.5, 13.5 and 27.2%. Recent Hispanic and Asian immigrant families followed a distinctly parabolic pattern. Hispanic poverty declined from 35.6 to 24.8% between 1959 and 1969, but sharply increased to 32.5% by 1979. Recent Asian immigrant poverty virtually halved over the 1960s (35.7 down to 17.7%), but showed an impressive increase by 1979 (26.1%). On balance, these results offer further support for assertions of increasing poverty among the newest immigrants. Due to their importance to the thrust of this study, recent immigrant families are examined more closely below.

Table 4.2 provides two additional series of comparisons. The first series speaks to the same questions of assimilation addressed in reference to Table 4.1. Briefly, the vertical comparisons in the last four rows of Table 4.2, which represent synthetic immigrant cohorts, indicate a decline in poverty with time spent in the United States. Focusing on the only real immigrant cohort comparisons available in these tables (diagonally comparing those residing in the United States 0–5 and 6–10 years as of 1969 to those in this country 11–20 years as of 1979), there is evidence of a sizable decline in poverty among whites (whose rates decline from roughly 10.1 to 6.3%) and Asians (15.6 down to 5.0%). No similar evidence of assimilation is indicated for Hispanics (17.9 up to 18.4%) or blacks (10.8 up to 13.2%), both of which revealed *greater* poverty rates in 1979 compared to ten years prior.

It is noteworthy that the selectivity bias and aging effects inherent in interpreting these results as evidence of assimilation work in the direction of decreasing the poverty rate of those here longer. For example, immigrants in this country a longer period of time will tend to be older. Because age is negatively associated with poverty, these immigrants should have lower poverty rates. That poverty should have *increased* by 1979 among those who immigrated during the 1960s is, thus, all the more surprising. In that it is immigrants of color—blacks and Hispanics—who show this pattern, these results square with the work of Milton Gordon (1964) and others who assert that race can inhibit assimilation.

The second series of comparisons monitors changes between 1969 and 1979 in the prevalence of poverty among immigrants who have the same duration of residence in the United States. I refer to the horizontal comparisons in the last four rows of Table 4.2. Again, distinct patterns emerge for the four race groups.

Beginning with black families, poverty rates increased for all duration categories. In general these differences were comparatively sharp, reflecting a marked deterioration in the economic status of black immigrants between 1969 and 1979. For example, the poverty rate for black immigrant families who arrived 6–10 years before the census rose from 8% in 1969 to 16% in 1979. While the majority of black immigrants were from the West Indies, the immigration of African-origin blacks increased dramatically between 1968 and 1984 (Reid 1986). If anything, a greater concentration of black immigrants from Africa would suggest *lower* poverty rates among them, because they are more apt to take advantage of occupational preference categories than their West Indian counterparts.[6] Moreover, this country-of-origin shift cannot explain the increase in poverty among all duration categories of black immigrants.

Hispanic family poverty rates decreased for those who resided in the United States 11 or more years, but increased among those with 0–10 years of residence in the United States. Thus, defining recent immigrants more broadly as those who arrived *10* or fewer years before the census, these results show a marked rise in poverty among recent Hispanics in 1980 as opposed to their counterparts in 1970. This rise offset a decrease between 1970 and 1980 among those with 11 or more years in the United States. These divergent trends resulted in little intercensal change in poverty rates among *all* Hispanic immigrants.

Among Asian immigrant families, poverty rates generally declined for these specific years-since-immigration categories. A glaring exception is the sharp increase in poverty between 1969 and 1979 among recent Asian immigrants. This reflects the sizable flows of Indo-Chinese refugees who entered after the 1975 fall of the U.S.-backed government in South Vietnam. Finally, white immigrant families showed a haphazard pattern of change between 1969 and 1979. On balance, these comparisons corroborate the notion that poverty among immigrants increased between 1969 and 1979 mostly because of higher rates among the more recent arrivals. I now examine these most recent immigrants in more detail.

Table 4.3 presents poverty rates for recent immigrants by race and year. It also includes the relative racial composition of recent immigrants under the column headed "Percent of Recent Immigrants." This table establishes the effect of the changing racial composition of recent immigrants on the overall increase of poverty among them. The tabulations reveal a number of reasons why poverty increased continuously between 1959 and 1979 for families with recent immigrant heads. First, despite the fact that they represent a decreasing proportion of all recent immigrants, the poverty rate for recent white immigrants increased monotonically over time. This outcome supports Charles Keely's (1975) assertion of a gradual decline in the economic viability of white immigrants. Because white families comprised a sizable proportion of all recent immigrant families as late as 1980 (31%), their increase had a strong positive impact on the poverty rate for all recent immigrants.

That the increase in poverty among recent white immigrant families was an important contributor to the increase among *all* recent immigrant families is seen in the following exercise. Replacing the 1979 white poverty rate (23.7%) with their rate in 1959 (7.6%) yields a weighted average for all recent immigrants in 1979 of only 22.5%, which compares to the actual value of 27.7%. In other words, regardless of the shift in the racial composition of immigrants, had poverty among recent white immigrants not increased, then poverty among *all* recent immigrants in 1979 would have been almost 20% less. There is evidence also that the effects of the sudden increase in poverty among recent white immigrants was offset by their declining representation among all recent arrivals. Applying the 1979 poverty rates to the 1959 racial distribution of recent immigrants yields an overall rate of 26.4%, not appreciably different from the actual 1979 rate of 27.7%. In other words, while some decry the shift toward Third World countries of origin, had the origin composition *not* changed since 1959, poverty rates among recent immigrants would still have increased to the levels they eventually did. Again, this is largely due to the sudden increase in poverty among all recent immigrants—whites included.

A second reason why poverty increased among recent immigrants between 1959 and 1979 is compositional. Despite the fact that poverty *decreased* between 1959 and 1969 for Hispanic and Asian families, these groups (especially Hispanics) had comparatively high poverty rates and comprised twice the share of all recent immigrants in 1969 than they did in 1959. Finally, it should be stressed that poverty increased between 1969 and 1979 among all four race groups of recent immigrants.

To summarize, Tables 4.1, 4.2 and 4.3 document a general decline in absolute poverty levels in the United States between 1959 and 1979. This decline appeared to be sharpest during the 1960s. By disaggregating poverty rates according to nativity, Table 4.1 shows that natives participated more in the overall decline than did immigrants. In fact, poverty increased for im-

Table 4.3
Absolute Poverty Rate for Families with Recent Immigrant Heads[a]

	1959		1969		1979	
	Percent in Poverty	Percent of Recent Immigrants	Percent in Poverty	Percent of Recent Immigrants	Percent in Poverty	Percent of Recent Immigrants
White	7.6	66.3	10.7	46.4	23.7	31.5
Black	12.5	1.2	13.5	4.9	27.2	5.6
Hispanic	35.6	29.1	24.8	39.9	32.5	34.5
Asian	35.7	3.4	17.7	8.7	26.1	28.4
	16.7	100.0	17.1	99.9[b]	27.7	100.0

Source: U.S. Bureau of the Census. 1960, 1970 and 1980 Public Use Samples. Table first published in Jensen (1988).

[a]Includes Puerto Ricans.

[b]Does not sum to 100 due to rounding error.

migrants between 1969 and 1979. Lending some credence to arguments that the new immigration has been characterized by an increased flow of impoverished immigrants, Table 4.1 shows that much of the increase in poverty among immigrant families between 1969 and 1979 is due to the sharply greater deprivation among the most recent arrivals. Among recent arrivals, the sharpest rise in absolute poverty between 1969 and 1979 is seen among white families with blacks not far behind. This dispels, somewhat, the impression that Latin American immigrants have been the prime contributors to rising poverty among immigrants. To be sure, among recent immigrant families, Hispanics have the highest poverty rates, but their increase between 1969 and 1979 was considerably less than that seen among Asians, blacks and whites.

Finally, an increase in poverty among recent immigrants would be less cause for concern if there were evidence to demonstrate their rapid rise out of poverty that presumably typified previous immigrants (Segalman and Basu 1981). While our interest in the outcome of the 1970–1980 cohort awaits the 1990 PUS, Table 4.2 revealed a *rise* in poverty among black and Hispanic immigrants after ten years of U.S. residence. These immigrants may be experiencing a more chronic form of poverty, in which case close monitoring is required in the years ahead.

AN ALTERNATIVE DEFINITION: RELATIVE POVERTY

To this point, I have analyzed trends in absolute poverty, which reflect changes in the percent of families who lack the income necessary to achieve a minimum standard of living. As discussed in chapter 3, an alternative definition of poverty compares family income to the average income in the population—relative poverty. In this analysis, and in general terms, I define relative poverty as annual family income below 44% of white median annual income. This definition has been used elsewhere (Ross, et al. 1987) and is detailed in chapter 3.

The social, psychological, microeconomic and macroeconomic costs of widespread absolute poverty are well studied (Ferman, et al. 1976). These include, for example, inadequate diet and health care, which lead to lower productivity and lower intelligence in children; poor housing and education facilities; and diminished chances for upward intragenerational and intergenerational mobility. Less well known are the distinct costs of relative poverty. These may include feelings of alienation, frustration, low self-esteem and pessimism (Kerbo 1983; Simpson and Yinger 1985). It is for this reason that relative poverty should be of concern to policymakers and why I document immigrant-native differentials in relative poverty here.

Relative poverty is not a mere transformation of absolute poverty. The trends and patterns of each measure can differ due to changes in the level of income inequality over time or due to differences between groups in mean income. Groups with lower aggregate income are more likely to reveal differences between their absolute and relative rates due to greater sensitivity to slight poverty threshold changes. Compared to absolute poverty, I expect the rise in relative poverty among recent immigrants to be more pronounced—that the new immigration has swelled the ranks of the relative poor faster than it has the absolute poor.

Table 4.4 presents relative poverty rates in the same format as that of Table 4.2. Because the level of income inequality in the United States remained remarkably stable between 1959 and 1979 (Kerbo 1983), relative poverty declined much more slowly than did absolute poverty. For example, while the absolute poverty rate for all white families declined from 15.0 to 8.0 to 6.4% in 1959, 1969 and 1979, respectively (see Table 4.2), the corresponding figures for relative poverty were 12.9, 11.2 and 11.0%. Also, whereas absolute poverty for Hispanic families declined monotonically, relative poverty declined slightly between 1959 and 1969, but then increased by 1979. Thus, although a greater percent of families were able to achieve the minimum standard of living by 1969, because income inequality changed little between 1959 and 1969, those at the bottom of the income distribution were no closer to acquiring the lifestyles of families at the middle and upper income percentiles. These results suggest that the progress against poverty of the 1960s was due more to a rise in real income in the entire population, than from any narrowing of income inequality. If anything, it was the middle and upper income groups who disproportionately benefited from the rise in real income.

The 20 years under study also witnessed a divergence in the level of absolute versus relative poverty. Nonetheless, many of the patterns of differences in absolute poverty between immigrant cohorts and across time are also seen in the relative poverty rates. For example, Asian immigrant relative poverty exceeds that for their native counterparts and relative poverty rates tend to be lower among those immigrant families who have been in the United States a longer period of time.

However, there are some informative differences in the patterns of absolute versus relative poverty. Because black and Hispanic families have lower incomes (Tienda and Jensen 1988), the increase in relative poverty over time among recent black and Hispanic immigrant families is far more pronounced. These groups slid further behind the average income of whites over time. While absolute poverty among recent black immigrant families roughly doubled between 1959 and 1979, the relative rates show a nearly ninefold increase (4.2 to 37.6%). Among recent Hispanic families, absolute poverty declined overall between 1959 and 1979, but their relative poverty increased steadily over the period. In fact, nearly half (46.5%) of all recent Hispanic immigrant families were poor in 1979 according to the relative definition.

Recent white and Asian immigrants also show a somewhat steeper rise in

Table 4.4
Relative Poverty Rates for Families by Immigration Cohort, Year and Race

Head's Nativity and Years Since Immigration	White			Black			Hispanic			Asian		
	1959	1969	1979	1959	1969	1979	1959	1969	1979	1959	1969	1979
All Families[a]	12.9	11.2	11.0	45.1	38.5	36.5	32.2	29.8	31.4	11.9	11.6	15.7
All Natives[a]	13.1	11.0	10.9	45.4	38.8	36.8	33.6	27.9	27.6	6.8	8.0	8.3
All Immigrants[a]	11.1	13.6	12.4	15.9	20.8	27.3	30.5	32.4	35.3	18.6	16.0	18.7
0-5 Years[a]	6.2	14.8	31.6	4.2	21.1	37.6	32.6	33.7	46.5	30.0	21.6	34.4
Over 5 Years[a]	11.4	13.5	10.5	16.7	20.6	25.1	30.2	32.1	33.3	17.4	14.2	10.2
0-5 Years	--	14.8	31.6	--	21.1	37.6	--	31.6	44.5	--	21.6	34.4
6-10 Years	--	13.6	14.6	--	14.8	26.1	--	20.3	35.9	--	17.4	10.7
11-20 Years	--	6.5	10.4	--	7.1	18.8	--	28.5	29.6	--	16.1	9.6
Over 20 Years	--	15.4	10.2	--	21.3	33.4	--	32.2	24.9	--	12.4	10.3

Source: U.S. Bureau of the Census. 1960, 1970 and 1980 Public Use Samples.

[a] Includes Puerto Ricans.

their relative as compared to absolute poverty between 1959 and 1979. Recent Asian families experienced declines in absolute rates between 1959 and 1979 (35.7 down to 26.1%) while their relative poverty increased (30.0 to 34.4%).

To summarize, while the percent of recent immigrant families who lack the income needed to subsist has increased, the percent of recent immigrant families with less than average annual income increased considerably faster—especially among minorities. Thus, the rise in poverty among recent immigrants to the United States is far more pronounced when considered in relative rather than absolute terms. Arguably, the rise in absolute poverty is a more pressing problem because the standard of living affordable at the absolute poverty threshold is dangerously meager (Schiller 1980). The social and economic implications of relative poverty are less well understood, yet its increase among recent immigrants over the past 20 years warrants careful consideration. Perhaps more alarming than the aggregate increase in relative poverty among immigrants is the notion that there may be a large component of the immigrant stream that is quite destitute in relative terms. This possibility is supported by evidence showing a distinct bifurcation in the occupational skills of the newest arrivals (Tienda, et al. 1984).

MULTIPLE EARNERS AND POVERTY: A DESCRIPTIVE TREATMENT

Various theories explaining the existence and nature of poverty have been put forward over the years. Harold Kerbo (1983) suggests four basic views of poverty—popular, culture-of-poverty, situational and structural—that differ with respect to the causal primacy placed on individual versus social structural factors. Proponents of all these views would concur, however, that participation in the labor force is perhaps the single most important determinant of poverty. As Herbert Gans (1982, p. 312) writes, "the best remedy for poverty is a large supply of jobs."

The spread of work across family members is an important strategy for making up income shortfalls. A family's battle against poverty can hinge on its ability to fully utilize its labor force potential. This highlights the importance of considering the earnings of family members other than the head—referred to herein as "multiple earners"—in determining family poverty.

Families with more complex nonnuclear structures, particularly those with extended adults, have greater flexibility in allocating domestic and labor market responsibilities among its members (Tienda and Jensen 1986; Tienda and Angel 1982; Angel and Tienda 1982). Because I find that immigrant families, particularly those with recent heads, are more likely to have extended adult family members present, it is reasonable to assume that the ameliorative impact of multiple earners will be greater for immigrant than native families.

To address this issue, Table 4.5 presents one-earner poverty rates, that is, the hypothetical absolute poverty rates that would obtain if the earnings of family members other than the head were subtracted from total family income. Like Table 4.2, the rates are conditioned on years since immigration, year and race. That these constrained poverty rates are higher than the actual rates reported in Table 4.2 is neither surprising nor interesting—clearly family poverty would increase if some of their earnings were eliminated. More informative are the differences between the race and immigrant groups in the degree to which these hypothetical one-earner poverty rates exceed the corresponding actual absolute rates. Accordingly, rather than discuss Table 4.5, I focus on Table 4.6.

The cell entries in Table 4.6 represent the percentage increase in poverty that would obtain if the earnings of those other than the head were subtracted from family income. Thus, an entry of 100 signifies a 100% increase in (or doubling of) absolute poverty if only the head's earnings is counted. Examination of the second and third rows of this table (the overall immigrant-native comparison) reveals that for all three census years, immigrants show greater increases in poverty when nonhead's earnings are ignored. The presence of multiple earners is of greater importance in keeping immigrant families out of poverty compared to natives. To take an example, in 1969, the absolute poverty rate for white immigrant families was 9.3% while the one-earner poverty rate was 16.9%, or 81.7% greater. By contrast, for white native families in 1969, the corresponding figures are 8.0% (absolute) and 13.3% (one-earner), or 66.2% greater. The finding that multiple earners are more important to immigrant than native families for achieving subsistence-level family income obtains for white, black and Hispanic families, although there are differences between these race groups in the degree to which this is true.

Asians stand as an exception to this generalization. In 1959 and 1979, it is the Asian *native* families who reveal a greater percentage increase in absolute poverty when nonhead's earnings are disregarded. In 1969, Asian families are consistent with the other three race groups; relatively more immigrant families are kept above poverty due to the contributions of multiple earners.

The first row of Table 4.6 reveals that the ameliorative effects of multiple earners for keeping families above poverty are especially strong among Asians. This is consistent with the high labor force participation and industriousness that have been the cornerstones of Asian success in the U.S. economy. That native Asians should benefit more in this regard squares with the findings of Robert Gardner, et al. (1985), who document that labor force participation rates among native-born Asian women are generally higher than those of their foreign-born counterparts.

Because of the disruptive effects of international migration and the profound social and economic adjustments required, recent immigrant families

Table 4.5
One-Earner Poverty Rates[a] for Families by Immigration Cohort, Year and Race

Head's Nativity and Years Since Immigration	White 1959	White 1969	White 1979	Black 1959	Black 1969	Black 1979	Hispanic 1959	Hispanic 1969	Hispanic 1979	Asian 1959	Asian 1969	Asian 1979
All Families[b]	22.1	13.5	11.4	60.8	43.5	39.3	47.2	31.1	32.8	27.6	17.0	19.9
All Natives[b]	21.7	13.3	11.3	61.1	43.7	39.5	44.0	28.7	28.5	17.6	10.7	10.4
All Immigrants[b]	26.7	16.9	13.1	39.2	27.4	32.6	51.2	34.2	37.2	40.7	24.5	23.7
0-5 Years[b]	15.7	18.0	34.7	45.8	28.1	49.7	52.2	36.2	51.2	45.7	28.0	39.4
Over 5 Years[b]	27.2	16.8	11.0	38.8	27.2	29.0	51.1	33.8	34.8	40.2	23.4	15.2
0-5 Years	--	18.0	34.7	--	28.1	49.7	--	35.1	50.0	--	28.0	39.4
6-10 Years	--	13.3	14.5	--	22.7	30.7	--	23.8	37.8	--	19.7	15.7
11-20 Years	--	8.4	11.7	--	13.1	23.9	--	30.5	29.9	--	19.8	12.5
Over 20 Years	--	19.1	10.5	--	26.8	34.7	--	40.2	30.8	--	26.2	17.7

Source: U.S. Bureau of the Census. 1960, 1970 and 1980 Public Use Samples.

[a] One-earner poverty rate is obtained by comparing family income minus earnings of family members other than the head to the absolute poverty line.

[b] Includes Puerto Ricans.

Table 4.6
Percentage Increase in Poverty Rates for Families When Earned Income of Family Members Other Than Head Is Ignored[a]

Head's Nativity and Years Since Immigration	White			Black			Hispanic			Asian		
	1959	1969	1979	1959	1969	1979	1959	1969	1979	1959	1969	1979
All	52.4	68.8	78.1	26.4	44.5	51.7	35.2	42.7	51.8	100.0	93.2	91.3
Native	47.6	66.2	79.4	26.2	44.2	50.8	22.6	41.4	46.2	122.8	81.4	103.9
Immigrant	110.2	81.7	84.5	121.5	80.3	74.3	51.9	44.3	57.0	90.2	100.8	88.1
Recent Immigrant	106.6	68.2	46.4	266.4	108.1	82.7	46.6	46.0	57.5	28.0	58.2	51.0

Source: Tables 4.2 and 4.5.

[a]Calculated as: ((one-earner poverty - total income poverty)/total income poverty) x 100.

are frequently vulnerable to periods of economic hardship. Their ability to have multiple earners can be crucial for keeping family income above the subsistence (poverty) level. On the whole, I anticipate a greater effect of non-head's earnings on poverty for recent immigrants as compared to immigrants generally. The data in Table 4.6 offer only partial support for this expectation. The effects are greater for recent immigrants than previous immigrants, but only among Hispanic and black families in all three years and white families in 1959.

Group differences in the relative size of the disparity between absolute poverty and one-earner poverty can result from many causes. One possible explanation for why multiple earners keep a greater percentage of immigrant white, black and Hispanic families out of poverty when compared to their native counterparts is that immigrants are clustered at the low end of the income distribution.

To control for income, Table 4.7 presents the percent of families *above* the poverty line who would be poor without nonhead earnings. In other words, restricting the analysis to families who are poor without multiple earners, what percent are above absolute poverty with multiple earnings added back into total family income?

The rates in Table 4.7 reinforce the conclusion that multiple earners lift a greater share of immigrant than native families out of poverty. Again, this result obtains for all but Asian families, among which natives enjoy the greater impact of multiple earners in 1959 and 1979. For white and black families, immigrants enjoy the greater ameliorative effect. However, this gap declines over time, owing both to an increase for natives and decrease for immigrants.

The decline over time in the ameliorative effect of multiple earners among white immigrant families is particularly steep among recent immigrants. While the cause of this decline is unclear, it helps explain the sudden increase in poverty among white families with recent immigrant heads. Among black immigrant families, there is a similarly sharp decline among recent arrivals. However, even by 1979, recent black immigrants show the greatest poverty-reducing impact of multiple-earner income strategies compared to other black immigrants or to black natives. Except in 1969, when there was little difference, Hispanic immigrants benefited from multiple earners more than Hispanic natives.

On balance, these findings suggest that immigrant families strive to earn at least a subsistence-level income by capitalizing on their labor force potential. This serves to dispel stereotypes that immigrants are content to survive on the largess of the state. These results also highlight the importance of controlling for labor force commitment when predicting poverty among families. Using a multivariate framework, I again address the economic benefits of multiple earners in the following chapter.

Table 4.7
Percent of Families above Poverty among All Families below Poverty When Earned Income of Family Members Other Than Head Is Ignored

Head's Nativity and Years Since Immigration	White			Black			Hispanic			Asian		
	1959	1969	1979	1959	1969	1979	1959	1969	1979	1959	1969	1979
All Families	34.3	40.3	44.1	21.0	30.8	33.8	26.0	30.0	34.4	50.1	48.6	47.7
All Natives	32.4	40.0	44.0	20.8	30.7	33.5	18.3	29.2	31.8	54.8	45.6	50.5
All Immigrants	52.4	44.9	45.6	54.8	44.3	42.6	34.2	30.9	36.4	47.5	50.2	47.2
Recent Immigrants	51.7	40.6	32.0	72.7	51.9	44.9	31.9	31.5	36.6	21.9	37.0	34.1

Source: U.S. Bureau of the Census. 1960, 1970 and 1980 Public Use Samples

SUMMARY AND CONCLUSIONS

The goal of this chapter was to establish, in a broad and descriptive fashion, trends in the level of poverty among immigrant and native families during the 1960–1980 period. A motivating question guiding the analysis was whether poverty among immigrants was higher among the third wave. These descriptive results were disaggregated along two key stratifying dimensions: race and years since immigration. I now highlight the most important findings of this chapter.

Absolute poverty among U.S. families declined precipitously during the 1960s, but this decline was far less impressive among immigrant families. Poverty among all families continued to decline between 1969 and 1979, but increased slightly among immigrant-headed families during this decade. While poverty roughly halved among native families between 1959 and 1979, it declined by only 10% among immigrant-headed families.

Poverty increased among immigrant families between 1969 and 1979. Results for specific years-since-immigration categories revealed that recent immigrants—those who arrived five or fewer years before the census—had by far the sharpest rise in poverty. Because poverty among those who had been in the United States from 6–10 to 11–20 years before the census also increased somewhat, I conclude that the post–1965 immigrants are primarily responsible for the rise in immigrant poverty between 1969 and 1979. Poverty among immigrants *did* increase as the new immigration proceeded.

That poverty among the most recent arrivals increased considerably between 1969 and 1979 among all four race groups calls into question inferences about how changes in the race and national-origin composition of immigrants has contributed to a deterioration in their economic status. Some assert that part of the deterioration in the economic status of succeeding waves of immigrants is due to the changing racial composition of immigrants—the hallmark of the new immigration. My results reveal, however, that recent white immigrant families were a prime contributor to the overall rise in poverty among recent arrivals.

Although poverty among recent immigrants is a cause for concern, assimilation theory predicts a decline in poverty as social and economic adjustments are made. Comparisons between synthetic immigrant cohorts support this expectation of declining poverty rates with duration in the United States, although lingering biases prevent me from placing great weight on these results. An examination of a real immigrant cohort showed the following. Immigrants of color (black- and Hispanic-headed families), who immigrated during the 1960s, had *higher* poverty rates in 1979 than they did in 1969. Because the elimination of any remaining bias would result in even greater poverty rates in 1979, the deterioration in the economic status of these immigrant black and Hispanic families is robust.

Absolute poverty decreased overall due to a rise in real income. However, because the degree of income inequality was stable between 1959 and 1979, improvement in relative poverty—the degree to which families have annual incomes less than half the median—was far less impressive. When viewed in relative terms, the increase in poverty among immigrants, particularly recent immigrants, between 1969 and 1979 was far more rapid. This tendency was more pronounced among recent black and Hispanic immigrant families. While the distinct implications of rising relative poverty are unclear, those concerned with immigration and immigration policy should be aware of this more rapid increase in relative as opposed to absolute poverty.

An additional goal of this chapter was to document immigrant-native differentials in the ameliorative impact of multiple earners for lifting families above the poverty line. These results show that the earnings of family members other than the head bring a greater percentage of immigrant than native families above the poverty line. This result obtained for all but Asian families.

To conclude, these descriptive tables firmly document that poverty among immigrants *did* increase and that much of this rise is due to the sharp rise among recent arrivals. The disaggregation of these tables by race was performed to determine the degree to which this was due to the changing racial composition of immigrants. Of course, there are several other factors that could account for this increase. These include individual factors, such as age and education; family characteristics, such as headship configuration and economic dependency; and locational factors such as rural versus urban residence. I consider these factors in the next chapter using a multivariate framework.

NOTES

1. Due to differences in family need, poverty thresholds are adjusted by household composition. To take account of inflation, the absolute poverty thresholds are adjusted by the Consumer Price Index (CPI). See chapter 3 for more details on the computation of absolute poverty.

2. The operational definitions of the race groups, along with information on intercensal comparability issues, appear in chapter 3.

3. At first blush, one might speculate that part of the rapidity of this decline may be accounted for by the strong economy and very low unemployment rate in 1969. Unemployment in 1969 was only 3.5% (Ehrenberg and Smith 1982). However, the 1959 and 1979 unemployment rates were likewise rather low (5.5 and 5.8%, respectively). Unfortunately, I do not have nativity-specific poverty rates for the intercensal periods and thus cannot determine the linearity of the decline in poverty over the 1960s.

4. That those here over 20 years in 1969 had a higher poverty rate than all but the most recent arrivals probably reflects the large number of aged heads among them. Analyses in chapter 5 will show that while age and poverty are negatively related, the effect is curvilinear, suggesting that poverty increases somewhat among the elderly. We know immigration was greatly curtailed during the 1930s and 1940s, so it seems

reasonable that the over 20 year group in 1969 contains many aged second-wave arrivals. By 1979, immigrant families here 20 years or more are more likely composed of younger immigrants who arrived after 1950, when immigration began to increase. Moreover, it is likely that by 1980, surviving aged second-wave arrivals would be widowed or in group quarters (thus dropping out of my sample) or living with their children (thus joining a native family).

5. The operational definitions of these groups are specified in chapter 3.

6. I base this assertion on INS statistics (Immigration and Naturalization Service 1984, Table 2.1). While their data are not broken down by race of immigrant, about 11% of West Indian immigrants entered under the occupational preference categories in 1984. This compares to about 25% of those from all African countries (I excluded Egypt and South Africa due to the likely preponderance of nonblacks among them).

5

Poverty among Immigrants: Multivariate Models

The descriptive tabulations in the previous chapter documented the degree of poverty among immigrant and native families in the United States between 1960 and 1980. I found several differences in poverty rates between nativity and race groups both within years and across time. For example, (1) poverty among recent immigrants was generally greater than that among previous arrivals, (2) poverty among recent immigrants increased considerably over the period and (3) immigrants benefit more than natives from multiple earners, but this advantage declined over time.

In this chapter, I use multivariate logistic regression analysis to pursue two broad goals. The first is to confirm these and other conclusions drawn from the descriptive analyses of the previous chapter. The second is to go beyond these simple models and explore the effects of immigrant status as one among a number of individual, family and contextual determinants of poverty.

The opening section of this chapter presents a series of very simple multivariate models of absolute poverty among families. By simultaneously controlling for race, year and nativity, these models establish whether poverty among recent U.S. immigrants is higher than that for earlier arrivals and, most importantly, whether poverty among recent immigrants increased among successive immigrant cohorts. I parameterize logistic regression models so as to establish the statistical significance of these possibilities.

Race and immigrant status are only two of many factors that affect poverty among families. The third section of this chapter builds the conceptual framework for more comprehensive and complex models of family poverty. These models, which employ logistic regression to estimate the probability

that a family will be poor, establish the nature of immigrant status as a determinant of poverty.

In the fourth section, I introduce and operationalize the independent
variables, justify their inclusion and state their hypothesized effects on
family poverty. The following section presents the estimates of these more
complex models of poverty among families. Initially, I discuss a model that
is pooled across race groups. This is followed by a series of models for white,
black, Hispanic and Asian families separately.

The previous chapter established, in descriptive fashion, the extent to
which multiple earners keep families above the poverty level. In the con-
cluding analytic section of this chapter, I take a closer look at this finding. I
model the probability that a family will be above the absolute poverty
threshold among those families who would be poor without the earnings of
family members other than the head. Both pooled and race-specifc models
are estimated, to provide a more rigorous treatment of immigrant-native differentials in the ameliorative effects of multiple earners.

ESTIMATION OF THE EFFECTS OF YEAR OF
OBSERVATION, NATIVITY AND RACE ON POVERTY

In chapter 4, I documented that absolute poverty among immigrants to
the United States declined slowly between 1959 and 1969, but then increased by 1979. Much of the increase of the 1970s was due to the rapid rise
in poverty among recent immigrants, that is, those who arrived five or fewer
years before the census. These descriptive tables offered tentative support
for the argument that poverty among immigrants increased as the new immigration unfolded. To subject these observations to a more definitive
statistical test, I estimate models of family poverty that use the same predictors appearing in Table 4.2—race, immigrant status and year.

The first multivariate models appear in Table 5.1. Before discussing them,
I briefly review the statistical methodology employed.[1] Because the dependent variable is a dichotomy—a family either is or is not in poverty—logistic
regression analysis is used.[2] Unlike ordinary least squares regression, logistic
regression provides unbiased and efficient estimates for equations with
dichotomous dependent variables (Hanushek and Jackson 1977).

The parameter estimates of logit models reflect the effect of a unit change
in the independent variable on the log of the odds of being in poverty. To
provide more intuitively meaningful results, these logit coefficients are
transformed to reflect the effect of a unit change in the independent variable
on the *probability* of being poor (Petersen 1985).

To test whether immigrant poverty increases significantly over time, net of
changes in cohort composition, I estimate models that are pooled across
year of observation. That is, data from the 1960, 1970 and 1980 family files
were concatenated to form a single data file. Year of observation is then in-

cluded in these models as a predictor with the year 1960 serving as the omitted reference category. The desired test inheres in the interaction terms between year of observation and nativity status.

Immigrant status is defined somewhat differently here than in Table 4.2. Because of the lack of detail on years since immigration in the 1960 Census, a three-category nativity variable is employed. The reference group is all families with native heads. To them I compare immigrant families with heads who arrived more than five years before the census (Immigrant, Not Recent) and those who arrived five or fewer years before (Recent Immigrants). Race is defined as in chapter 4, that is, determined by the race of the head. In these multivariate models, white families are the reference category.

Turning to Model 1 in Table 5.1, the negative estimates for year of observation confirm that families were less likely to be poor in 1969 and 1979 than they were in 1959.[3] That the coefficient for the 1980 Census is not appreciably greater than that for 1970 is consistent with the rapid decline in poverty during the 1960s and abated decline during the 1970s. An example will illustrate interpretation of the transformed logit coefficients under column *P*. The probability that a family was poor in 1969 was 0.053 less than in 1959, after controlling for immigrant status.

Model 1 also shows that, controlling for the overall decline in poverty over the 1960 to 1980 period, recent immigrants were significantly *more* likely and all other immigrants were significantly *less* likely than natives to be in poverty. This squares with the image of immigrants starting from humble origins, but enjoying upward socioeconomic mobility as they adjust to the U.S. economy.

Model 2 in Table 5.1 includes the main effects for race. Compared to white families, black- and Hispanic-headed families were far more likely to be poor. This offers further support for the disadvantages of color first established in Table 4.2. Reflecting their general economic prosperity, Asian-American poverty rates were not significantly different from those of whites. This model agrees with earlier results that show that recent immigrants are more likely and all other immigrants less likely to be poor than natives. In Model 2, the effect for Recent Immigrant changes little from its value in Model 1. Thus the greater concentration of nonwhites among recent immigrants does not explain why they are more likely than natives to be poor.

The descriptive tables revealed a sharp increase over the years in poverty among recent immigrants. Model 3 in Table 5.1 addresses this by introducing the interaction terms between year of observation and immigrant status. These interactions determine whether immigrants in 1970 and 1980 are significantly more likely to be poor than their counterparts in 1960, after controlling for the main effects of year, race and immigrant status.

The last four coefficients in Model 3 confirm the observation that poverty

Table 5.1
Logistic Regression of Absolute Poverty on Year of Observation, Immigrant Status and Race

	Model 1		Model 2		Model 3		Model 4	
	L	p	L	p	L	p	L	p
Intercept	-1.01 (.04)		-1.77 (.05)		-1.77 (.05)		-1.81 (.06)	
Main Effects								
1970	-.57 (.05)	-.053	-.62 (.05)	-.056	-.65 (.06)	-.059	-.66 (.07)	-.059
1980	-.80 (.05)	-.068	-.78 (.06)	-.067	-.79 (.07)	-.068	-.78 (.07)	-.067
Immigrant, Not Recent	-.15 (.05)	-.016	-.15 (.06)	-.016	-.14* (.10)	-.015	-.01* (.14)	-.001
Recent Immigrant	.53 (.09)	.073	.51 (.10)	.070	.10* (.23)	.012	.77 (.34)	.115
Black			1.51 (.06)	.276	1.52 (.06)	.278	1.63 (.07)	.305
Hispanic			1.15 (.06)	.193	1.16 (.06)	.195	1.19 (.07)	.202
Asian			.11* (.11)	.013	.08* (.11)	.009	-.41 (.19)	-.040
Interaction Terms								
Immigrant, Not Recent, 1970					.15* (.13)	.018	.14* (.13)	.017
Recent Immigrant, 1970					.12* (.28)	.014	.08* (.28)	.009

Variable	Model 1 L (SE)	Model 1 P	Model 2 L (SE)	Model 2 P	Model 3 L (SE)	Model 3 P	Model 4 L (SE)	Model 4 P
Immigrant, Not Recent, 1980	-.16* (.13)	-.017					-.08* (.13)	-.009
Recent Immigrant, 1980	.75 (.27)	.112					.43* (.28)	.058
Black Immigrant, Not Recent							-.94 (.22)	-.076
Hispanic Immigrant, Not Recent							-.08* (.14)	-.009
Asian Immigrant, Not Recent							.34* (.27)	.044
Recent Black Immigrant							-1.40 (.40)	-.096
Recent Hispanic Immigrant							-.75 (.28)	-.065
Recent Asian Immigrant							.69 (.35)	.101
-2 log (likelihood ratio)	13210		12380		12360		12290	
Degrees of Freedom	13985		13982		13978		13972	

Note: L = Logit Coefficient (standard errors in parentheses); P = Probability Change (reflects the change in the probability of being poor resulting from a unit change in the independent variable) computed at P̂ = .1323 (see Petersen 1985).

*Parameter estimate not significant at .05.

among recent immigrants increased over the 1960–1980 period. The only statistically significant term involving immigrant status is that for recent immigrant families in 1980. Substantively, this term indicates that compared to their counterparts in 1959, recent immigrant families in 1979 were particularly likely to be in poverty, other things being equal. The effects for other immigrants are all insignificant, indicating little change over time in the net propensity of previous immigrant families to be poor. These models were not, therefore, sensitive enough to confirm the observation that poverty among Immigrant, Not Recent families increased over time in comparison to native families (see discussion of Tables 4.1 and 4.2). However, this model offers strong support for the conclusion that poverty among recent immigrants was particularly great in 1979.

Model 4 in Table 5.1 introduces the interaction terms between immigrant status and race. This model shows that much of the reason why poverty is greater among recent immigrants in general is because of the comparatively high risks of poverty among recent white and Asian immigrant families. Because of the race-immigrant status interaction, the main effect for Recent Immigrant is that for the reference group, whites. The positive signs for this term and the Recent Asian Immigrant term reflects the particularly strong propensity of these groups to be poor. The negative effects for both groups of black immigrants confirms the generally lower poverty among black immigrants compared to black natives. The negative and significant effect for Recent Hispanic Immigrants is noteworthy because they are a group that has sparked some of the greatest concern over the new immigration.[4]

To summarize, the logistic regression models in Table 5.1 confirm that (1) poverty declined among families between 1959 and 1979, but more steeply during the 1960s; (2) families with black and Hispanic heads have much greater poverty rates than their white and Asian counterparts; (3) over the entire period, recent immigrants had higher poverty rates than natives and previous immigrants had lower poverty rates than natives; (4) the overall effect for Recent Immigrants was *comparatively* strong for white and Asian families and weak for black and Hispanic families and (5) recent immigrants in 1979 (as compared to recent immigrants in 1959 or 1969) were especially likely to be poor.

CONCEPTUAL BACKGROUND FOR A MULTIVARIATE MODEL OF POVERTY AMONG FAMILIES

The models in the preceding section were less concerned with explaining poverty among families than with confirming some simple patterns of poverty across race and immigrant status categories. In this section, I elaborate the conceptual foundation beneath more comprehensive models of poverty among families. In addition to nativity and race, these models take into account the effects of other individual, family and contextual variables that influence poverty risks.

The causes and appropriate cures for poverty in the United States represent a most fundamental debate in the social sciences and among the general public. Numerous scholars (Feagin 1975; Schiller 1980; Kerbo 1983) envision a rough dichotomy between individualists, those who place primary blame for poverty on individual deficiencies among the poor, and structuralists, those who regard poverty as resulting from a lack of economic opportunity (for the able) or adequate social provisions (for the disabled).

Throughout American history, public sentiment has leaned toward the former, or individualistic, explanation of poverty (Feagin 1975). To be sure, most would agree that individual characteristics such as low education or subemployment have much to do with why people and families are poor. Disagreement surrounds the causes of these individual characteristics. Individualists would posit a lack of discipline and initiative while structuralists would suggest prejudice, discrimination and other structural barriers to employment and education.

My models of family poverty draw on the status attainment (Blåu and Duncan 1967) and human capital (Becker 1975; Mincer 1974) perspectives of socioeconomic attainment. I assume that employment is the primary source of family income and that there is a market for labor in which people are remunerated in direct proportion to their productivity. This value is determined by a person's skill, education and other so-called human capital characteristics. In the context of poverty, I assume that, *ceteris paribus,* people with less human capital will be more likely than others to be in poverty.

By stressing the importance of human capital attributes, I am not dismissing structural explanations for poverty. As will become apparent in my description of the variables to be included, I acknowledge the structural barriers that can prevent individuals from attaining the human capital needed to lift them out of poverty. To deny the importance of human capital for earnings determination would err in the opposite direction. Such characteristics, therefore, warrant inclusion in models of poverty. In the analyses below, I restrict my consideration to the individual characteristics of the head of the family.

The unit of analysis in this study is the family. While the salience of the human capital characteristics of the head is recognized, other family characteristics are likewise key determinants of economic well-being. For example, family poverty can hinge on the family's ability to commit additional workers to the labor force. Thus, in addition to the family head's characteristics, I include variables monitoring family structure. In order to assess the macroeconomic context, I have also included two variables that describe the place of residence.

To summarize, I assume that poverty is a condition shared and endured by families, who in turn develop strategies to ameliorate its effects. Various individual characteristics of the family head can determine income and hence, the likelihood of family poverty. I also assume that family structure and place of residence have important direct effects on poverty.

INDEPENDENT VARIABLE DEFINITIONS AND
HYPOTHESIZED EFFECTS

This section provides additional technical and theoretical background to the forthcoming multivariate models of poverty among families. I operationalize the independent variables and discuss their expected effects. I consider, in order, individual, family-level and contextual determinants of poverty. A summary of their operational definitions appears in Table 5.2.

Individual-Level Variables

A number of individual characteristics of the family head are used to estimate the probability that a family will be poor. Age of head is simply a continuous variable indicating age in completed years. Those who are under 18 are excluded from the analysis, and any heads who are 100 or more years of age are recoded to 99. Earnings and total income tend to increase with age (Ehrenberg and Smith 1982). Older workers frequently have greater experience and skill than younger workers and their pay rises in accordance with this increase in human capital. Net of other factors, age of head should lower poverty among families.[5] In addition to the head's earnings effect, older families are less apt to be poor because, often with reduced child care demands and more working-age children, they may be able to commit multiple workers to the labor market. It is especially important to control for age in the context of this research, so as to differentiate between aging and assimilation effects.

The typical age-earnings profile is not linear, but parabolic downward. While income generally increases with age, it tends to decline among the aged for well-documented reasons (Atchley 1978). Retirement, whether mandatory or voluntary, brings a reliance on public and private pensions that are frequently inadequate. Widowhood usually means the loss of a breadwinner and frequently presages below-poverty income (Lopata 1973; Smith 1988). I expect that poverty will, conversely, increase among the aged compared to their prime-aged counterparts. To capture this nonlinear effect, I introduce the square of head's age (age-squared). In order to bring the mean for this variable in line with those of the other independent variables employed, head's age-squared is divided by 1,000. I expect this term to have a positive effect, meaning that poverty is greater among families with aged heads than among families with prime-aged heads. I should note that a reduced need for income among the aged has been factored into the absolute poverty lines used here (Orshansky 1965). Other things being equal, households with aged heads have lower poverty thresholds than those headed by the nonaged. That is, while income may decline with old age, so do poverty thresholds. Nonetheless, I anticipate a positive and significant effect of age-squared on poverty.

Formal education has a strong and positive impact on status and earnings attainment (Blau and Duncan 1967; Sewell, et al. 1970; Sewell and Hauser 1975). Education increases individual knowledge and skill, thus improving the wage-bargaining position in the labor market. Net of what people learn in the classroom, individuals with high school or college degrees are regarded by employers as being more diligent and organized just for having graduated (Schiller 1980). Conflict theorists question whether employers are truly concerned about the content of education or whether they use the diploma as a convenient way to exclude lower-class job applicants (Kerbo 1983). The ill-educated also suffer from higher rates of unemployment and layoffs (Schiller 1980). For these reasons, I expect education to significantly lower poverty risks, so that families with better-educated heads are less likely to be poor, *ceteris paribus*.

Changing background characteristics—lower education in particular—make the issue of educational effects especially interesting. Part of the argument as to why immigrants have become more likely to be poor, is because of a deterioration in the background characteristics of new arrivals. Controlling for education is crucial if I am to explain the effects of immigrant status on family poverty.

In this analysis, education is measured in completed grades. For example, a value of 0 means the head, at best, never completed first grade and a value of 12 signifies a high school graduate with no completed years of college. The maximum value of this variable is 20.

The variable race has already been defined and discussed. In addition to the four-category version in Table 5.1, three additional refinements are employed. These differ from the four-category version only to the extent that Hispanics and Asians are decomposed into three ethnic groups each. Hispanics are subdivided into Mexicans, Puerto Ricans and Other Hispanics, and Asians into Japanese, Chinese and Other Asian. Thus the eight-category version of race identifies whites (the reference category), blacks and the three Hispanic and Asian groups.

The more refined specifications of race are used only in estimations based on separate subsamples of Hispanics and Asians. The first identifies Other Hispanics (the reference category), Mexicans and Puerto Ricans. The second defines Other Asians (the reference category), Japanese and Chinese. Some of the hypothesized effects for these variables have already been tested. Black and Hispanic families have higher poverty rates than whites or Asians. While part of this is due to lower human capital characteristics, some also is due to discrimination in education and employment (Schiller 1980). Thus, I expect the effects for Hispanic and black families to be significant, even after controlling for other determinants of poverty. Looking within the Hispanic and Asian categories, I expect that, compared to Other Hispanics (which includes Cubans, Central and South Americans and any residual group not clearly identified as Mexican or Puerto Rican), Puerto Rican families will be

Table 5.2
Definitions of Variables Used in Multivariate Analyses of Poverty

Variable	Definition
Family Head Characteristics	
Age	Age of head in years, 18-99
Age Squared	Head's age squared, divided by 1000
Education	Grades of schooling completed by head
Secondary Occupation	Head has secondary labor market occupation[a] coded 2; 1 otherwise
Race (4 categories)	1 = Head is Non-Hispanic White 2 = Head is Non-Hispanic Black 3 = Head is Hispanic 4 = Head is Non-Hispanic Asian
Race (8 categories)	1 = Head is Non-Hispanic White 2 = Head is Non-Hispanic Black 3 = Head is Mexican 4 = Head is Puerto Rican 5 = Head is Other Hispanic 6 = Head is Japanese 7 = Head is Chinese 8 = Head is Other Asian
Hispanic Ethnicity	1 = Head is Other Hispanic 2 = Head is Mexican 3 = Head is Puerto Rican
Asian Ethnicity	1 = Head is Other Asian 2 = Head is Japanese 3 = Head is Chinese
Nativity	1 = Head is Native 2 = Head is Immigrant, Not Recent (immigrated over five years before) 3 = Head is Recent Immigrant (immigrated up to 5 years before)
Family Characteristics	
Headship Configuration	1 = Family, both spouses present 2 = Spouse absent family
Extended Family	Adult Relative of Head (except spouse or child) present coded 2; 1 otherwise
Dependency Rate	Number of non-working family members as a percent of total family members

Table 5.2 (*continued*)

Variable	Definition
Other Independent Variables	
Southern Residence	Family resides in Southern state coded 2; 1 otherwise (where Southern states are AL, AR, DE, DC, FL, GA, KY, LA, MD, MS, NC, OK, SC, TN, TX, VA and WV)
Non-metropolitan Residence	Family resides in a non-metropolitan area coded 2; 1 otherwise
Year of Observation	1 = 1960 2 = 1970 3 = 1980
Dependent Variables	
Absolute Poverty	Total family income less than poverty threshold coded 1, 0 otherwise
Multiple-Earner Non-Poor (MENP)	Total family income at or above absolute poverty threshold coded 1, 0 otherwise[b]

[a]Based on Osterman's (1975) definition of secondary labor market occupation.

[b]This variable is used only in analyses which are restricted to families who would be poor without the earnings of family members other than the head.

significantly more likely to be poor. The economic destitution of Puerto Ricans is a deep and emergent problem, which is gaining recognition (Tienda 1984; Massey and Bitterman 1985; Tienda and Jensen 1988). While Mexican-Americans are known to have higher than average poverty rates (Tienda and Jensen 1988), I have no *a priori* reason to expect them to be more deprived than Other Hispanics.[6] Compared to families headed by Other Asians, Japanese should exhibit far lower poverty rates, as this group has prospered the most compared to other Asian groups (Gardner, et al. 1985).

Part of the argument about why poverty has increased since the new immigration is that the emphasis on family reunification and the shift in the racial composition of the new arrivals has increased the prevalence of immigrants with the most marginal occupations (Lamm and Imhoff 1985). Dual labor market theory (Doeringer and Piore 1971) classifies such jobs as secondary labor market occupations. This theory dichotomizes occupations into primary and secondary sectors. Secondary labor market occupations pay poorly, are unstable, have poor working conditions and, most importantly, offer little opportunity for advancement. I hypothesize that, *ceteris paribus,* families of heads with secondary occupations will have a higher probability of being poor than those whose heads are not so employed (Schiller 1980).

My operationalization of secondary labor market occupation is based on Paul Osterman's (1975) classification. He carefully considered wages, stability of employment, working conditions, degree of autonomy and opportunities for upward mobility in assigning each five-digit census occupation to either (1) the upper tier of the primary sector, (2) the lower tier of the primary sector or (3) the secondary sector. My variable is coded 2 if the head has a secondary occupation and 1 otherwise. Selected examples of secondary jobs include bootblacks, carpenters' helpers, charwomen, messengers, gardeners, hucksters and peddlers, kitchen workers, laborers, porters and waiters.

The final individual-level independent variable is head's nativity, which is used to define the nativity of the entire family. This is the same as that appearing in Table 5.1. Families with native heads serve as the reference category, and to them I compare families with recent immigrant heads and families with immigrant heads who arrived more than five years before the census.

Family Characteristics

Aside from these individual-level variables, several family characteristics directly influence the economic vitality of families. Three of these are headship configuration, extended family structure and economic dependency. Tying these indicators together is the fundamental assumption that employment—the ability and tendency for families to commit workers to the labor force—is of overwhelming importance in determining families' poverty risks (Gans 1982).

Headship configuration is singularly important among the family variables that define poverty risks. For a variety of reasons, families headed by married couples are far less apt to be poor than those headed by a single parent (Schiller 1980). This fact has become all the more obvious with the trend toward one-parent families (O'Hare 1985; Ross, et al. 1987). Often burdened with child-care responsibilities, single parents have much greater difficulty committing workers to the labor force. Moreover, because most single-parent families are headed by women, they are doubly jeopardized due to gender discrimination in the market, which lowers their own earning prospects (Schiller 1980). I hypothesize that spouse-absent families will reveal higher poverty rates, *ceteris paribus,* than intact families. Spouse-absent families, those in which the head either is separated, widowed, divorced or never married, are coded 2, while those headed by married couples are coded 1.

Extended families, those in which there are adult relatives of the head present (other than spouse or children), have greater flexibility in allocating labor resources (Tienda and Angel 1982; Angel and Tienda 1982). Such families have an enhanced ability to commit workers to the labor force. This variable is coded 2 if extended adults are present and 1 otherwise. Thus, I hypothesize a negative effect of extended family status on poverty.

Families will be poor in direct proportion to their economic dependency, that is, to the degree that a large number of family members depend on the income produced by a small number of workers. In the multivariate models of poverty to follow, I include a dependency rate, defined as the number of nonworkers as a percent of total family size. In order to bring the range of this variable in line with the others in the models, the dependency rate is multiplied by 100. I expect this variable to have a negative direct effect on family poverty.

Other Independent Variables

In addition to head and family characteristics, these models include three contextual variables. The first indicates whether the family resided in a southern state.[7] Compared to the other three census regions (Northeast, Midwest and West), the South has perennially had a higher overall poverty rate. Reasons for this include (1) its rurality, (2) a comparative lack of economic and social infrastructure development, (3) less human capital among residents and (4) a higher concentration of blacks (Ornati 1966; Ghelfi 1986; Schiller 1980). While I control for a number of these factors, I expect Southern Residence to have a positive net effect on poverty among families.

A second contextual variable is Nonmetropolitan (Nonmetro) Residence. For a variety of reasons, poverty is greater in rural than urban United States (Morrissey 1985). These reasons include (1) a lack of employment opportunities due to urban bias in economic development initiatives, (2) agricultural labor displacement due to mechanization and the move toward large, corporate-owned farms, (3) a lack of rural economic development owing to the move to preserve wilderness areas, (4) the loss to urban areas of better-educated youngsters, (5) greater age dependency and (6) a lack of knowledge about or reluctance to apply for cash assistance and in-kind transfer programs (Carlson, et al. 1981).

An area is considered metropolitan if it lies within the confines of a standard metropolitan statistical area (SMSA). The definition of the SMSA is rather complex (Shryock, et al. 1976) and need not be detailed here. In essence, it is a county with a central city (a city of 50,000 or more people) plus surrounding counties that are metropolitan in character and tied economically and socially to the central county. This definition changed little between the censuses used in this analysis. Most of the growth of existing SMSAs and most of the increase in the number of SMSAs between 1950 and

1980 has been the result of metropolitanization (U.S. Bureau of the Census 1982). For my purposes, nonmetropolitan areas lie outside of SMSAs; the reference consists of families within SMSAs.[8] I hypothesize that nonmetro families will experience higher poverty risks.

The final variable to be defined is one that has already been discussed and used extensively, year of observation. Families in 1970 and 1980 are compared to the reference group, families in 1960. Negative effects are expected for these dummy variables.

The descriptive statistics for these variables appear in Table 5.3. While these statistics are provided as a point of reference, some differences between natives, recent immigrants and previous immigrants are worth highlighting.

Nativity differences for mean education show that immigrants were less well educated in the aggregate than were the native born. The education of recent immigrants is substantially above that of other immigrants (10.7 versus 9.4 completed grades), partly reflecting the younger age composition of recent immigrants (see means for age). This also implies that most recent immigrants would have obtained their educations in a era when the schooling opportunities were greater.

The distributions of the race variables across these immigrant statuses underscore the preponderance of whites among the native-born population and the greater prevalence of minorities among immigrants—recent immigrants in particular. Whites were only half as well represented among recent immigrants (42%) than among natives (87%).

Recent immigrants occupied secondary labor market occupations more so than the other two groups. Because this variable is coded 1 or 2, the mean of 1.25 for recent immigrants suggests that fully 25% of recent immigrant heads had secondary occupations. This figure compares to only 13% among natives and 15% among other immigrants.

Looking next at the family and contextual variables, there is little difference between immigrants and natives in the prevalence of spouse-absent families. However, families headed by immigrants, especially recent immigrants, were more likely to be extended than those of natives. Recent immigrant families had lower economic dependency rates in the aggregate compared to either previous immigrant or native families. Immigrant families also were less likely to live in the South and in nonmetro areas. While 31% of natives resided in nonmetro areas, only 6% of recent immigrant families did.

Having discussed the conceptual background and variables to be used in these multivariate models of poverty, I now present the estimates of these models.

MULTIVARIATE MODELS OF POVERTY AMONG FAMILIES

In this section, several models of poverty among families are presented and discussed. I begin with a series of models that are pooled across race

Table 5.3
Distribution of Variables Used in Multivariate Analyses of Poverty[a]

Variable	Total	Native	Immigrant Not Recent	Recent Immigrant
Family Head Characteristics				
Age	46.6 (15.5)	46.2 (15.3)	53.8 (16.8)	37.4 (12.3)
Age Squared	1.91 (1.60)	1.86 (1.56)	2.68 (1.86)	1.04 (1.10)
Education	10.9 (3.72)	11.1 (3.59)	9.4 (4.72)	10.7 (5.17)
Secondary Occupation	1.14 (.34)	1.13 (.34)	1.15 (.36)	1.25 (.43)
Race/Ethnicity				
White	85.19	86.78	69.07	41.66
Black	9.83	10.43	2.32	4.09
Hispanic	4.15	2.43	23.39	37.10
Mexican	2.15	1.53	9.23	13.85
Puerto Rican	0.61	0.10	6.75	6.82
Other Hispanic	1.39	0.81	7.41	16.43
Asian	0.83	0.35	5.22	17.15
Japanese	0.27	0.23	0.64	1.79
Chinese	0.23	0.07	1.88	3.73
Other Asian	0.33	0.06	2.70	11.63
Nativity				
Native	92.34			
Immigrant, Not Recent	6.82			
Recent Immigrant	0.84			
Family Characteristics				
Spouse absent family	1.16 (.37)	1.16 (.37)	1.17 (.37)	1.16 (.37)
Extended Family	1.11 (.31)	1.11 (.31)	1.14 (.34)	1.21 (.41)
Dependency Rate	55.2 (29.9)	55.1 (29.8)	56.5 (31.1)	51.7 (30.8)
Other Independent Variables				
Southern Residence	1.30 (.46)	1.32 (.47)	1.13 (.34)	1.19 (.39)
Non-metropolitan Residence	1.29 (.46)	1.31 (.46)	1.11 (.31)	1.06 (.24)
Year of Observation				
1960	29.1	29.1	31.0	16.0
1970	32.7	32.8	31.4	29.4
1980	38.2	38.1	37.6	54.6

Source: 1960, 1970 and 1980 Public Use Samples of the U.S. Census.

[a] Means of continuous variables (standard deviations in parentheses) and percentage distributions of discrete variables.

categories. These models are followed by separate estimates for white, black, Hispanic and Asian families.

Table 5.4 presents a progression of four hierarchical models of poverty among families pooled across race groups. Model 1 in Table 5.4 replicates Model 1 in Table 5.1. To recapitulate, these results show that families were less likely to be poor in 1969 and 1979 as compared to 1959 and that recent immigrants were significantly *more* likely and all other immigrants significantly *less* likely to be poor compared to natives.

Throughout I have speculated about the reasons for the higher poverty among recent arrivals. The results of Table 5.1 indicated that the shift in the racial composition of immigrants is not a key explanatory factor. Alternative explanations are that recent immigrants tend to be younger, less well educated and, thus, more apt to have secondary labor market occupations.

To account for these possibilities Model 2 includes race, education, secondary occupation, age and age-squared. The effects for the eight-category race variable conform with expectation. Compared to families with white heads (the reference group), blacks, Mexicans, Puerto Ricans, Other Hispanics and Other Asians were significantly more likely to be poor. This effect is especially pronounced among blacks and Puerto Ricans. As expected, among Hispanics, Puerto Ricans have comparatively high poverty rates. No groups were significantly less likely than whites to be poor (the negative terms for Japanese and Chinese families failed to reach significance).

The effects for the other independent variables also generally conform to expectation. Families with heads who were older and better educated were less likely to be in poverty, other things being equal. Moreover, the positive and significant effect for age-squared supports the hypothesis that, while the probability of poverty generally decreases with age, it increases among the aged. Interestingly, head's secondary labor market occupation had no significant effect on poverty. The most important result of Model 2, however, is that the inclusion of race, education and age does not explain the positive effect on poverty for recent immigrants. Despite some attenuation, the coefficient for recent immigrant status remains positive and significant. Along with the negative term for other immigrants, Model 2 continues to show that recent immigrants were more likely and all other immigrants were less likely than their native counterparts to be poor. This result is consistent with assimilation theory, which posits an initial period of economic adjustment, during which immigrants are more prone to poverty.

Model 3 in Table 5.4 introduces the family and contextual variables discussed in the previous section. These include the family's dependency rate, headship configuration (whether the spouse is absent) and extension. It also includes the two contextual variables: whether the place of residence is in a nonmetro area and whether it is in the South.

The effects of these variables on family poverty likewise conform to expectation. Families with greater economic dependency—with a greater percent of nonworkers—were significantly more likely to be poor. In terms of family structure, families with the spouse of head absent were more likely and extended families were less likely to be in poverty. The former effect is particularly strong. Other things being equal, the probability that a family was poor increased by 0.236 if it was *not* headed by a married couple.

Finally, the two contextual terms also behave as expected. Families living in the South and those in nonmetro areas were significantly more likely to be poor, *ceteris paribus*. Both these effects are of similar magnitude, increasing the probability of poverty by about 0.10.

Model 3 reveals a suppression of the effect for recent immigrants. Adding the family and contextual terms to the equation produces a sizable *increase* in the positive effect of recent immigrant status on poverty. This result is explained by the means for recent immigrants on the five family and contextual variables (see Table 5.3). Recent immigrants, in comparison to natives, had lower economic dependency, were more likely to be in extended families and were less likely to live in the South and in nonmetro areas, all of which reduce poverty risks.

The suppression effect means that if recent immigrants did not differ from natives in their dependency as well as their propensity to be extended, to live in the South and to live in nonmetro areas, recent immigrant poverty would be that much higher. Controlling for these variables increases the main effect for recent immigrants. Separate analyses (not shown) revealed that dependency and extension were largely responsible for the suppression. This implies that the extended family structures and the greater proportionate labor force commitment that typify recent immigrants are important for keeping many families out of poverty.

A similar story holds for previous immigrants as well (those who arrived over five years prior to the census). The main effect for Immigrant, Not Recent in Model 2 is negative and significant, suggesting that previous immigrants were *less* likely to be in poverty than natives, after controlling for the individual characteristics of the family head. When the five family and contextual terms are entered (Model 3), the main effect for Immigrant, Not Recent attenuates to zero. Table 5.3 documents that these immigrant families were somewhat more likely than natives to be in extended families, and were far less apt to live in the South and in nonmetro areas (they did not differ with respect to dependency or headship). Again, because these characteristics tend to reduce poverty risks, they help explain the lower poverty among previous immigrants compared to natives.

The final model in Table 5.4 introduces the interaction between nativity status and year of observation. The intent of this model is to determine whether recent immigrants in the most recent period are particularly likely to be poor, net of the other variables in the equation. Model 4 is analogous to Model 3 in Table 5.1, which showed that poverty risks of recent immigrants had increased over time.

Table 5.4
Logistic Regression of Absolute Poverty: Pooled by Race[a]

	Model 1 L	p	Model 2 L	p	Model 3 L	p	Model 4 L	p
Intercept	-1.01 (.04)		2.08 (.22)		-2.51 (.30)		-2.52 (.28)	
1970	-.57 (.05)	-.053	-.51 (.06)	-.048	-.72 (.06)	-.063	-.74 (.08)	-.064
1980	-.80 (.05)	-.068	-.51 (.06)	-.048	-.69 (.07)	-.061	-.70 (.08)	-.062
Family Head Variables								
Immigrant, Not Recent	-.15 (.05)	-.016	-.35 (.06)	-.035	-.00* (.07)	-.000	.02* (.12)	.002
Recent Immigrant	.53 (.09)	.073	.31 (.10)	.040	1.04 (.12)	.169	.54* (.29)	.075
Black			1.20 (.06)	.204	1.01 (.08)	.163	1.02 (.08)	.165
Mexican			.73 (.08)	.108	.64 (.09)	.092	.64 (.09)	.092
Puerto Rican			1.01 (.12)	.163	1.03 (.14)	.167	1.05 (.14)	.171
Other Hispanic			.54 (.09)	.075	.40 (.10)	.053	.42 (.10)	.056
Japanese			-.17* (.20)	-.018	-.00* (.22)	.000	-.00* (.22)	-.000

Chinese	-.01* (.20)	-.001	.21* (.22)	.026	.19* (.22)	.023
Other Asian	.65 (.15)	.094	.64 (.16)	.092	.57 (.17)	.080
Education	-.15 (.01)	-.016	-.12 (.01)	-.013	-.12 (.01)	-.013
Secondary Occupation	.02* (.06)	.002	.32 (.06)	.041	.32 (.06)	.041
Age	-.09 (.01)	-.010	-.04 (.01)	-.005	-.04 (.01)	-.005
Age^2	.82 (.08)	.125	.23 (.10)	.029	.23 (.10)	.029
Family and Contextual Variables						
Dependency Rate			.04 (.00)	.005	.04 (.00)	.005
Spouse Absent			1.34 (.06)	.236	1.34 (.06)	.236
Extended Family			-.68 (.08)	-.061	-.69 (.08)	-.061
Southern Residence			.69 (.06)	.101	.69 (.06)	.101
Non-metropolitan Residence			.73 (.06)	.108	.73 (.06)	.108

Table 5.4 (continued)

	Model 1 L	P	Model 2 L	P	Model 3 L	P	Model 4 L	P
Interaction Terms								
Immigrant, Not Recent, 1970							.07* (.15)	.008
Recent Immigrant, 1970							.35* (.34)	.046
Immigrant, Not Recent, 1980							-.13* (.16)	.014
Recent Immigrant, 1980							.74 (.32)	.110
-2 log (likelihood ratio)	13210		11590		9338		9329	
Degrees of Freedom	13985		13974		13969		13965	

Note: L = Logit Coefficient (standard errors in parentheses); P = Probability Change (reflects the change in the probability of being in poverty resulting from a unit change in the independent variable) computed at P' = .1323 (see Petersen 1985).

*Parameter estimate not significant at .05.

Model 4 of Table 5.4 includes several human capital, family and contextual variables that could account for the higher incidence of poverty in the later period. However, the interaction term for Recent Immigrant 1980 is positive and significant. Compared to recent immigrants in 1960 or 1970, those in 1980 were particularly likely to be poor. This effect obtains even after controlling for the other variables in the model, indicating that neither a deterioration in immigrant "quality" nor an increase in the percent of nonwhites accounts for the disproportionately high poverty rates among recent immigrants in 1980.

Table 5.5 examines the question of changes in immigrant poverty over time separately for the four race groups. Among white families, Table 5.5 upholds previous findings that poverty among recent immigrants increased substantially over time. The terms for Recent Immigrants in both 1970 and 1980 are positive and significant; other things being equal, recent white immigrants in 1969 and 1979 were more likely to be in poverty than their statistical counterparts in 1959.

A similar conclusion applies to black families. The strong and positive interaction terms for Recent Immigrant, 1970 and Recent Immigrant, 1980 suggest recent black immigrant families have become increasingly likely to be poor, controlling for many factors affecting poverty. Here, however, poverty among previous black immigrants (Immigrant, Not Recent) likewise increased over time. This substantiates the conclusion, drawn from the descriptive tabulations (Table 4.2), that poverty risks of black immigrants increased over time, irrespective of their duration of U.S. residence. Moreover, this secular increase is not explained by a deterioration in the background characteristics of black immigrants, because they have been purged of the influence of education and secondary labor market occupation.

The previous chapter documented that Hispanic immigrant families were *not* largely responsible for the steady increase in poverty among recent immigrants over the past 20 years. This finding is important, because Hispanics have been identified as most of "the immigrant problem" (Cafferty, et al. 1983). Results from the logit model of poverty among Hispanic families (Table 5.5) confirm this conclusion. Recent Hispanic immigrants were significantly more likely than their native counterparts to be poor (as evidenced by the main effect for Recent Immigrants). However, none of the interaction terms between immigrant status and year of observation reached significance. Unlike white and black families, recent Hispanic immigrant families did not experience a steady increase in poverty, other things being equal. This model also reveals that compared to Mexicans and Other Hispanics, Puerto Ricans were significantly more likely to be in poverty.

The model for Asian families in Table 5.5 shows that Asian immigrant families, particularly recent arrivals, were more likely to be poor than Asian natives. This result is manifest in the positive and significant main effects for

Table 5.5
Logistic Regression of Absolute Poverty: White, Black, Hispanic and Asian Families[a]

	White		Black		Hispanic		Asian	
	L	P	L	P	L	P	L	P
Intercept	-2.28 (.43)		-1.49 (.31)		-2.17 (.27)		-1.45 (.40)	
1970	-.71 (.11)	-.050	-.92 (.08)	-.169	-.69 (.09)	-.101	-.29* (.17)	-.023
1980	-.70 (.12)	-.049	-1.08 (.08)	-.190	-.52 (.10)	-.080	-.17* (.17)	-.014
Family Head Variables								
Immigrant, Not Recent	-.00* (.20)	-.000	-.86 (.32)	-.160	.13* (.10)	.024	.74 (.17)	.089
Recent Immigrant	-1.19* (1.05)	-.070	-4.93 (2.40)	-.335	.59 (.19)	.121	1.54 (.33)	.242
Mexican					.06 (.06)	.011		
Puerto Rican					.43 (.09)	.086		
Japanese							-.36 (.10)	-.028
Chinese							.05* (.09)	.005
Education	-.14 (.01)	-.012	-.13 (.01)	-.028	-.14 (.01)	-.024	-.11 (.01)	-.010
Secondary Occupation	.57 (.12)	.056	.38 (.07)	.089	.42 (.06)	.083	.44 (.09)	.047
Age	-.04 (.01)	-.004	-.04 (.01)	-.009	-.04 (.01)	-.007	-.09 (.01)	-.008
Age^2	.26* (.14)	.027	.23 (.11)	.053	.19* (.10)	.036	.68 (.14)	.080

Family and Contextual Variables	L	P	L	P	L	P	L	P
Dependency Rate	.04 (.00)	.004	.04 (.00)	.009	.04 (.00)	.007	.04 (.00)	.004
Spouse Absent	1.47 (.11)	.231	1.37 (.06)	.330	1.33 (.06)	.302	1.04 (.09)	.140
Extended Family	-.83 (.14)	-.056	-.55 (.08)	-.110	-.46 (.07)	-.072	-.50 (.10)	-.037
Southern Residence	.33 (.09)	.035	.69 (.07)	.166	.80 (.06)	.171	.36 (.11)	.038
Non-metropolitan Residence	.77 (.08)	.096	.87 (.08)	.211	.60 (.07)	.124	.09* (.10)	.008
Interaction Terms								
Immigrant, Not Recent, 1970	.06* (.25)	.006	.94 (.41)	.229	-.05* (.13)	-.009	-.50 (.23)	-.037
Recent Immigrant, 1970	2.48 (1.12)	.477	5.62 (2.43)	.655	.16* (.24)	.030	-.29* (.39)	-.023
Immigrant, Not Recent, 1980	-.39* (.28)	-.031	1.19 (.35)	.289	-.03* (.14)	-.005	-.87 (.21)	-.056
Recent Immigrant, 1980	2.84 (1.12)	.561	5.83 (2.41)	.656	.09* (.25)	.017	-.10* (.35)	-.009
-2 log (likelihood ratio)	4251		7148		9854		5794	
Degrees of Freedom	8849		8268		11939		11945	

Note: L = Logit Coefficient (standard errors in parentheses); P = Probability Change (reflects the change in the probability of being in poverty resulting from a unit change in the independent variable) computed at P' = .1038 for whites; .3382 for blacks; .2344 for Hispanics; and .1006 for Asians (see Petersen 1985).

*Parameter estimate not significant at .05.

immigrant status. Other things being equal, the probability that a recent Asian immigrant family was in poverty exceeded that among natives by 0.242. All four interaction term estimates are negative, but only those between year of observation and previous immigrants are statistically significant. This suggests that after controlling for numerous determinants of poverty, there was no temporal increase in the propensity of recent Asian immigrant families to be poor. As first documented in the preceding chapter, however, previous Asian immigrants were less likely to be poor in 1969 and 1979 compared to 1959.

Other variables, such as Education, Age and Secondary Occupation, behaved as expected in these models. Parameter estimates for family economic dependency, headship configuration, extended structure and Nonmetro and Southern Residence likewise confirmed my hypotheses.

To summarize, Tables 5.4 and 5.5 presented multivariate models of poverty among families. The intent was to examine the relative influence of immigrant status as one among a number of individual, family and contextual determinants of poverty. In so doing I documented the net propensity of immigrant families to be poor and determined whether a secular increase in poverty could be confirmed in this multivariate context. I also established how these findings differed across the four race groups considered here.

These models showed that, other things being equal, (1) families with heads who were better educated and older (but not aged) were less likely to be poor; (2) families with heads who had a secondary occupation or who were black, Mexican, Puerto Rican and Other Asian (compared to white) were more likely to be poor; (3) families with single heads, nuclear (versus extended) structures, southern and nonmetropolitan residence or with higher economic dependency ratios were more likely to be poor; (4) recent immigrants had higher poverty rates than natives; (5) poverty among recent immigrants would be even higher were it not for their lower dependency rates, greater prevalence of extended structure and residence outside southern and nonmetropolitian areas, compared to natives; (6) Immigrant, Not Recent families were less likely than natives to be poor, but this was likewise accounted for by their family structure and residential preference; (7) recent immigrants in 1979 were particularly likely to be poor and (8) this increase over time in the net propensity of recent immigrant families to be poor obtained for white and black families.

TREADING WATER: MULTIPLE EARNERS AND FAMILY POVERTY

In this section I examine the extent to which the earnings of family members other than the head keep families from being poor. I addressed this issue in a descriptive and general way in the previous chapter. Table 4.7 showed that multiple earners (i.e., family members other than the head with positive earnings) are a more effective poverty response among immigrant versus native families. This result obtained for all but Asian families.

The finding that the intrafamily spread of work keeps a larger share of immigrant families out of poverty is a key insight because it suggests that immigrants more successfully rely on their labor, as opposed to welfare, as a means of escaping poverty. While questions of welfare utilization are addressed in subsequent chapters, this result begins to dispel the impression that immigrants prefer welfare to work as a means of escaping poverty or that they arrive expecting to take advantage of lucrative public assistance benefits. These initial results imply that low-income immigrant families are more committed to the labor force as an income-maintenance strategy.

There are several possible explanations for why immigrant families derive a greater ameliorative effect from multiple earners. I have already shown, for example, that immigrant families were more likely to be extended and that extension reduces poverty. The present section subjects the findings to a more rigorous statistical test. Here I use logistic regression to estimate the probability that total family income will be above the poverty threshold among those families that are below the poverty line when the earnings of secondary workers are subtracted from total family income.

In the ensuing analyses, I refer to this dependent variable as Multiple Earner, Nonpoor (MENP). It is coded 1 for families brought above poverty by multiple earnings and 0 otherwise.

Table 5.6 presents a series of models of multiple earner, nonpoor. Model 1 estimates the probability of being above poverty from year of observation and immigrant status. The main effects of year of observation show that, net of immigrant status, low income families were brought above the poverty line via multiple earnings to an *increasing* degree over time. The ameliorative effect of multiple earners was greater in 1969 than 1959 and even more pronounced in 1979. This model also confirms that immigrant families, both recent and not recent, derived a greater ameliorative impact of multiple earners than did native families. The effect was greater among those immigrant groups with more than five years of U.S. residence than recent immigrants, which highlights the barriers confronted by recent immigrants in mobilizing the human resources to increase their incomes.

The following two models in Table 5.6 introduce controls for various individual, family and contextual variables. The intent is to determine whether the greater ameliorative effect of multiple earners enjoyed by immigrants can be explained by other factors correlated with economic well-being.[9] Because MENP is the inverse of poverty, these variables should have signs opposite those obtained when predicting poverty.

Model 2 in Table 5.6 introduces controls for additional family head characteristics. These include race, education, age and age-squared. None of these variables attenuates the positive effects of immigrant status on being above poverty. To a greater extent than native families, earnings of family

Table 5.6
Logistic Regression of Multiple Earner, Nonpoor: Pooled by Race[a]

	Model 1		Model 2		Model 3		Model 4	
	L	P	L	P	L	P	L	P
Intercept	-1.04		-4.09		-3.85		-3.87	
	(.03)		(.20)		(.21)		(.21)	
1970	.28	.067	.24	.057	.32	.076	.46	.111
	(.05)		(.05)		(.05)		(.06)	
1980	.49	.119	.44	.106	.48	.116	.60	.146
	(.05)		(.05)		(.06)		(.07)	
<u>Family Head Variables</u>								
Immigrant, Not Recent	.40	.096	.38	.091	.24	.057	.50	.121
	(.04)		(.05)		(.06)		(.09)	
Recent Immigrant	.17	.040	.27	.064	-.01*	-.002	.54	.131
	(.08)		(.09)		(.09)		(.22)	
Black			-.28	-.062	-.29	-.064	-.30	-.066
			(.06)		(.06)		(.06)	
Mexican			-.20	-.045	-.26	-.057	-.29	-.064
			(.07)		(.07)		(.07)	
Puerto Rican			-.43	-.092	-.57	-.118	-.66	-.134
			(.11)		(.11)		(.12)	

	(1)	(2)	(3)	(4)	(5)	(6)
Other Hispanic	-.22 (.08)	-.049	-.29 (.08)	-.064	-.29* (.08)	-.064
Japanese	.28* (.16)	.067	.25* (.17)	.059	.21* (.17)	.050
Chinese	.33 (.14)	.079	.19* (.14)	.045	.18* (.14)	.042
Other Asian	-.07* (.12)	-.016	-.17* (.13)	-.038	-.14* (.13)	-.032
Education	.06 (.01)	.014	.05 (.01)	.012	.05 (.01)	.011
Age	.10 (.01)	.023	.10 (.01)	.023	.10 (.01)	.023
Age^2	-.72 (.07)	-.145	-.75 (.07)	-.150	-.74 (.07)	-.148

Family and Contextual Variables

			(3)	(4)	(5)	(6)
Spouse Absent			-.59 (.05)	-.122	-.60 (.05)	-.124

Table 5.6 (*continued*)

	Model 1		Model 2		Model 3		Model 4	
	L	P	L	P	L	P	L	P
Extended Family					1.19 (.05)	.289	1.20 (.05)	.291
Southern Residence					-.26 (.05)	-.057	-.26 (.05)	-.057
Non-metropolitan Residence					-.47 (.05)	-.100	-.47 (.05)	-.100
Interaction Terms								
Immigrant, Not Recent, 1970							-.45 (.12)	-.096
Recent Immigrant, 1970							-.61 (.26)	-.126

				L (S.E.)	P
Immigrant, Not Recent, 1980				-.31 (.12)	-.068
Recent Immigrant, 1980				-.70 (.25)	-.141
-2 log (like-lihood ratio)	14700	14070	13370	13350	
Degrees of Freedom	11666	11656	11652	11648	

Note: L = Logit Coefficient (standard errors in parentheses); P = Probability Change (reflects the change in the probability of being above poverty resulting from a unit change in the independent variable) computed at P' = .3588 (see Petersen 1985).

*Parameter estimate not significant at .05.

members other than the head raise immigrant families above the poverty threshold, irrespective of duration. This finding is not accounted for by systematic differences by race, education or age. The main effects for race are as expected. Black- and Hispanic-headed families were less likely than whites to rise above poverty due to multiple earnings. Puerto Ricans were particularly unlikely to do so, a result that squares with evidence of their declining labor market experiences. Interestingly, Chinese families were significantly *more* likely than whites to benefit from multiple earners. While families with older heads were more likely to be multiple earner, nonpoor, the effect was nonlinear; families with aged heads were less likely than those with prime-aged heads to be multiple earner, nonpoor.

Model 3 introduces controls for the family and contextual variables. All these effects are significant and in the expected direction. Southern and rural families were less likely to rise above poverty due to multiple earnings, compared to their nonsouthern and metropolitan counterparts. Extended families were far more likely to rise above poverty than nuclear families, probably owing to their greater flexibility to commit workers to the labor force (Angel and Tienda 1982; Tienda and Angel 1982; Tienda and Glass 1985). Conversely, spouse-absent families are less able to cover both domestic and labor force responsibilities, a circumstance reflected in the negative effect of Spouse Absent.

The inclusion of this block of family and contextual variables completely attenuates the positive direct effect of being in a recent immigrant family; this effect declines from a significant 0.27 in Model 2, to an insignificant −0.01 in Model 3. As for the models of poverty, this attenuation largely results from differences between immigrants and natives in the means for family and contextual characteristics (not shown). That is, among families that would be poor without multiple earners, families headed by recent immigrants were less likely to be spouse absent, more likely to be extended and less likely to reside in the South or in nonmetro areas compared to native families. All these factors contribute to lower poverty risks among recent immigrants. Thus, controlling for these family and contextual characteristics attenuates the positive impact of being in a recent immigrant family on MENP.

A major conclusion drawn from Tables 4.6 and 4.7 was that the greater ameliorative effect of multiple earners on poverty enjoyed by immigrants versus natives was declining over time for whites and blacks. Model 4 in Table 5.6 includes the interaction terms between immigrant status and year of observation. These estimates, all negative and significant, suggest this conclusion is generalizable to the entire population. Compared to their counterparts in 1959, immigrants (both recent and previous) in 1969 and 1979 were *less* likely to rise above poverty due to multiple earnings.

Models 3 and 4 are disaggregated by race in Tables 5.7a and 5.7b. The models in Table 5.7a predict MENP separately for white and black families, while those in Table 5.7b cover Hispanic and Asian families. The intent is (1) to determine whether, within race groups, there is evidence of a greater ameliorative affect of multiple earners for immigrant versus native families and, if so, (2) whether this effect changed over time.

Model 1 for white families contains the main effects for head, family and contextual variables. This model shows that, net of other determinants of economic well-being, recent immigrants were significantly less likely, and other immigrants significantly more likely than white native families to be multiple earner, nonpoor. Model 2 for whites includes the interactions between immigrant status and year of observation. This model reveals some deterioration over time in the ameliorative impact of multiple earnings for white immigrants who have been here more than five years. The interaction effects for recent white immigrants show no consistent pattern over time. The overall negative effect for recent white immigrants in Model 1 is uniform across census years.

Model 1 for blacks reveals that both groups of immigrant families enjoyed a greater poverty ameliorating effect of multiple earners than did their native counterparts. That is, the main effects of both immigrant status terms are positive and significant. However, the immigrant status by year interactions (Model 2) show that this ameliorative impact *deteriorated* considerably over time. All four interaction terms in Model 2 are negative and significant, and the effects for recent immigrants in 1970 and 1980 are particularly strong. While relatively more black immigrant families are lifted above poverty due to multiple earnings than are native black families, the advantage was apparent in 1960 only.

Hispanic families reveal a pattern identical to that of blacks. Model 1 shows positive and significant effects on Multiple Earner, Nonpoor for both immigrant groups. Among Hispanic families overall, immigrants benefit more from multiple earners compared to natives, other things being equal. However, all four interaction terms are negative and significant, suggesting the net ameliorative impact of multiple earners also declined over time for this group.

Model 1 for Asians shows that, overall, recent Asian immigrant families are significantly less likely than natives to be lifted above poverty owing to multiple earnings. The interaction terms in Model 2 show that this effect is no different in 1970 and 1980 than it was in 1960. Again, this result is due less to a lack of labor force commitment among recent Asian immigrants than to the very strong commitment seen among Asian natives (see Table 4.7). Finally, there is evidence of an improvement over time in the ameliorative effect of multiple earners among all but recent immigrants, as evidenced by the positive and significant estimate for Immigrant, Not Recent, 1980.

To recapitulate, the models in Tables 5.6, 5.7a and 5.7b estimated the probability of being above poverty via the earnings of family members other than the head (multiple earners) among those families that are below

Table 5.7a
Logistic Regression of Multiple Earner, Nonpoor: White and Black Families[a]

	Whites				Blacks			
	Model 1		Model 2		Model 1		Model 2	
	L	p	L	p	L	p	L	p
Intercept	-3.08 (.22)		-3.12 (.22)		-4.90 (.23)		-4.89 (.23)	
1970	.24 (.06)	.058	.32 (.07)	.078	.59 (.06)	.133	.64 (.06)	.145
1980	.33 (.06)	.081	.43 (.08)	.106	.67 (.06)	.153	.75 (.06)	.172
Family Head Variables								
Immigrant, Not Recent	.19 (.06)	.046	.49 (.10)	.121	.27 (.09)	.058	1.03 (.19)	.242
Recent Immigrant	-.36 (.14)	-.081	-.26* (.44)	-.060	.38 (.14)	.083	1.97 (.70)	.456
Education	.03 (.01)	.007	.03 (.01)	.007	.08 (.01)	.017	.08 (.01)	.017
Age	-.09 (.01)	-.021	.08 (.01)	.019	.12 (.02)	.025	.12 (.02)	.025
Age^2	-.70 (.08)	-.148	-.69 (.08)	-.147	-.97 (.08)	-.153	-.96 (.08)	-.152
Family and Contextual Variables								
Spouse Absent	-.20 (.05)	-.046	-.20 (.05)	-.046	-.99 (.05)	-.156	-1.00 (.05)	-.157

	L	P	L	P	L	P	L	P
Extended Family	1.07 (.07)	.261	1.07 (.07)	.261	1.17 (.05)	.277	1.17 (.05)	.277
Southern Residence	-.24 (.05)	-.055	-.23 (.05)	-.053	-.14 (.05)	-.028	-.13 (.05)	-.026
Non-metro Residence	-.47 (.05)	-.104	-.46 (.05)	-.102	-.52 (.06)	-.093	-.51 (.06)	-.092
Interaction Terms								
Immigrant, Not Recent, 1970			-.43 (.13)	-.096			-.98 (.27)	-.154
Recent Immigrant, 1970			.25* (.50)	.061			-1.55 (.77)	-.206
Immigrant, Not Recent, 1980			-.45 (.15)	-.100			-.95 (.22)	-.151
Recent Immigrant, 1980			-.40* (.49)	-.090			-1.74 (.72)	-.219
-2 log (likelihood ratio)	10330		10310		12000		11980	
Degrees of Freedom	8152		8148		11331		11327	

Note: L = Logit Coefficient (standard errors in parentheses); P = Probability Change (reflects the change in the probability of being in poverty resulting from a unit change in the independent variable) computed at P' = .3877 for whites; and .2841 for blacks (see Petersen 1985).

*Parameter estimate not significant at .05.

Table 5.7b
Logistic Regression of Multiple Earner, Nonpoor: Hispanic and Asian Families[a]

	Hispanics				Asians			
	Model 1		Model 2		Model 1		Model 2	
	L	P	L	P	L	P	L	P
Intercept	-3.90 (.20)		-4.00 (.20)		-4.12 (.48)		-3.76 (.50)	
1970	.20 (.05)	.044	.60 (.08)	.140	.11* (.14)	.027	-.25* (.23)	-.062
1980	.41 (.05)	.094	.65 (.08)	.153	.48 (.14)	.120	.02* (.23)	.005
Family Head Variables								
Immigrant, Not Recent	.25 (.05)	.056	.61 (.08)	.143	.11* (.12)	.027	-.35* (.21)	-.086
Recent Immigrant	.24 (.07)	.054	.71 (.14)	.168	-.73 (.14)	-.173	-1.18 (.48)	-.260
Mexican	.12 (.05)	.026	.05* (.05)	.011				
Puerto Rican	-.26 (.07)	-.053	-.37 (.08)	-.073				
Japanese					.12* (.14)	.030	.12* (.14)	.030

102

Chinese					.20* (.11)	.050	.17* (.11)	.042
Education	.06 (.01)	.013	.06 (.01)	.013	.05 (.01)	.012	.05 (.01)	.012
Age	.08 (.01)	.017	.08 (.01)	.017	.11 (.02)	.027	.11 (.02)	.027
Age^2	-.53 (.08)	-.101	-.53 (.08)	-.101	-.78 (.17)	-.183	-.75 (.17)	-.177
<u>Family and Contextual Variables</u>								
Spouse Absent	-.60 (.05)	-.113	-.61 (.05)	-.114	-.67 (.11)	-.160	-.67 (.11)	-.160
Extended Family	1.29 (.05)	.310	1.29 (.05)	.310	1.07 (.11)	.248	1.06 (.11)	.246
Southern Residence	-.44 (.05)	-.086	-.44 (.05)	-.086	-.56 (.15)	-.135	-.56 (.15)	-.135
Non-metro Residence	-.48 (.06)	-.093	-.48 (.06)	-.093	.12* (.13)	.030	.10* (.13)	.025

Table 5.7b (continued)

	Hispanics				Asians			
	Model 1		Model 2		Model 1		Model 2	
	L	P	L	P	L	P	L	P
Interaction Terms								
Immigrant, Not Recent, 1970			-.67 (.11)	-.124			.45* (.30)	.111
Recent Immigrant, 1970			-.83 (.18)	-.147			.89* (.55)	.213
Immigrant, Not Recent, 1980			-.42 (.11)	-.082			.77 (.27)	.186
Recent Immigrant, 1980			-.50 (.18)	-.096			.58* (.51)	.142
-2 log (like- lihood ratio)	14470		14430		2958		2946	
Degrees of Freedom	13062		13054		2419		2415	

Note: L = Logit Coefficient (standard errors in parentheses); P = Probability Change (reflects the change in the probability of being in poverty resulting from a unit change in the independent variable) computed at P' = .3119 for Hispanics; and .4838 for Asians (see Petersen 1985).

*Parameter estimate not significant at .05.

poverty without multiple earners. I documented that (1) controlling for individual characteristics of the family head, families headed by recent immigrants and other immigrants were more likely than their native counterparts to be brought above the poverty line due to multiple earners; (2) this positive effect for recent immigrant families was explained completely by their greater tendency than natives to be nuclear, extended, nonsouthern and metropolitan; (3) after controlling for individual, family and contextual variables, the positive and significant effect for previous immigrants persists and (4) white, black and Hispanic immigrant families reveal a marked deterioration over time in the ameliorative impact of multiple earners on poverty status.

SUMMARY AND CONCLUSIONS

Poverty among new immigrants to the United States increased substantially as the new immigration proceeded. This finding first obtained in the descriptive analyses of chapter 4, where I found a steady increase in absolute poverty among recent immigrants between 1960 and 1980. This surge in poverty among recent white, black, Hispanic and Asian immigrant families was particularly sharp during the 1970s. One of the goals of the present chapter was to solidify these findings in a multivariate context.

The first models presented (Table 5.1) confirmed that poverty among recent immigrants increased. That is, after controlling for year of observation and race, recent immigrants in 1979 were significantly more likely to be poor than their counterparts in 1969 or 1959. Furthermore, this surge was not explained by a shift in the racial composition of immigrants.

A justification for the more comprehensive models of absolute poverty was to determine whether the rise in recent immigrant poverty could be explained by household head, family and residence characteristics. The pooled models (Table 5.4) revealed that recent immigrants in 1979 were more likely to be poor than natives, even after controlling for these socioeconomic variables. Disaggregating by race, a significant increase in absolute poverty was indicated for white and black recent immigrant families, but not Hispanic and Asian recent immigrant families. While much of the clamor over the new immigration has been in reaction to a flood of Hispanic and Asian immigrants, both my descriptive and multivariate models show that white and black recent immigrant families had the sharpest increase in poverty.

Low-income families are faced with alternative strategies to improve their economic situation. One option is to try to place additional workers in the labor force. This can be costly, both in terms of time away from family and an increase in total (occupational and domestic) work load for the individuals involved. Nonetheless, for many families, the earnings of secondary workers can spell the difference between being above or below the poverty threshold. Therefore, I first assessed the ameliorative impact of multiple earners on poverty in chapter 4, where I showed that proportionately more immigrants than natives are brought above poverty via multiple earners.

In this chapter, I presented several multivariate models examining the ameliorative effect of secondary workers on family poverty. Again, I found that immigrants, both recent and previous, gain a significantly greater benefit from multiple earners. This effect was explained, to varying degrees, by the propensity of immigrants to live in extended and married-couple families and to live outside southern and rural areas. Still, even after controlling for numerous socioeconomic factors, the greater poverty ameliorating effect enjoyed by immigrants obtained for black and Hispanic families. However, while low-income immigrants were lifted over the poverty line due to multiple earners to a greater degree than natives, I found that this advantage declined significantly over time among white, black and Hispanic families. Asians immigrants never enjoyed this advantage compared to Asian natives.

Overall, results in this chapter reinforce the robustness of my finding that poverty among recent immigrants to the United States increased as the new immigration proceeded. It obtained in both my descriptive and multivariate results, lending support to alarmist claims that the United States is admitting too many impoverished immigrants. As noted in my historical review in chapter 2, throughout U.S. immigration history this country has consistently sought to turn away poor immigrants. However, the abiding concern then, and now, is not the immigration of impoverished individuals per se but the immigration of those who are likely to become a "public charge."

A rise in immigrant poverty is less detrimental if they are unlikely to turn to public assistance and other social services. Thus, while they are difficult to disentangle, the complaint that the United States has become a haven for the world's poor is not voiced as much as the complaint that we are admitting too many immigrants destined for the welfare rolls. As noted in chapter 1, this fear is widespread. Almost half of all adult Americans believe that *most* immigrants wind up on welfare (Pear 1986). Given the dramatic increase in the poverty rates among recent arrivals one might accede to alarmist claims that the new immigration has considerably swelled the welfare rolls. However, this assumes a one-to-one correspondence between poverty and welfare utilization. That poverty necessarily entails use of welfare benefits is an assumption held by many Americans (Feagin 1975). It is not, however, a valid generalization. Whether because of the negative social stigma linked to welfare use (Feagin 1975), ignorance or other reasons, many people do not take advantage of benefits they are entitled to receive (Ross, et al. 1987). Others prefer informal sources of support in times of need (Tienda 1980). Nonetheless, the sudden rise in poverty among recent immigrants is cause for some concern about welfare utilization. Accordingly, in the following two chapters I deal with the question of immigrant-native differentials in public assistance utilization.

Notes

1. See chapter 3 for more details on methodological issues.

2. Maximum likelihood estimates of logit parameters were computed using the GLIM system (Baker and Nelder 1978).

3. I remind the reader that although the years of observation were 1960, 1970 and 1980, because poverty status is based on family income in the previous year, families would have been poor in 1959, 1969 and 1979, respectively.

4. I have opted not to present the results of the saturated model because it merely reproduces perfectly the pattern of poverty rates in the appropriate rows of Table 4.2.

5. Note that many of the hypothesized effects in this section are based on previous research on status and income attainment. Because income is negatively related to poverty, I hypothesize that most of the significant predictors of income will likewise be significant for poverty, but of opposite signs.

6. Cuban-Americans have been quite economically successful (Portes and Bach 1985). If the Other Hispanic category were composed primarily of these groups, I would expect them to have lower poverty rates than Mexicans. However, only about 19% of this group were Cuban in 1980. The balance were from other Central and South American countries (U.S. Bureau of the Census 1983, Fig. 13).

7. Southern states include Alabama, Arkansas, Delaware, the District of Columbia, Florida, Georgia, Kentucky, Louisiana, Maryland, Mississippi, North Carolina, Oklahoma, South Carolina, Tennessee, Texas, Virginia and West Virginia.

8. To protect the anonymity of the respondents in the 1960 and 1970 censuses, certain states had areas in which the metro-nonmetro variable was missing. Where possible, I assigned the nonmetro code to those living in rural areas and the metro code to those living in urban areas. Urban areas are those incorporated cities, boroughs, etc., with 2,500 or more inhabitants; densely settled areas outside of urbanized areas and other large or densely populated areas. In states where both the urban-rural and metro-nonmetro variables were suppressed, I assigned all residents of that state to either the metro or nonmetro groups. These included Rhode Island and Delaware (metro) and Hawaii, Nevada, North Dakota and Utah (nonmetro). In 1980, there was no suppression on the metro-nonmetro variable. This operationalization maximized comparability given existing data constraints.

9. Because the dependent variable is largely a measure of family labor force commitment, I have not included predictor variables that are related to occupation or employment. Thus, unlike the models of poverty, these models exclude head's secondary occupation and economic dependency.

6

Public Assistance Utilization among Immigrants: The Probability of Receipt

As established in chapter 2, the United States has persistently sought to exclude poor immigrants on the grounds that they are likely to become an economic burden. The evolution of the welfare state during the twentieth century has only raised the potential cost of immigration due to pauperism. The extreme position on this issue, articulated by Lamm and Imhoff (1985, p. 185), points alarmingly toward the potential drain of public assistance resources by the new immigrants.

We have been blinded to the problems ahead of us by the motto on the Statue of Liberty and by our own past success. But America of the 1980s is vastly different from the America of the 1880s. Now we have social service and welfare programs that are easy to deceive and exploit. We have a cash-wage economy with high unemployment, vastly different from the empty frontier that greeted previous immigrants. And we have a new social phenomenon wherein all groups can 'demand' almost instant entry into the American middle class, not as a result of hard work but as a matter of entitlement.

There are several reasons—both theoretical and statutory—to expect gross differentials between immigrants and natives in their receipt of public assistance income.[1] Theoretically, due to unresolved assimilation, immigrants (especially recent immigrants) may experience periods of economic hardship and need. This would increase public assistance receipt rates if economically unsuccessful immigrants relied on welfare rather than returning to their country of origin (Cafferty, et al. 1983). On the other hand, there is general ad hoc agreement that immigrants come to the United States in search of employment (Tienda 1983) and that they may be an economically select group (Chiswick 1979). Other research has shown that many immigrants prefer informal sources of support (Tienda 1980; Browning and Rodriguez 1985), and it is plausible that others are unaware of programs for which they qualify or may be uninformed about how to apply for them. Finally, "being on welfare" may run contrary to the desire to comply with American values; seeking acceptance, the stigma of welfare use may be stronger for immigrants. On balance, however, whether immigrants are more or less likely than natives to use public assistance is an empirical question.

Statutory proscriptions regarding immigrant welfare utilization also deserve mention. If immigrants in general, and recent arrivals in particular, are prohibited from using welfare by law, their rates of welfare receipt will be greatly affected. Technically, under the provisions of the Immigration and Nationality Act, legal immigrants who use public assistance within five years of entry are considered a "public charge," and are subject to deportation (Select Commission on Population 1978). Exceptions include those immigrants on welfare for reasons that arose after their entry (e.g., a disability). There is reason to doubt, however, whether this law has much affect on welfare receipt among recent immigrants. To quote from the Select Commission on Population (1978, p. 33),

At first blush, it would seem that the risk of deportation would deter recent immigrants from receiving welfare assistance. However, the public-charge provisions are no deterrent at all, since the Federal courts have consistently held that an immigrant who receives public assistance cannot be deported under the act unless the assistance program requires repayment and the immigrant fails to pay. Few public assistance programs require repayment. Hence, in the 15 years between 1961 and 1976, only 29 immigrants were deported under the public-charge provision of the law.

Despite the theoretical ambiguity on this matter, many Americans assume that immigrants are disproportionately dependent on transfers (Pear 1986) and that this dependency has become particularly pronounced since the legislative reforms of 1965. This assumption shaped the amnesty provisions of the Immigration Reform and Control Act of 1986.[2] Amnesty, which offered legal alien status and eventually citizenship to (otherwise qualified) undocumented immigrants, was denied to any applicants who had received public assistance in the past or who appeared likely to become a public charge in the future. In addition, those granted amnesty were ineligible for welfare for five years.

Given the pervasiveness and influence of the assumption that immigrants are welfare prone, it has received surprisingly little attention in the research literature. "Immigrants undoubtedly have an effect on the cost of providing a whole range of public services including welfare. . . . Few of these effects, however, have received more than cursory attention by immigration researchers or by the administrators of these public services" (Select Commission on Population 1978, p. 32). As such, it has been easy for policy opponents to justify their positions with anecdotal evidence. In the following two chapters I fully explore immigrant use of public assistance programs. I do this in two phases. The present chapter examines the propensity of immigrant families to receive welfare income. In chapter 7, I consider welfare recipients only and analyze the amount of transfer income received.

These analyses parallel the study of poverty in the previous two chapters. In the first analytic section of this chapter, I describe aggregate patterns of public assistance receipt among families in 1969 and 1979.[3] Rates of receipt—the percent of families that received public assistance income in the year before the census—are presented for the entire population and are disaggregated with respect to immigrant status and race. These data establish the gross differences between immigrants and natives in the propensity to receive welfare benefits. These tables also provide baseline data to inform the multivariate analyses that come later.

The subsequent section presents the conceptual framework behind multivariate models of public assistance receipt among families. Like the models of poverty (chapter 5), these consider numerous individual, family and locational characteristics as determinants of welfare receipt.

The next section presents estimates of these multivariate models of welfare receipt. Initial specifications provide empirical confirmation for conclusions drawn from the descriptive tables. These multivariate models also document the net effect of immigrant status on welfare receipt. I establish (1) whether immigrants are particularly likely to receive welfare as some observers assert, (2) whether recent immigrants are more or less likely to receive welfare compared to natives or previous immigrants and (3) whether there are any significant differences between 1969 and 1979 in probabilities of welfare receipt.

In the final analytic section, I re-estimate these models but include a predictor indicating whether the family's prewelfare income is below the poverty line. This determines if economically destitute immigrants are less likely than their native counterparts to receive welfare benefits.

PUBLIC ASSISTANCE RECIPIENCY RATES: DESCRIPTIVE TABLES

In this section I present a series of tables describing aggregate rates of public assistance receipt for all families combined and disaggregated by immigrant status and race. A family is defined here as a recipient if any family member received one or more dollars of income from public assistance programs in the year prior to the census.

Tabular Results

Table 6.1 presents public assistance receipt rates in 1969 and 1979 for all families and according to selected immigrant status categories. The figures for all families show that the proportion receiving benefits is actually rather low, though these increased between 1969 (5.5%) and 1979 (8.5%). This increase partly reflects the weaker economy and higher poverty rate in the latter period (Ross, et al. 1987). Other important factors include programmatic changes that broadened the pool of eligible families, a growth in female-headed families, the success of outreach programs designed to inform the poor of the availability of assistance and a dulling of the stigma attached to being on welfare (Levitan 1985). Most of this increase occurred during the early 1970s.

It is noteworthy that the percent receiving welfare is considerably below the percent in poverty (see Table 4.1). In fact, in 1969, family welfare receipt was roughly half the percent in poverty (5.5 versus 10.6%).

Table 6.1
Public Assistance Receipt Rates for Families by Immigration Cohort and Year

Head's Nativity and Years Since Immigration	1969	1979
All Families[a]	5.5%	8.5
All Natives[a]	5.4	8.4
All Immigrants[a]	6.8	10.4
0-5 Years[a]	7.0	11.3
Over 5 Years[a]	6.8	10.2
0-5 Years	6.0	9.5
6-10 Years	6.2	9.5
11-20 Years	4.6	9.1
Over 20 Years	5.3	7.5

Source: U.S. Bureau of the Census. 1960, 1970 and 1980 Public Use Samples.

[a]Includes Puerto Ricans.

Gross differences in welfare receipt (Table 6.1, rows two and three) show higher rates of welfare use among immigrant families compared to natives in both years, although the percentage point differences were not great (1.4 and 2.0% in 1969 and 1979, respectively). Further comparison of Tables 4.1 and 6.1 reveals that, in relative terms, poverty rates exceeded public assistance receipt rates by a considerable amount in 1969 for both immigrants (90%) and natives (93%).[4] By 1979, however, this excess had declined precipitously among natives (6%), but less so among immigrants (35%). In relation to poverty rates then, use of public assistance increased much more for native than immigrant families between 1969 and 1979. On the whole, however, these baseline data show that immigrant families *were* marginally more likely to receive public assistance income than native families in both years.

Theoretically, years since immigration has both positive and negative influences on the propensity to use public assistance. The concept of assimilation suggests that recent immigrants, because of their lack of integration with the economy, might experience initial periods of labor market dislocation and hardship. This implies a higher rate of welfare receipt initially following immigration, but one that would diminish with structural assimilation. Moreover, the biases discussed in previous chapters (selective emigration and shifting immigrant cohort quality) would inflate the welfare receipt of recent immigrants. That is, those with longer periods of U.S. residence may be selected on economic success, and recent arrivals may have less human capital (Borjas 1985). The above factors imply a negative effect of years since immigration on welfare receipt. On the other hand, additional U.S. experience could increase receipt of welfare through greater knowledge of and familiarity with social programs. Also, individuals with longer periods of U.S. residence will be older and, *ceteris paribus,* more apt to be eligible for Supplemental Security Income.

Turning to the differences between recent immigrants and earlier arrivals (Table 6.1, rows four and five), welfare receipt among recent arrivals was only minutely greater in both years. This gap increased slightly between 1969 (7.0 versus 6.8%) and 1979 (11.3 versus 10.2%).

The final four rows of Table 6.1 present a more refined look at years since immigration. Here I consider those immigrant families whose head arrived 0–5, 6–10, 11–20 and over 20 years before the census.[5] Compared to previous immigrants (i.e., those who arrived 6–10 years before the census), the more recent arrivals were no more likely to receive welfare. While the patterns across these years-since-immigration categories are not systematic, there is some evidence that immigrants who arrived 0–10 years before the census were somewhat more likely than earlier arrivals to receive public assistance, but these differences were modest. In 1969, receipt among those here 0–10 years averaged slightly over 6%, while that for earlier arrivals was on the order of 5%. Thus, while there is some evidence of declining welfare participation with years since immigration, the magnitude of these aggregate differences precludes solid conclusions.

Comparing across rows, the rise in public assistance utilization between 1969 and 1979 is seen for all years-since-immigration categories. For example, those with 11–20 years of U.S. experience received welfare at rates of 4.6 and 9.1% in 1969 and 1979, respectively. These interdecade cohort increases are commensurate with those of the population as a whole. Hence, these comparisons offer little support for the notion that immigrant dependence has become more acute in the most recent period, particularly among recent immigrants.

Finally, these tables allow for a comparison of rates for one real immigrant cohort over time. Specifically, the welfare receipt rate among those with 0–10 years of U.S. residence as of 1969 (about 6.1%) compares to a rate of 9.1% ten years later. This runs decidedly counter to assimilation theory, which would predict lower receipt rates for those immigrants with ten years of U.S. experience. However, this increase coincides with a period when public assistance receipt increased for the population as whole.

Tables 6.2a and 6.2b present these same welfare receipt rates separately for white, black, Hispanic and Asian families. First, comparing public assistance receipt rates across these race categories reveals a pattern similar to that seen among the poverty rates in chapter 4. That is, white and Asian families have far lower rates of receipt than black and Hispanic families. Asian receipt of public assistance is slightly greater than that for whites, while Hispanic receipt is somewhat less than that for blacks.

For white families, natives rather than immigrants reveal the greater average welfare receipt rates. While the differences are slight, they were greater in 1979 than 1969. In 1979, 6.0% of families headed by white natives received public assistance income as compared to 5.5% for immigrant white families. Considering next the differences between years-since-immigration groups, both within years and across time, the last four rows of Table 6.2a reveal that recent white immigrant families do not exhibit the greatest public assistance receipt rates. The patterns based on aggregate tabulations are too haphazard to warrant speculation on the effect of years since immigration on welfare receipt. For example, the most recent groups (0–5 and 6–10 years) showed the greatest interdecade increase. White families who immigrated 0–5 years before the census had receipt rates of 2.1 and 5.3% in 1969 and 1979, respectively. However, only one of these eight groups, those with 6–10 years of U.S. residence as of 1979, had higher welfare receipt than native white families.

Among black families, a similar picture emerges, except that, in comparison to whites, the differentials observed are more pronounced. Native black welfare receipt rates greatly exceed those of their immigrant counterparts. This echoes a similar difference found for poverty rates. In 1979, for example, native receipt stood at 25.2% as compared to only 10.7% among

Table 6.2a
Public Assistance Receipt Rates by Immigration Cohort and Year: White and Black Families

Head's Nativity and Years	White		Black	
Since Immigration	1969	1979	1969	1979
All Families	3.8%	6.0	18.3	24.7
All Natives	3.8	6.0	18.4	25.2
All Immigrants	3.7	5.5	7.1	10.7
0-5 Years	2.1	5.3	3.8	9.6
Over 5 Years	3.8	5.5	8.5	11.0
0-5 Years	2.1	5.3	3.8	9.6
6-10 Years	3.3	7.2	3.4	8.9
11-20 Years	3.1	5.2	8.3	9.5
Over 20 Years	4.1	5.4	7.7	15.6

Source: U.S. Bureau of the Census. 1960, 1970 and 1980 Public Use Samples.

black immigrants. The increase in welfare utilization among all immigrant cohorts was largest for the most recent arrivals. Receipt among recent immigrants increased from 3.8 to 9.6% over the period. Also, welfare receipt was generally greater among black families with more than ten, rather than less than ten years in the United States, contrary to the predictions of assimilation theory. However, none of the years-since-immigration groups displayed welfare receipt rates as high as those of black native families. This reflects that fact that black immigrants, though few in number, are generally highly skilled and enter under those preference categories requiring labor certification.

Among Hispanics, a greater percent of immigrant than native families received some public assistance income in both 1969 and 1979, in contrast to results for blacks and whites. This difference was considerable in 1969, when 11.0% of Hispanic natives used welfare as compared to 16.6% of immigrants. Owing to a sizable increase in welfare receipt among Hispanic natives between censuses, the immigrant-native differential was smaller in 1979 (15.5% for natives versus 17.6% for immigrants). Thus, among His-

panics, the most sizable increase in welfare utilization during the 1970s occurred for natives rather than immigrants. This result also emerges in the
differences between years-since-immigration groups (Table 6.2b, rows six
through nine). Hispanic immigrants with 0–5, 6–10 and over 20 years of
U.S. residence show far less interdecade increase than their native counterparts.[6] Most of the rise in welfare receipt among Hispanics is due to an increase among natives. In fact, receipt among recent arrivals *declined* between
1969 (12.5%) and 1979 (9.3%).

Like Hispanics, immigrant Asian families also reveal greater use of public
assistance than their native counterparts. However, whereas among Hispanics the utilization gap converged between 1969 and 1979, among Asians
it increased. In 1969, 3.6% of natives and 5.0% of immigrants received
welfare, rates that compare to 5.8 and 9.7%, respectively, in 1979. That Asian
immigrant receipt increased and that they constituted a greater percentage
of all Asian families in 1979 compared to 1969 partly explains the interdecade doubling of Asian public assistance receipt rates (4.3 to 8.6%). Like

Table 6.2b
**Public Assistance Receipt Rates by Immigration Cohort and Year: Hispanic
and Asian Families**

Head's Nativity and Years Since Immigration	Hispanic		Asian	
	1969	1979	1969	1979
All Families[a]	13.4%	16.6	4.3	8.6
All Natives[a]	11.0	15.5	3.6	5.8
All Immigrants[a]	16.6	17.6	5.0	9.7
0-5 Years[a]	14.1	14.3	5.9	14.5
Over 5 Years[a]	17.1	18.2	2.1	7.2
0-5 Years	12.5	9.3	2.1	14.5
6-10 Years	10.6	12.5	2.8	6.0
11-20 Years	9.8	13.2	4.6	7.1
Over 20 Years	16.2	16.4	7.6	8.9

Source: U.S. Bureau of the Census. 1960, 1970 and
1980 Public Use Samples.
[a]Includes Puerto Ricans.

black families, the greatest increases in welfare receipt among Asian immigrants occurred for recent arrivals. Clearly, the most recent arrivals, those arriving five or fewer years before the census, experienced the most impressive increase (2.1 up to 14.5%). This increase reflects the presence of many Indo-Chinese refugees among recent immigrants in 1979.

As noted previously, many Vietnamese and Kampuchean refugees entered the United States after the fall of Saigon in 1975 (Goza 1987). Refugees, almost by definition, are less motivated by economic pull factors and thus stand a greater chance of labor market dislocation and economic hardship (Todaro 1969). I documented in chapter 4 that poverty among recent Asian immigrants in 1979 was significantly greater than that for recent Asian immigrants in 1969. Consequently, their welfare utilization rates should be greater. In addition, their refugee status entitled them to relaxed eligibility for several public assistance programs (Department of Health and Human Services 1983). Both factors—the increase in poverty and easier access to assistance programs—help explain the sudden surge in welfare utilization among recent Asian immigrants.

Summarizing my descriptive tabulations, in the aggregate (across race and years-since-immigration categories), immigrant families received public assistance income at slightly higher rates than natives. However, race-specific tabulations showed this generalization obtained only for Hispanic and Asian families. For white and (especially) black families, welfare receipt among the native born was higher than that for their immigrant counterparts. Still, in the aggregate, there is evidence of marginally higher welfare utilization among immigrants.

For the total foreign-born population, recent immigrants (those arriving five or fewer years before the census) had slightly greater rates of public assistance receipt than earlier arrivals. This aggregate generalization conceals substantial racial variation; among black, white and Hispanic immigrants, recent arrivals had *lower* welfare utilization than previous immigrants. Thus, the marginally higher average welfare recipiency of recent immigrants reflects the preponderance of Asians among persons who arrived five years prior to the census. Over time, public assistance receipt rates among recent immigrant families did increase, but at a slower rate than for the population as a whole. Disaggregating by race showed that welfare utilization rates rose sharply for black and Asian immigrants between 1969 and 1979. Despite this surge, in 1979 welfare receipt for foreign blacks remained below that for black natives. For Asians, the rise in receipt among recent immigrants is explained by the large number of Indo-Chinese refugees among them.

On the whole, these tables offer little support for the notion that immigrants, particularly recent arrivals, pose a substantial burden on public assistance programs. These results certainly refute the conventional wisdom, held by some 47% of Americans, that *most* immigrants wind up on welfare.

This stereotype springs from the more general but unproven assumption that immigrants are disproportionately likely to use welfare. In the following section, I test this assumption by controlling for numerous factors that determine need and eligibility for public assistance.

MULTIVARIATE MODELS OF PUBLIC ASSISTANCE RECEIPT: CONCEPTUAL BACKGROUND

In this section I analyze the propensity of immigrants to utilize public assistance based on a conceptualization by Francine Blau (1984) and expanded by Marta Tienda and Leif Jensen (1986). Blau assumed that a family's propensity to receive welfare income is based on individual and family characteristics that determine need and eligibility. Controlling for these characteristics allows for the exploration of the unique influence of nativity on receipt of welfare. In this way, the assumption that immigrants are particularly likely to receive transfer payments can be examined empirically. Using the 1976 Survey of Income and Education (SIE), Blau found that, other things being equal, immigrants are in fact *less* likely than natives to receive transfer payments.

Tienda and Jensen (1986) utilized this framework to explore data from a Public Use Microdata Sample of the 1980 Census. The larger sample size allowed for analyses within basic racial categories. The authors corroborate Blau's finding for white, black and Hispanic families by showing a negative effect of immigrant status on public assistance receipt. However, a positive net effect of immigrant status obtained for Asian families.

The present endeavor goes beyond previous research on this topic by analyzing data from 1970 and 1980 simultaneously. That is, the parallel data files used in the preceding sections were concatenated and year of observation (1970 versus 1980) is introduced as an independent variable. This approach helps establish whether the net negative effect of immigrant status on public assistance utilization also obtained in 1970. More importantly, I can determine whether recent immigrants in 1980 were any more likely to receive public assistance than recent immigrants in 1970. This comparison is critical in view of the assertion that poverty and dependence increased as the new immigration developed.

I assume that the propensity to receive public assistance is determined by several individual and household characteristics reflecting a family's need and eligibility for assistance. The variables chosen to model public assistance receipt appear in Table 6.3, along with their operational definitions. As many of these variables are identical to those used in modeling family poverty (chapter 5), I do not elaborate on their definitions. Instead, I focus on the additional variables used to predict welfare receipt. As in the tabular analyses above, the dependent variable is binary and flags those families in which at least one family member had positive public assistance income for the year prior to the census.[7]

Table 6.3

Definitions of Variables Used in Multivariate Analyses of Public Assistance Receipt

Variable	Definition
Family Head Characteristics	
Age	Age of head in years, 18-99
Age Squared	Head's age squared, divided by 1000
Education	Grades of schooling completed by head
Race (4 categories)	1 = Head is Non-Hispanic White 2 = Head is Non-Hispanic Black 3 = Head is Hispanic 4 = Head is Non-Hispanic Asian
Race (8 categories)	1 = Head is Non-Hispanic White 2 = Head is Non-Hispanic Black 3 = Head is Mexican 4 = Head is Puerto Rican 5 = Head is Other Hispanic 6 = Head is Japanese 7 = Head is Chinese 8 = Head is Other Asian
Hispanic Ethnicity	1 = Head is Other Hispanic 2 = Head is Mexican 3 = Head is Puerto Rican
Asian Ethnicity	1 = Head is Japanese 2 = Head is Chinese 3 = Head is Other Asian
Nativity	1 = Head is Native 2 = Head is Immigrant, Not Recent (immigrated over five years before) 3 = Head is Recent Immigrant (immigrated up to 5 years before)
Family Characteristics	
Headship Configuration	1 = Family, both spouses present 2 = Spouse absent family
Extended Family	Adult Relative of Head (except spouse or child) present coded 2; 1 otherwise
Dependency Rate	Number of non-working family members as a percent of total family members

Table 6.3 (*continued*)

Variable	Definition
Other Income	Total annual family non-earned, non-transfer income in thousands of 1979 dollars
Pre-Welfare Poor	Total family income minus total family welfare income less than poverty threshold, coded 2; 1 otherwise

Other Independent Variables

Variable	Definition
Southern Residence	Family resides in Southern state coded 2; 1 otherwise (where Southern states are AL, AR, DE, DC, FL, GA, KY, LA, MD, MS, NC, OK, SC, TN, TX, VA and WV)
Non-metropolitan Residence	Family resides in a non-metropolitan area coded 2; 1 otherwise
State Average[a] AFDC Payment	Average monthly AFDC payment per family for family's home state in hundreds of 1980 dollars
Year of Observation	1 = 1960 2 = 1970 3 = 1980

Dependent Variable

Variable	Definition
Public Assistance Receipt	Total family Public Assistance income greater than 0 coded 1; 0 otherwise

[a]U.S. Bureau of the Census (1981b, p. 345)

Race is defined as it was in the multivariate models of the previous chapter. That is, in the models pooled by race, I compare to white-headed families (the reference group), blacks, Mexicans, Puerto Ricans, Other Hispanics, Japanese, Chinese and Other Asians. Based on the results of the multivariate analyses of poverty and the tabular results of the preceding section, I expect families with black, Mexican, Puerto Rican, Other Hispanic and Other Asian heads to be more likely, *ceteris paribus,* than those with white heads to receive public assistance income. I then present models for the four race groups separately. The models for Hispanic families include an ethnic variable identifying Mexicans, Puerto Ricans and Other Hispanics (the reference category). Unlike the models of poverty, however, for Asians I use the Japanese as the reference group, to whom I compare families headed by Chinese and Other Asian heads. These models thus include terms for Other Asians, a group I suspect has much to do with the overall increase in welfare receipt among Asian immigrant families.

Other characteristics of the household head that I hypothesize have an effect on welfare receipt are Age, Age-squared and Education. These variables are all defined as they were in chapter 5. I expect the greatest need for public assistance income to be felt by families with young heads and thus hypothesize a negative affect of age on the probability of public assistance receipt. To capture the fact that families with aged heads are more likely to be eligible for Supplemental Security Income, the models include a quadratic term. I expect age-squared to have a positive effect on public assistance receipt. As a rough proxy for labor market potential, education should depress welfare receipt.

In addition to these characteristics of the head, variables describing the nature of the family household as a whole are included. I anticipate single-headed families to display greater use of public assistance, other things being equal, than families headed by a married couple. In the previous chapter, I concluded that single-headed families were far more likely to be poor. Also, certain public assistance programs, such as Aid to Dependent Children (AFDC) are frequently not available to families headed by a married couple. To measure labor market commitment, the proportion of family members not working (dependency) is included and is expected to have a positive net effect on receipt. That is, families with greater economic dependency should exhibit higher rates of public assistance receipt, other things being equal. A variable not appearing in the models of poverty (chapter 5) measures alternative financial resources. Total family nonearned, nontransfer income is expected to have a negative effect on welfare receipt, other things being equal. Finally, extended family structure, defined as the presence of one or more adult relatives of the head (other than spouse or children), should lower welfare receipt. This more complex family arrangement increases the flexibility of families in coping with and overcoming deprivation (see Angel and Tienda 1982; Tienda and Glass 1985). The poverty-ameliorating effect of extended family structure found in the previous chapter reinforces this expectation.

Finally, I evaluate the influence of three contextual variables in these models of welfare receipt. The first is Southern Residence. As was documented in the previous chapter, poverty and economic hardship are significantly greater in the South than in the other three census regions (North, Midwest and West). For this reason, I expect higher welfare receipt in the South.

The second contextual variable, also used in the multivariate analysis of poverty, is Nonmetropolitan (Nonmetro) Residence. That poverty was greater in metropolitan (metro) compared to nonmetro areas, other things being equal, suggests a positive effect of nonmetro residence on public assistance receipt. However, others have documented that nonmetro residents underutilize welfare programs compared to their metro counterparts (Carlson et al. 1981). The net effect is an empirical question.

Despite the psychological costs due to the stigma of welfare receipt (Feagin 1975), utilization will be more attractive in direct proportion to the benefit levels for one's area of residence. To capture this, State Average AFDC Payment per family is included.[8] This final contextual variable is expected to have a positive direct effect on receipt.

Table 6.1 showed that public assistance recipiency rates were greater in 1979 than 1969. Thus, the variable denoting the 1980 census is expected to have a positive effect, other things being the same.

MULTIVARIATE MODELS OF PUBLIC ASSISTANCE RECEIPT: EMPIRICAL RESULTS

With the preceding conceptual discussion in mind, in this section I estimate logistic regression models of family public assistance receipt. The first series of models is pooled across categories of race (Table 6.4), but then estimates for white, black, Hispanic and Asian families are presented separately (Tables 6.5a to 6.5c). Finally, I estimate a number of models that include as an independent variable a flag for families that are prewelfare poor. These are likewise presented pooled (Table 6.6) and disaggregated by race (Table 6.7).

Results

Model 1 in Table 6.4 estimates family welfare receipt from year of observation, immigrant status and race. This specification speaks to some of the conclusions drawn from the descriptive tables (Tables 6.1, 6.2 and 6.3). As expected, the positive and significant estimate for year of observation indicates that, net of immigrant status and race, families were more likely to receive public assistance in 1979 than in 1969.

Compared to white families, black, Mexican, Puerto Rican, Other Hispanic and Other Asian families were significantly more likely to receive welfare income. Blacks and Hispanics continue to be among America's most disadvantaged minority groups (Tienda and Jensen 1988), and Other Asians include many refugees. The significant hardship faced by Puerto Rican families manifests itself in a very strong positive effect on welfare utilization. Although the term fails to reach significance, Japanese-headed families appear to be somewhat less likely that whites to receive assistance. The Chinese differ little from whites in this regard.

Of greater relevance to this research, however, are the effects for immigrant status. First, they show that Immigrant, Not Recent families were significantly less likely than natives to receive welfare benefits. Second, recent immigrants were more likely than previous arrivals to receive welfare, a finding consistent with the notion that new immigrants are more likely to experience economic disruption and hardship. Third, families headed by a recent immigrant do not differ significantly from natives in their propensity to receive welfare income. (This term was negative, but failed to reach significance.)

Model 2 of Table 6.4 introduces the main effects for the characteristics of the family head, the family and its residence location. Many of these effects were consistent with expectation. For example, education had a negative and significant effect on the probability of welfare receipt. Other things being equal, families with better-educated heads were less likely to receive welfare than those with less-educated heads. Spouse-absent families were significantly more likely than otherwise comparable married-couple families to receive public assistance, as were families with greater economic dependency (lower labor force participation per capita). Finally, families with more nonearned, nontransfer income—a resource that diminishes economic need—were significantly less likely to receive welfare, compared to those with less Other Income.

A number of terms failed to reach significance. These included Age, Age-squared, State Average AFDC Payment and Nonmetropolitan Residence. The latter two terms are not surprising, because they had theoretically equivocal effects on welfare receipt. The lack of an effect for average AFDC payment suggests that, net of characteristics that determine need and eligibility, higher benefits are not by themselves strong determinants of welfare use among families. That age and age-squared had no significant effect on welfare is more surprising, especially in view of the finding that poverty declines linearly with age and increases with old age (chapter 5).

One result highly contrary to expectation is the effect of extended family structure. The presence of one or more adult relatives of the head (other than spouse or children) had a strong and positive effect on receipt of public assistance. I predicted that because extended structure provides families with greater flexibility to cover both domestic and labor force responsibilities, it would *decrease* need for public assistance. This reasoning followed, in part, from the results of the previous chapter; extended families were significantly less likely to be poor, other things being equal. While extended family members would not affect a family's eligibility for AFDC, they might have disabilities that would increase their eligibility for Supplemental Security Income.

The most important outcome of Model 2, however, is the persistently negative and significant effect for Immigrant, Not Recent families and the negative (but insignificant) effect for recent immigrant families. These estimates imply that, after controlling for numerous family characteristics that determine need and eligibility for public assistance, previous immigrants were less likely to receive welfare than natives.

In the previous chapter, I determined that the aggregate national improvement in poverty between 1969 and 1979 was not enjoyed by immigrants. In fact, poverty among recent immigrants increased dramatically between censuses. This rise in the level of economic hardship among recent immigrants could foreshadow a similar rise in the level of public assistance receipt. To address this possibility, Model 3 in Table 6.4 includes the in-

Table 6.4
Logistic Regression of Public Assistance Receipt: Pooled by Race[a]

	Model 1		Model 2		Model 3	
	L	P	L	P	L	P
Intercept	-3.11 (.07)		-4.99 (.38)		-4.92 (.38)	
1980	.33 (.05)	.025	.54 (.08)	.044	.57 (.09)	.047
Family Head Variables						
Immigrant, Not Recent	-.19 (.07)	-.011	-.41 (.08)	-.022	-.35 (.12)	-.020
Recent Immigrant	-.01* (.11)	-.001	-.09* (.13)	-.056	-.06* (.21)	-.004
Black	1.55 (.07)	.191	1.07 (.09)	.110	1.08 (.09)	.111
Mexican	1.06 (.09)	.108	.65 (.10)	.056	.65 (.10)	.056
Puerto Rican	2.17 (.14)	.327	1.62 (.16)	.205	1.61 (.16)	.203
Other Hispanic	.90 (.10)	.086	.81 (.12)	.074	.81 (.12)	.074
Japanese	-.43* (.25)	-.023	-.21* (.26)	-.012	-.21* (.26)	-.012
Chinese	.10* (.22)	.007	.26* (.23)	.019	.27* (.23)	.020

Variable						
Other Asian	.58 (.15)	.048	.72 (.17)	.064	.73 (.17)	.065
Education			-.09 (.01)	-.006	-.09 (.01)	-.006
Age			.01* (.01)	.001	.01* (.01)	.001
Age^2			-.06* (.11)	-.004	-.06* (.11)	-.004

Family and Contextual Variables

Variable				
Dependency Rate	.03 (.01)	.002	.03 (.01)	.002
Spouse Absent	1.33 (.07)	.151	1.34 (.07)	.153
Extended Family	.71 (.08)	.063	.71 (.08)	.063
Other Income	-.06 (.01)	-.004	-.06 (.01)	-.004
Southern Residence	-.27 (.11)	-.016	-.27 (.11)	-.016
Non-metro Residence	.03* (.09)	.002	.03* (.09)	.002
State Average AFDC Payment	.00* (.04)	.000	.00* (.04)	.000

Table 6.4 (*continued*)

	Model 1		Model 2		Model 3	
	L	P	L	P	L	P
Interaction Terms						
Immigrant, Not Recent, 1980					-.10* (.14)	-.006
Recent Immigrant, 1980					-.06* (.26)	-.004
-2 log (likeli-hood ratio)	9046		7363		7362	
Degrees of Freedom	14610		14600		14598	

Note: L = Logit Coefficient (standard errors in parentheses); P = Probability Change (reflects the change in the probability of receiving public assistance resulting from a unit change in the independent variable) computed at P' = .0697 (see Petersen 1985).

*Parameter estimate not significant at .05.

teraction terms between immigrant status and year of observation. If the rise in poverty among recent arrivals brought about a similar rise in welfare receipt rates, these interactions should be positive and significant. However, these multiplicative terms are neither positive nor significant; previous immigrants were less likely than statistically comparable natives to receive welfare in both 1969 and 1979. More importantly, the rise in poverty among recent immigrants did not presage a commensurate rise in public assistance receipt.

The results in Table 6.4 suggest that immigrants are not a disproportionate burden on welfare resources. However, the descriptive tables revealed considerable differences in the patterns of public assistance receipt across race groups. For example, the propensity of black immigrant families to receive welfare was far below that of black native families. Among Asian families, the opposite pattern emerged, with recent Asian immigrants revealing appreciably greater welfare receipt rates. To examine these issues with more rigor, I now present models of welfare receipt for white, black, Hispanic and Asian families separately.

In Table 6.5a, Model 1 for whites includes the main effects for individual, family and contextual variables. The estimates are similar to those that obtained for the population as a whole. For example, Education had a negative effect and having an absent spouse had a positive impact on welfare receipt, other things being equal. Also, the surprising positive effect of extended family structure obtains among these white families. None of the contextual variables (Southern and Nonmetro Residence and State AFDC Payments) are statistically significant.

Most importantly, the effects for immigrant status were the same as those for the entire population. All but recent white immigrant families were less likely than their native counterparts to receive welfare income, other things being equal. This negative effect of immigrant status obtained for recent white immigrants, but failed to reach significance. Vis-à-vis otherwise comparable natives then, white immigrants appear to eschew welfare as an income-maintenance strategy.

In chapters 4 and 5, I documented a considerable rise over time in poverty among white immigrants, recent arrivals in particular. This may portend increasing welfare utilization as well. However, the interactions between year and immigrant status in Model 2 for whites refute the notion that public assistance receipt likewise increased between 1969 and 1979. Both terms are negative and insignificant, meaning that, relative to white natives, the lower likelihood of white immigrants to receive welfare remained the same between censuses.

Parallel models for black families, also reported in Table 6.5a, reveal a unique pattern of effects. For example, southern blacks were considerably less likely than their nonsouthern counterparts to receive transfers, but nonmetro residents were more likely to do so. The most important differences

Table 6.5a
Logistic Regression of Public Assistance Receipt: White and Black Families[a]

	Whites				Blacks			
	Model 1		Model 2		Model 1		Model 2	
	L	p	L	p	L	p	L	p
Intercept	-3.32 (.60)		-3.36 (.60)	.047	-3.24 (.39)		-3.25 (.39)	-.138
1980	.65 (.14)	.040	.73 (.15)	.047	.68 (.09)	.138	.68 (.08)	-.138
Family Head Variables								
Immigrant, Not Recent	-.46 (.13)	-.017	-.28* (.18)	-.011	-.79 (.12)	-.106	-.79 (.29)	-.106
Recent Immigrant	-.64* (.41)	-.022	-.25* (.60)	-.010	-1.11 (.26)	-.135	-1.93 (.72)	-.181
Education	-.11 (.02)	-.005	-.11 (.02)	-.005	-.11 (.01)	-.018	-.11 (.01)	-.018
Age	-.01* (.02)	-.000	-.01* (.02)	-.000	.00* (.01)	.000	.00* (.01)	.000
Age^2	.06* (.17)	.003	.06* (.17)	.003	-.04* (.11)	-.007	-.04* (.11)	-.007
Family and Contextual Variables								
Dependency Rate	.02 (.00)	.001	.02 (.00)	.001	.03 (.01)	.005	.03 (.01)	.005
Spouse Absent	1.28 (.11)	.105	1.28 (.11)	.105	1.41 (.07)	.316	1.41 (.07)	.316

	L (SE)	P	L (SE)	P	L (SE)	P	L (SE)	P
Extended Family	.85 (.13)	.057	.86 (.13)	.058	.44 (.08)	.085	.44 (.08)	.085
Other Income	-.09 (.02)	-.004	-.09 (.02)	-.004	-.07 (.02)	-.012	-.07 (.02)	-.012
Southern Residence	-.24* (.19)	-.010	-.24* (.19)	-.010	-.43 (.11)	-.065	-.42 (.11)	-.064
Non-metro Residence	-.03* (.13)	-.001	-.03* (.13)	-.001	.22 (.09)	.040	.22 (.09)	.040
State Average AFDC Payment	.04* (.07)	.002	.03* (.07)	.001	-.02* (.05)	-.003	-.02* (.05)	-.003
Interaction Terms								
Immigrant, Not Recent, 1980			-.03* (.23)	-.013			.00* (.32)	.000
Recent Immigrant, 1980			-.07* (.80)	-.022			1.00* (.77)	.214
-2 log (likelihood ratio)	3083		3072		6147		6145	
Degrees of Freedom	8901		8898		8320		8318	

Note: L = Logit Coefficient (standard errors in parentheses); P = Probability Change (reflects the change in the probability of receiving public assistance resulting from a unit change in the independent variable) computed at P' = .0478 for whites and .2199 for blacks (see Petersen 1985).

*Parameter estimate not significant at .05.

rest with immigrant status, however. Compared to native blacks, immigrants, particularly recent immigrants, were significantly less likely to receive welfare income. This is consistent with the notion, supported in the poverty analyses, that immigrant blacks are in a better economic position compared to black native families.

Model 2 for blacks includes the interaction terms between immigrant status and year of observation. These reveal that, *ceteris paribus,* black immigrants in 1979 were no more likely than their counterparts in 1969 to receive welfare. Compared to black natives, the lower likelihood of receipt among immigrants was constant between 1969 and 1979.

Table 6.5b presents a series of models for Hispanic families. Model 1 includes the main effects for all individual, family and locational variables. Among these is an ethnic identifier that compares Mexicans and Puerto Ricans to Other Hispanics (the reference category). The estimates for these dummy variables reveal that compared to Other Hispanics, Mexican families were significantly less likely and Puerto Rican families were much more likely to receive welfare benefits. Thus, while Mexicans have been the focus of an appreciable amount of the concern regarding the new immigration (Cafferty, et al. 1983), among all Hispanics they reveal the lowest likelihood of welfare use.

Regarding immigrant status, the results for Hispanic families parallel those for whites, blacks and the population as a whole. Hispanic immigrants (except recent arrivals) were significantly less likely to receive public assistance, other things being equal, than their native counterparts. The sign for Recent Immigrants was also negative, but this term was statistically insignificant.

Model 2 for Hispanics includes the immigrant status by year-of-observation interactions. Both of these terms are negative and significant suggesting the following. The lower likelihood of Hispanic immigrants to receive welfare compared to natives was unique to 1979. This runs contrary to popular fears that Hispanic immigrants in the most recent period are particularly likely to be welfare dependent. In the final model for Hispanics (Model 3), I include the interactions between immigrant status and ethnicity. Note that both terms for Mexican immigrants are negative and significant while the main effect for Mexicans becomes positive and insignificant. This suggests that most of the reason why Mexicans had relatively low rates of public assistance receipt on the whole, was because of the particularly low receipt among Mexican *immigrants*.

The descriptive tables revealed that, in the aggregate, recent Asian immigrant families were far more likely than Asian natives to receive welfare. The models in Table 6.5c subject this observation to multivariate scrutiny. Model 1 estimates family public assistance receipt from a host of variables, including Asian ethnicity. As expected, compared to Japanese families, both Chinese and Other Asian families were significantly more likely to receive welfare income. This effect is far stronger for the Other Asian category. Many of the other estimates conform to expectation. Education has a negative and significant effect, while economic dependency and single headedness both have positive effects. Two of the contextual variables reached significance for Asians. Asian families living in nonmetro areas were significantly less likely to receive, while those living in states with higher benefits were, *ceteris paribus,* more prone to welfare receipt. Again, contrary to expectation, extended structure *increased* the likelihood of welfare receipt.

With respect to immigrant status, all but recent Asian immigrant families were as likely as natives to receive welfare. However, recent Asian immigrant families were markedly more likely to receive welfare benefits than natives, net of the other determinants of need and eligibility. The descriptive tables revealed a sharp increase in the rate of welfare receipt among recent Asian immigrants. Model 2, which includes the interaction between nativity and year of observation, confirms this result. Net of other factors, recent Asian immigrants in 1979 were far more likely to receive assistance when compared to their counterparts in 1969. Above, I speculated that this was due to the presence of Indo-Chinese refugees among recent arrivals. Model 3 offers some support for this contention. This model includes the two-way interaction between immigrant status and ethnicity. The terms for recent Chinese and Other Asian immigrants—groups that are predominantly Indo-Chinese refugees (Goza 1987)—are both strong and positive.

By way of summary to this section, I stress the following results. I found that (1) for the population as a whole, immigrant families (except recent immigrants) were significantly *less* likely to receive welfare benefits than otherwise comparable natives; (2) this seeming aversion to public assistance among all but recent immigrants obtained for white, black, Hispanic and Asian families, although this effect was not statistically significant for latter; (3) disregarding race, recent immigrants were *not* more likely than natives to use welfare; (4) recent black immigrants were significantly less likely and recent Asian immigrants were significantly more likely than their respective native counterparts to receive welfare, while recent white and Hispanic immigrants differed little from natives; (5) despite the increase in poverty between 1969 and 1979, only recent Asian immigrants revealed a significantly greater propensity toward welfare receipt in 1979; (6) Hispanic immigrants appeared increasingly reluctant to use public assistance over time compared to Hispanic natives and (7) Mexican immigrants, compared to other Mexicans and Hispanics in general, were less likely to receive welfare benefits. On balance, far from evidence of an immigrant proclivity toward public assistance utilization, these findings would seem to support an immigrant aversion to welfare. These results offer strong evidence against the notion that the new immigration poses a serious drain on public assistance resources. Still, a more definitive answer to this question awaits the results of

Table 6.5b
Logistic Regression of Public Assistance Receipt: Hispanic Families[a]

	Model 1		Model 2		Model 3	
	L	P	L	P	L	P
Intercept	-5.03 (.36)		-5.06 (.37)		-5.06 (.37)	
1980	.50 (.07)	.075	.69 (.10)	.109	.64 (.10)	.010
Family Head Variables						
Immigrant, Not Recent	-.24 (.07)	-.028	-.12* (.09)	-.015	.27 (.13)	.037
Recent Immigrant	-.12* (.11)	-.015	.28 (.14)	.039	.66 (.17)	.104
Mexican	-.19 (.07)	-.022	-.19 (.07)	-.022	.16* (.10)	.021
Puerto Rican	.52 (.10)	.078	.50 (.10)	.075	.78 (.23)	.127
Education	-.06 (.01)	-.007	-.06 (.01)	-.007	-.06 (.01)	-.007
Age	.02* (.01)	.003	.01* (.01)	.001	.01* (.01)	.001
Age^2	.02* (.10)	.003	.03* (.10)	.004	.07* (.10)	.009

Family and Contextual Variables

	Model 1			Model 2			Model 3		
Dependency Rate	.03	(.00)	.004	.03	(.00)	.004	.03	(.00)	.004
Spouse Absent	1.32	(.06)	.246	1.32	(.06)	.246	1.32	(.06)	.246
Extended Family	.87	(.07)	.145	.88	(.07)	.147	.87	(.07)	.145
Other Income	-.09	(.02)	-.011	-.09	(.02)	-.022	-.09	(.02)	-.011
Southern Residence	-.18*	(.11)	-.021	-.19*	(.11)	-.022	-.27	(.11)	-.031
Non-metro Residence	-.14*	(.09)	-.017	-.13*	(.09)	-.016	-.09*	(.10)	.011
State Average AFDC Payment	.03*	(.04)	.004	.03*	(.04)	.004	.01*	(.04)	.001
Interaction Terms									
Immigrant, Not Recent, 1980				-.24	(.12)	-.028	-.22*	(.12)	-.026
Recent Immigrant, 1980				-.89	(.21)	-.082	-.70	(.22)	-.069

Table 6.5b (*continued*)

	Model 1		Model 2		Model 3	
	L	P	L	P	L	P
Mexican Immigrant, Not Recent					-.59 (.14)	-.060
Mexican Immigrant, Recent					-.99 (.26)	-.087
Puerto Rican Immigrant, Not Recent					-.42* (.26)	-.046
Puerto Rican Immigrant, Recent					-.39* (.38)	-.043
-2 log (likeli-hood ratio)	8131		8113		8088	
Degrees of Freedom	12605		12603		12599	

Note: L = Logit Coefficient (standard errors in parentheses); P = Probability Change (reflects the change in the probability of receiving public assistance resulting from a unit change in the independent variable) computed at P' = .1482 (see Petersen 1985).

*Parameter estimate not significant at .05.

the following chapter. For now, I offer a final additional analysis of immigrant-native differentials in the propensity to use welfare.

WELFARE UTILIZATION CONDITIONED BY PREWELFARE POVERTY STATUS

Throughout this work, I have cited research showing that immigrants prefer informal sources of support in times of need (Tienda 1980; Massey 1986). This view is consistent with the notion of the process of immigration as occurring because of, and in turn reinforcing, a social network of immigrants (Findley 1977; Sassen-Koob 1979). This line of research paints an image of immigrants who respond to economic hardship differently than natives— turning not to welfare, but to each other.

Some empirical support for this possibility has already been documented in this volume. That is, while immigrant poverty generally exceeded native poverty by a considerable degree, public assistance receipt among immigrants did not exceed that of natives to the same degree. For example, in 1979, while immigrant poverty surpassed that of natives by some 57% (14.0 versus 8.9%), immigrant public assistance receipt exceeded that for natives by only 24% (10.4 versus 8.4%).

To shed more light on this issue, I re-estimated the models of the preceding section, taking into account prewelfare poverty status. This variable is computed as follows. If prewelfare family income (total family income minus welfare income) is less than the poverty threshold, Prewelfare Poverty is coded 2, otherwise it is assigned the value 1.

By controlling for a common state of economic destitution, I can determine whether immigrants in need are less likely than similarly destitute natives to turn to public assistance as an income maintenance strategy. Such a determination is particularly warranted in view of the rise in immigrant poverty as the new immigration unfolded.

Models of public assistance receipt for families with Prewelfare Poverty as a predictor appear in Tables 6.6 and 6.7. The first of these tables presents models pooled across categories of race. The latter presents models for white, black, Asian and Hispanic families separately.

That prewelfare poor families were far more prone to welfare receipt is documented in Model 1 of Table 6.6. The estimate for this term is very strong and positive. Other things being equal, the probability of welfare receipt increased by 0.20 if the family was prewelfare poor.

This result is neither surprising nor interesting. More important is the interaction between prewelfare poverty and immigrant status. If, in fact, immigrants are less apt to turn to public assistance in times of economic hardship compared to natives, then these interaction terms should be negative. Model 2 shows that both of these parameter estimates are negative, but only that for recent immigrants is significant. Compared to otherwise similar

Table 6.5c
Logistic Regression of Public Assistance Receipt: Asian Families[a]

	Model 1		Model 2		Model 3	
	L	P	L	P	L	P
Intercept	-5.92 (.60)		-5.83 (.60)		-5.95 (.61)	
1980	.85 (.14)	.072	.63 (.20)	.048	.62 (.20)	.047
Family Head Variables						
Immigrant, Not Recent	-.15* (.12)	-.008	-.22* (.21)	-.012	-.27* (.28)	.018
Recent Immigrant	.48 (.13)	.034	-.67* (.42)	-.029	-4.86 (1.87)	-.061
Chinese	.36 (.14)	.024	.37 (.14)	.025	.44 (.21)	.031
Other Asian	.71 (.14)	.056	.71 (.14)	.055	.83 (.20)	.069
Education	-.06 (.01)	-.003	-.06 (.01)	-.003	-.06 (.01)	-.003
Age	-.00* (.02)	.000	-.00* (.02)	-.000	-.00* (.02)	.000
Age^2	.22* (.15)	.014	.23* (.15)	.015	.17* (.16)	.011

Family and Contextual Variables

	Model 1			Model 2			Model 3		
Dependency Rate	.02 (.00)		.001	.02 (.00)		.001	.02 (.00)		.001
Spouse Absent	.64 (.10)		.049	.64 (.10)		.049	.61 (.10)		.046
Extended Family	1.30 (.09)		.133	1.29 (.09)		.131	1.30 (.09)		.133
Other Income	-.05 (.01)		-.003	-.05 (.01)		-.003	-.05 (.01)		-.003
Southern Residence	.11* (.21)		.007	.13* (.21)		.008	.12* (.21)		.007
Non-metro Residence	-.53 (.16)		-.024	-.59 (.16)		-.026	-.60 (.16)		-.027
State Average AFDC Payment	.18 (.08)		.011	.19 (.08)		.012	.19 (.08)		.012

Interaction Terms

	Model 1			Model 2			Model 3		
Immigrant, Not Recent, 1980				.12* (.24)		.007	.16* (.24)		.010
Recent Immigrant, 1980				1.29 (.43)		.131	1.28 (.44)		.129

Table 6.5c (*continued*)

	Model 1		Model 2		Model 3	
	L	P	L	P	L	P
Chinese Immigrant, Not Recent					-.62 (.31)	-.027
Chinese Immigrant, Recent					4.33 (1.84)	.771
Other Asian Immigrant, Not Recent					-.62 (.30)	-.027
Other Asian Immigrant, Recent					4.13 (1.83)	.743
-2 log (likeli-hood ratio)	4302		4291		4269	
Degrees of Freedom	10148		10146		10142	

Note: L = Logit Coefficient (standard errors in parentheses); P = Probability Change (reflects the change in the probability of receiving public assistance resulting from a unit change in the independent variable) computed at P' = .0616 (see Petersen 1985).

*Parameter estimate not significant at .05.

Table 6.6
Logistic Regression of Public Assistance Receipt, Controlling for Prewelfare Poverty: Pooled by Race[a]

	Model 1		Model 2	
	L	P	L	P
Intercept	-5.22 (.39)		-5.29 (.39)	
1980	.59 (.09)	.049	.60 (.09)	.050
Family Head Variables				
Immigrant, Not Recent	-.40 (.08)	-.022	-.31 (.10)	-.018
Recent Immigrant	-.32 (.14)	-.018	-.01* (.19)	-.001
Black	.90 (.09)	.086	.88 (.10)	.085
Mexican	.54 (.11)	.044	.53 (.11)	.043
Puerto Rican	1.41 (.17)	.165	1.43 (.17)	.169
Other Hispanic	.73 (.12)	.065	.72 (.12)	.064
Japanese	-.30* (.27)	-.017	-.29* (.27)	-.017
Chinese	.10* (.24)	.007	.10* (.24)	.007
Other Asian	.57 (.18)	.047	.56 (.17)	.046
Education	-.06 (.01)	-.004	-.06 (.01)	-.004
Age	.02* (.01)	.001	.02 (.01)	.001
Age^2	-.10* (.11)	-.006	-.10* (.11)	-.006
Family and Contextual Variables				
Dependency Rate	.02 (.01)	.001	.02 (.01)	.001
Spouse Absent	1.01 (.07)	.101	1.00 (.07)	.100
Extended Family	.89 (.08)	.085	.89 (.08)	.085
Other Income	-.02* (.01)	-.001	-.02* (.01)	-.001

Table 6.6 (*continued*)

	Model 1		Model 2	
	L	P	L	P
Pre-Welfare Poor	1.61 (.08)	.203	1.72 (.09)	.225
Southern Residence	-.37 (.12)	-.020	-.37 (.12)	-.020
Non-metro Residence	-.08* (.09)	-.005	-.09* (.09)	-.006
State Average AFDC Payment	.03* (.05)	.002	.03* (.05)	.002
Interaction Terms				
Immigrant, Not Recent, Pre-Welfare Poor			-.21* (.14)	-.012
Recent Immigrant, Pre-Welfare Poor			-.55 (.24)	-.028
-2 log (likelihood ratio)	6920		6914	
Degrees of Freedom	14599		14597	

Note: L = Logit Coefficient (standard errors in parentheses); P = Probability Change (reflects the change in the probability of receiving public assistance resulting from a unit change in the independent variable) computed at P' = .0697 (see Petersen 1985).

*Parameter estimate not significant at .05.

natives, destitute recent immigrants were significantly *less* likely to receive public assistance benefits.

Table 6.7 re-estimates the latter model for each race group. Among white families, both interaction terms between prewelfare poverty and immigrant status are negative and significant. Compared to impoverished native white families, impoverished immigrants were much less likely to receive public assistance benefits, other things being equal. This effect was particularly strong for recent white immigrants.

As can be seen in Model 2 in Table 6.7, black immigrant families differ little from their native counterparts in this regard. That is, controlling for a common state of need, black immigrants were *not* less likely than native families to receive welfare.

Hispanic families reveal the same pattern as whites. The negative and significant interaction terms establish that, for a similar level of need, immigrants (both recent and earlier arrivals) were significantly less prone to receive welfare compared to Hispanic natives. When viewed in relation to the great concern over the Hispanic component of the new immigration, this finding is all the more striking.

Finally, among Asian families, the lower likelihood of receipt for immigrants in need (when compared to similarly situated natives), obtained for previous immigrants only. Recent immigrants also appeared less likely to receive public assistance income, but this term failed to reach significance.

In sum, while the patterns of relationships differ across race groups, the results reinforce the image of immigrants as eschewing formal sources of support to a greater degree than natives. This is consistent with my conclusion that a rise in immigrant poverty per se does not necessarily foster a commensurate increase in welfare utilization. This may reflect the fact that, in times of economic difficulty, immigrants rely on family and kin to a greater degree than natives. Unfortunately, more definitive support for this notion is not possible because these data do not detail interhousehold transfers of money or labor.

SUMMARY AND CONCLUSIONS

This chapter focused on one sensitive cost of immigration: the utilization of public assistance. Fearing that immigrants are prone to dependency, throughout our immigration history we have chosen to exclude persons who are likely to become paupers (Bennett 1963). The assertion that immigrants tend to be disproportionate users of welfare programs persists today, yet has gone largely untested by researchers. This chapter extended the work of Blau (1984) and Tienda and Jensen (1986) by examining the gross and net propensity of immigrants to receive public assistance income, and changes in these propensities during the 1960–1980 intercensal period.

The descriptive tables presented at the outset revealed that, in the aggregate, immigrant families had only minimally higher public assistance recipiency rates compared to native families. These differences were proportionately less than the excess of immigrant poverty over that of natives. Disaggregating these immigrant-native comparisons by race revealed that immigrants had greater welfare receipt among Hispanic and Asian families, while natives had higher receipt among white and black families. Except for the sizable excess of native receipt among black families, these aggregate differences were not considerable. At this general level, there was little evidence for the assertion that immigrants are prone to use public assistance.

A comparison (between 1969 and 1979) of the recipiency of cohorts who had been in the United States the same amount of time provided little support for the contention that recent immigrants in 1979 were disproportionately more likely than their counterparts in 1969 to receive assistance. Although the utilization rates increased, they did not do so in excess of the population-wide rise between 1969 and 1979. However, there were a few exceptions to this generalization. Recent Asian immigrants in 1979 were much more likely than recent Asian immigrants in 1969 to receive assistance, due

Table 6.7
Logistic Regression of Public Assistance Receipt, Controlling for Prewelfare Poverty: Within-Race Models[a]

	Whites		Blacks		Hispanics		Asians	
	L	p	L	p	L	p	L	p
Intercept	-3.91 (.61)		-3.77 (.40)		-5.27 (.39)		-6.46 (.62)	
1930	.69 (.15)	.043	.79 (.09)	.016	.68 (.10)	.107	.64 (.20)	.049
Family Head Variables								
Immigrant, Not Recent	-.19* (.15)	-.008	-.76 (.16)	-.103	.04* (.12)	.005	-.04* (.23)	-.002
Recent Immigrant	-.15* (.46)	-.006	-1.35 (.39)	-.152	.38 (.18)	-.042	-.80* (.43)	-.033
Mexican					-.22 (.07)	-.026		
Puerto Rican					.43 (.11)	.063		
Chinese							.30 (.15)	.020
Other Asian							.64 (.14)	.049
Education	-.08 (.02)	-.005	-.09 (.01)	-.015	-.03 (.01)	-.004	-.04 (.01)	-.002

Family and Contextual Variables

Age	-.00* (.02)	-.000	.01* (.01)	.002	.02 (.01)	.003	.02* (.02)	.001
Age^2	.01* (.17)	.000	-.08* (.11)	-.013	-.02* (.11)	-.003	.09* (.16)	.005
Dependency Rate	.01 (.00)	.000	.02 (.00)	.003	.02 (.01)	.003	.02 (.00)	.001
Spouse Absent	.92 (.12)	.064	1.10 (.07)	.239	.99 (.06)	.171	.46 (.10)	.033
Extended Family	1.11 (.13)	.084	.60 (.09)	.119	1.05 (.07)	.184	1.42 (.09)	.152
Other Income	-.05 (.02)	-.002	-.01* (.02)	-.002	-.04 (.01)	-.005	-.02* (.01)	-.001
Pre-Welfare Poverty	1.84 (.15)	.191	1.43 (.83)	.321	1.75 (.10)	.352	1.77 (.21)	.217
Southern Residence	-.25* (.19)	-.010	-.42 (.12)	-.064	-.37 (.11)	-.041	.06 (.21)	.004
Non-metro Residence	-.13* (.14)	-.006	.16* (.10)	.029	-.29 (.10)	-.033	-.54 (.16)	-.025
State Average AFDC Payment	.07* (.07)	.003	.06* (.05)	.010	-.02* (.05)	-.003	.19 (.08)	.012

Table 6.7 (*continued*)

	Whites		Blacks		Hispanics		Asians	
	L	P	L	P	L	P	L	P
Interaction Terms								
Im., Not Recent Pre-Welfare Poor	-.70 (.29)	-.023	-.05* (.23)	-.008	-.34 (.13)	-.038	-.55 (.26)	-.025
Recent Immigrant Pre-Welfare Poor	-2.08 (.90)	-.041	.16 (.52)	.029	-.48 (.21)	-.051	-.34* (.25)	-.017
Immigrant, Not Rec., 1980					-.28 (.13)	-.032	.09* (.25)	.005
Recent Immigrant, 1980					-.94 (.22)	-.085	1.20 (.44)	.117
-2 log (likelihood ratio)	2933		5813		7618		4128	
Degrees of Freedom	8898		8317		12600		10143	

Note: L = Logit Coefficient (standard errors in parentheses); P = Probability Change (reflects the change in the probability of receiving public assistance resulting from a unit change in the independent variable) computed at P' = .0478 for whites and .2199 for blacks, .1482 for Hispanics and .0616 for Asians (see Petersen 1985).

*Parameter estimate not significant at .05.

in part to the influx of Indo-Chinese refugees in the post–1975 period. Recent black immigrants were also disproportionately more likely to receive welfare than their 1969 counterparts. Finally, the descriptive tables documented a *decline* in the receipt of welfare by the most recent group of Hispanic immigrants.

Using multivariate logistic regression, I estimated the propensity of immigrants vis-à-vis natives to receive public assistance net of other determinants of need and eligibility. I determined that white and black families headed by immigrants were significantly *less* likely than their native counterparts to receive public assistance—a negative effect that was uniform between 1969 and 1979. For Hispanics, immigrant families were also less likely to receive welfare, other things being equal, but this effect was unique to 1979. Mexican immigrants were found to be particularly disinclined to use welfare. For Asian families, a positive net effect of immigrant status on welfare receipt was found, but this effect was unique to 1979. Again, this is consistent with the Indo-Chinese refugee flow.

Recent Hispanic immigrants in 1979 were particularly reluctant to use welfare, as were recent Mexican immigrants in both 1969 and 1979. One might speculate that part of the explanation for the reluctance of recent Hispanic immigrants to receive public assistance in 1979 lies in the surprising number of undocumented immigrants among them (Warren and Passel 1983; Bean, et al. 1986). As many as two-thirds of the Mexicans enumerated in the 1980 Census who entered between 1975 and 1980 may be illegal. Their disinclination to apply for public assistance (for fear of apprehension) coupled with their otherwise great need for assistance could greatly bias downward the net propensity of recent Hispanic (particularly Mexican) immigrants to receive public assistance.

However, two arguments can be made against this possibility. First, three-way interactions between ethnicity, nativity and year of observation (not shown) revealed that recent Mexican immigrants in 1979 were *not* more reluctant than Mexican immigrants generally to receive welfare. If the negative effect for Mexican immigrants is due to the large presence of undocumented persons among them and if there were substantially more undocumented persons included in the 1980 Census, then the interaction for recent Mexican immigrants in 1979 should have been negative and significant. Second, there is ample evidence that both legal (Tienda 1980) and illegal (Massey 1986) Mexican immigrants tend to rely heavily on friendship and kinship networks for support (particularly initially). A preference for such networks over government transfers would explain the negative effect of immigrant status on welfare receipt for Mexicans. Unfortunately, these census data can not adequately capture interhousehold support.

Recent Asian immigrants, those arriving less than five years prior to the census, were more likely than otherwise comparable natives to receive assistance. In part this was due to heavy welfare use among recent Chinese and Other Asian families.

Finally, I estimated a series of models that include family prewelfare poverty as a predictor. The intent was to determine whether immigrants and natives in a similar state of economic need revealed a differential propensity to use public assistance. On the whole, these models established that impoverished immigrants were significantly *less* likely than similarly destitute natives to turn to welfare. These results are consistent with the image of immigrants as preferring informal to formal sources of support.

To conclude, even some conservative observers concede that legal immigrants may not be disproportionate users of transfers. Lamm and Imhoff (1985, p. 161) write that "most social scientists would assume that legal immigrants would use social benefits in about the same way and in about the same proportion as their demographic peers among native-born Americans." On balance, my results show that their assumption is incorrect. Immigrant families were, in fact, significantly *less* likely than their native demographic peers to receive welfare income. This analysis casts doubt on the assumption, held by many Americans (Pear 1986), that immigrants have a penchant for transfer payment receipt. It should also provide some relief for those who fear that the amnesty program will spawn a rush on welfare offices.

My concern in this chapter has been with the probability of welfare receipt among families. While this propensity is an important component of the total cost to society of immigration, of equal relevance is the amount of public assistance received. To provide a more comprehensive picture of the burden of immigrants on public assistance resources, in the final analytic chapter I estimate total annual welfare receipt.

NOTES

1. Public assistance income includes payments under Aid to Families with Dependent Children (AFDC), general assistance and Supplemental Security Income (SSI). The latter includes Old-Age Assistance, Aid to the Blind and Aid to the Permanently and Totally Disabled. Taken together, public assistance is frequently termed welfare (Levitan 1985).

2. Senator Alan Simpson (R–WY) spearheaded several earlier attempts to pass similar legislation beginning in 1981. Being a politically delicate issue, each of these previous attempts failed. Part of the reason it passed in this instance was that national attention was diverted to a Soviet-American summit meeting in Iceland.

3. The 1960 Public Use Sample from the U.S. Census lacks the detail on income sources required to study public assistance. Therefore, in the following two chapters, I am forced to restrict my attention to welfare receipt in 1969 and 1979 only.

4. These figures represent, in percentage terms, the extent to which poverty rates exceed public assistance receipt rates. The 93% figure reflects the fact that in 1969, native poverty (10.4%) was nearly double native welfare receipt (5.4%).

5. Because island-born Puerto Ricans are technically citizens of the United States, they were not asked the detailed year-of-immigration question. Thus, they are excluded from the last four rows of the table. The differences in welfare receipt rates be-

tween recent immigrants with and without Puerto Rican families included highlights the profound economic destitution of this Hispanic group. For example, in 1979, welfare receipt among recent immigrants is 11.3 and 9.5% with and without Puerto Ricans, respectively. This difference is all the more surprising because these categories include all immigrant groups, not just Hispanics.

6. Arguably, this is an unfair comparison, because natives include Puerto Rican while the immigrant cohorts are purged of this group. However, because relatively few natives are Puerto Rican and the comparison between the more aggregated cohorts that include Puerto Ricans (rows 4 and 5) reveals a similarly slight increase, I stand by my assertion that most of the increase in public assistance receipt among Hispanic families between 1969 and 1979 is due to an increase among Hispanic natives.

7. Note that the public assistance income received by any household members who are not related to the head by blood, marriage or adoption is not considered.

8. State mean monthly AFDC payment per family in 1970 and 1980 was obtained from the Statistical Abstract of the United States (U.S. Bureau of the Census 1981b, p. 345).

7

Public Assistance Utilization among Immigrants: An Examination of Total Annual Receipt

One of the questions motivating this volume has been the economic impact of the "new immigration." A cost to society that has raised concern throughout U.S. history is immigrant use of social welfare programs. In the previous chapter, I approached this issue by estimating the net effect of immigrant status on the probability that a family received public assistance. My results documented that, by and large, immigrants were less likely than otherwise comparable natives to receive welfare. However, the mere propensity to receive welfare is only one component of the burden that a group can place on this social resource. Also important is the absolute *amount* of public assistance received.

Accordingly, in this chapter I address immigrant-native differentials in annual public assistance income received by families. In so doing, I restrict the following analysis to "welfare families"—those with positive public assistance income in the year prior to the census. Because the 1960 Census did not provide as detailed a breakdown of annual income by source as the two subsequent censuses did, I consider welfare receipt in 1969 and 1979 only.

I pursue a research strategy similar to that in the previous two chapters. The first analytic section of this chapter contains a series of tables presenting mean public assistance income among families by immigrant status and year of observation. The first of these is pooled by race. I then detail mean welfare receipt for white, black, Hispanic and Asian families separately. These tables establish gross differences in welfare receipt between immigrants and natives as well as between immigrant groups.

The subsequent section briefly builds the conceptual background behind a multivariate model of total public assistance receipt among families. I then use Ordinary Least Squares (OLS) regression to estimate the log of welfare receipt from individual, family and locational characteristics. These models are estimated for all welfare families and within the four race groups. The intent of these multivariate models is both to explain immigrant-native differences that obtain in the descriptive tables and to assess the place of immigrant status as one among a number of determinants of total receipt.

TOTAL PUBLIC ASSISTANCE RECEIPT: DESCRIPTIVE TABLES

To document broad differences between immigrants and natives in mean public assistance receipt, in this section I present a series of descriptive tables. The first of these (Table 7.1) presents mean receipt for all families, then separately for immigrant status categories. Tables 7.2a and 7.2b establish these patterns across the four race groups: whites, blacks, Hispanics and Asians. To derive comparable means across time, family welfare income in 1969 was converted to 1979 dollars via the Consumer Price Index (CPI).

Table 7.1 shows mean annual public assistance receipt for all welfare families by immigrant status and year of observation. Overall, this table documents a slight increase between 1969 and 1979 in average welfare benefits received by families.[1] Mean annual public assistance income increased from $2,418 in 1969 (in 1979 dollars) to $2,659 in 1979.

More important are the overall differences between immigrant and native families. Table 7.1 (rows 2 and 3) shows that immigrant families had greater mean public assistance receipt than natives in both 1969 and 1979. However, while mean receipt among natives increased over the decade, immigrant receipt remained about the same. In 1969, immigrant receipt ($3,159) exceeded that for natives ($2,347) by roughly 35%. By 1979, however, immigrant receipt ($3,156) exceeded native receipt ($2,606) by 21%. At this aggregate level then, there is evidence that immigrants draw from public assistance coffers to a greater degree than natives. However, rather than increasing as the new immigration proceeded and as their poverty rates increased, this gap narrowed somewhat over time.

Breaking immigrant families down into recent immigrants (those who arrived five or fewer years before the census) and all other immigrants reveals some divergence over time. That is, while mean receipt among all immigrant families was rather constant between 1969 and 1979, among recent immigrant families it increased substantially. Mean receipt among recent immigrants increased from $2,943 in 1969 to $3,271 in 1979. While this 11% increase over time for recent arrivals is commensurate with the 11% increase among all native families, it does suggest an increasing welfare burden by recent immigrants. In 1979, compared to other immigrants and natives, recent arrivals had the highest mean public assistance income.

The last four rows of Table 7.1 reveal a haphazard pattern of mean receipt

Table 7.1
Mean Annual Public Assistance Receipt (in 1979 dollars) for
Families by Immigration Cohort and Year

Head's Nativity and Years Since Immigration	1969	1979
All Families[a]	$2418	$2659
All Natives[a]	2347	2606
All Immigrants[a]	3159	3156
0-5 Years[a]	2943	3271
Over 5 Years[a]	3184	3135
0-5 Years	2623	3078
6-10 Years	2590	3177
11-20 Years	2933	2852
Over 20 Years	2434	2723

Source: U.S. Bureau of the Census. 1960, 1970 and
1980 Public Use Samples.

[a]Includes Puerto Ricans.

according to the duration of U.S. residence. However, three observations
can be made. First, there is some evidence that in 1979 the two more recent
groups (0-5 and 6-10 years) had slightly greater mean welfare income than
previous immigrants. Second, the group with the lowest mean receipt in
both 1969 and 1979 was that with 20 or more years of U.S. residence. This is
somewhat counterintuitive. Sar Levitan (1985) has documented that older
public assistance recipients tend to receive more benefits than the young
because they draw more often from Supplemental Security Income (SSI)
programs. SSI benefits are greater than those derived from the other two
principal components of public assistance: AFDC and general assistance.
Because immigrants with over 20 years in the United States tend to be older
than recent arrivals, their comparatively low mean receipt was unexpected.
Third, comparing the means for recent arrivals both with and without
Puerto Ricans (row five versus seven) highlights the sizable welfare utilization among recent Puerto Rican immigrants.

A key finding is the greater mean welfare receipt among immigrants vis-à-vis natives. To determine whether this and other observations obtain within race groups, I present this same pattern of conditional means separately for white, black, Hispanic and Asian families (Tables 7.2a and 7.2b).

Table 7.2a shows that among whites, immigrant families had greater receipt than natives in both 1969 and 1979. However, whereas receipt declined minutely between 1969 and 1979 for all immigrant families, mean receipt among white immigrant families *increased* substantially over the period. In percentage terms, the interdecade increase was, however, greater for native than immigrant white families. Turning next to the means for recent white immigrants, a striking increase is revealed. Whereas average receipt increased by 15% for all white immigrants between 1969 and 1979, for recent arrivals the increase was 61%. This finding joins previous results showing a substantial rise among recent white immigrants in both poverty rates (chapters 4 and 5) and the propensity to use public assistance (chapter 6).

In previous chapters, I documented that black immigrants were far less

Table 7.2a

Mean Annual Public Assistance Receipt (in 1979 dollars) by Immigration Cohort and Year: White and Black Families

Head's Nativity and Years Since Immigration	White		Black	
	1969	1979	1969	1979
All Families	$2127	$2530	$2725	$2719
All Natives	2105	2515	2724	2717
All Immigrants	2495	2861	2811	2850
0-5 Years	1914	3071	3946	2163
Over 5 Years	2517	2842	2607	2976
0-5 Years	1914	3071	3946	2163
6-10 Years	2394	3571	3399	3289
11-20 Years	3014	3037	2843	3166
Over 20 Years	2450	2699	3111	2591

Source: U.S. Bureau of the Census. 1960, 1970 and 1980 Public Use Samples.

likely to be poor or to receive public assistance than black native families. However, Table 7.2a reveals that among black welfare families, immigrants received slightly more transfer income on average than natives. While these differences were quite small, this divergence increased slightly between 1969 and 1979.

Interestingly, while the mean welfare receipt among black immigrants increased between censuses, receipt among recent black immigrants declined precipitously. In 1979, receipt among recent black arrivals was nearly half ($2,163) of what it had been ten years earlier ($3,946). Thus, it was previous black immigrants, not the most recent newcomers, who were principally responsible for the overall interdecade rise in black immigrant receipt.

Table 7.2b presents this pattern of conditional means for Hispanic and Asian families. Looking first at Hispanics, this table shows that immigrants received more annual public assistance income, on average, than did their native-born counterparts. In 1969, Hispanic immigrant receipt stood at $3,670, which exceeded that for natives ($2,840) by some 29%. By 1979, this

Table 7.2b
Mean Annual Public Assistance Receipt (in 1979 dollars) by Immigration Cohort and Year: Hispanic and Asian Families

Head's Nativity and Years Since Immigration	Hispanic		Asian	
	1969	1979	1969	1979
All Families[a]	$3276	$3140	$2267	$3060
All Natives[a]	2840	2927	2294	3068
All Immigrants[a]	3670	3330	2244	3059
0-5 Years[a]	3153	3546	933	3143
Over 5 Years[a]	3762	3301	2397	2968
0-5 Years	2794	3157	933	3143
6-10 Years	2640	3087	3069	2957
11-20 Years	2833	2734	2997	2956
Over 20 Years	2396	2737	2171	2989

Source: U.S. Bureau of the Census. 1960, 1970 and 1980 Public Use Samples.
[a]Includes Puerto Ricans.

gap converged to 14%, owing to the fact that immigrant receipt declined to $3,330 while that for natives increased slightly to $2,927. Although mean receipt declined among Hispanic immigrants, this decline did not occur for recent arrivals. Mean public assistance income for recent Hispanic immigrants increased from $3,153 to $3,546 between 1969 and 1979.

Asians are the only group to reveal greater mean receipt among natives rather than immigrants, but these differences are quite small. More noteworthy for Asians are the following observations. First, compared to other race groups, Asian families experienced the greatest increase in mean public assistance receipt (about 35%). Second, receipt among recent Asian immigrants in 1969 was quite low, only $933. By 1979, recent Asian immigrant receipt had tripled to $3,143. This increase was likely due to the heavy influx of Indo-Chinese refugees during the late 1970s. These refugees were granted relaxed eligibility for, and were encouraged to use, AFDC and other public assistance programs (Department of Health and Human Services 1983).

To summarize, these descriptive results have established that (1) mean receipt was greater among immigrants than natives (on the order of 28%), but this excess declined over time, and (2) while receipt decreased slightly for all immigrants between 1969 and 1979, it increased substantially for recent immigrants (though not in excess of a similar increase for natives). Breaking down the overall comparisons by race revealed considerably different patterns of mean welfare receipt between white, black, Hispanic and Asian families. I found that (1) except for Asian families, mean receipt among immigrants generally exceeded that for natives; (2) although Table 7.1 documented a convergence in the excess of immigrant over native receipt, this result obtained only among Hispanics and (3) mean receipt increased substantially among recent immigrants between 1969 and 1979 for all but black families.

To conclude, trends in mean welfare receipt among the new immigrants suggest an increasing burden of immigrants on public assistance resources. Despite the fact that Hispanic immigrants have borne the brunt of popular concern, the sharpest increases in mean public assistance receipt among recent immigrants were registered for white and Asian families. To examine these results in more detail, I now discuss the theoretical background for a multivariate model of welfare receipt among families.

MODELS OF TOTAL PUBLIC ASSISTANCE RECEIPT: CONCEPTUAL BACKGROUND

In the previous section, I documented that in the aggregate, immigrants receive more public assistance income, on average, than do natives. In the present section, I develop possible explanations for this result by building the conceptual framework behind a multivariate analysis of total family public assistance receipt. I present estimates of these models in the following section.

In the multivariate analyses of previous chapters, I assumed that the propensity of families to be poor and to receive welfare was shaped by individual, family and locational variables. Here again, I draw on this basic approach. I assume that many of those factors that contribute to a family being poor and receiving public assistance in the first place will also influence the total benefits drawn by program participants. I elaborate on these relationships before presenting multivariate results. First however, I acknowledge certain peculiarities that distinguish this analysis of total annual welfare income from the estimation of the probability of welfare receipt. These peculiarities arise from (1) the unique population under study and (2) the nature of the dependent variable.

By restricting the analysis to the subset of public assistance recipients, I have, de facto, limited attention to destitute families. Because these families are not random with respect to many of the individual and family characteristics used in previous analyses (e.g., education), the variances and predictive power of these variables may be drastically reduced. Also, because this analysis is restricted at the lower end of the income distribution, predictors of the probability of receipt for the entire population may have a different effect on amount received among recipients. Second, I recognize the peculiarities of total receipt as distinct from the mere propensity to receive. While, in general, I expect those factors that promote receipt to affect the amount received in the same direction, I pay attention to instances where this might not be the case.

To recapitulate, in the following models I assume that total annual public assistance receipt will be affected by a number of individual, family and locational characteristics. Operational definitions of these variables appear in Table 7.3.[2]

Key to this research is immigrant status. Tabular results documented greater utilization among immigrants in the aggregate. This would suggest a positive effect of immigrant status on total receipt. However, there are reasons to doubt whether such an effect will obtain once other variables are controlled. First, chapter 6 revealed that immigrants were less likely, *ceteris paribus,* to receive welfare income than natives. I anticipate that the same factors will operate to curtail total receipt among immigrant families. Second, a preference among immigrants, particularly new immigrants, for informal sources of economic assistance (Tienda 1980; Kritz and Gurak 1984; Browning and Rodriguez 1985), may diminish the need for public transfers. Third, the greater mean receipt among immigrants in the aggregate may be explained by their preference for states with high welfare benefits. States in which many immigrants concentrate, such as California, New York and Illinois, also have comparatively high welfare benefits (Levitan 1985). I pay close attention to the explanatory impact of State Average AFDC Payments per family. Finally, previous research suggests against greater net receipt among immigrants vis-à-vis natives. With data from the 1976 Survey of Income and Education (SIE), Francine Blau (1984) found that immigrants did

Table 7.3

Definitions of Variables Used in Multivariate Analyses of Total Public Assistance Receipt

Variable	Definition
Family Head Characteristics	
Age	Age of head in years, 18-99
Age Squared	Head's age squared, divided by 1000
Education	Grades of schooling completed by head
Race (4 categories)	1 = Head is Non-Hispanic White 2 = Head is Non-Hispanic Black 3 = Head is Hispanic 4 = Head is Non-Hispanic Asian
Race (8 categories)	1 = Head is Non-Hispanic White 2 = Head is Non-Hispanic Black 3 = Head is Mexican 4 = Head is Puerto Rican 5 = Head is Other Hispanic 6 = Head is Japanese 7 = Head is Chinese 8 = Head is Other Asian
Hispanic Ethnicity	1 = Head is Other Hispanic 2 = Head is Mexican 3 = Head is Puerto Rican
Asian Ethnicity	1 = Head is Japanese 2 = Head is Chinese 3 = Head is Other Asian
Nativity	1 = Head is Native 2 = Head is Immigrant, Not Recent (immigrated over five years before) 3 = Head is Recent Immigrant (immigrated up to 5 years before)
Family Characteristics	
Headship Configuration	0 = Family, both spouses present 1 = Spouse absent family
Extended Family	Adult Relative of Head (except spouse or child) present coded 1; 0 otherwise
Dependency Rate	Number of non-working family members as a percent of total family members
Other Income	Total annual family non-earned, non-transfer income in thousands of 1979 dollars
Pre-Welfare Poor	Total family income minus total family welfare income less than poverty threshold, coded 1; 0 otherwise

Table 7.3 (*continued*)

Variable	Definition
Other Independent Variables	
Southern Residence	Family resides in Southern state coded 1; 0 otherwise (where Southern states are AL, AR, DE, DC, FL, GA, KY, LA, MD, MS, NC, OK, SC, TN, TX, VA and WV)
Non-metropolitan Residence	Family resides in a non-metropolitan area coded 1; 0 otherwise
State Average AFDC Payment[a]	Average monthly AFDC payment per family for family's home state in hundreds of 1980 dollars
Year of Observation	0 = 1960 1 = 1970 2 = 1980
Dependent Variable	
Total Public Assistance Income	The natural logarithm of total family public assistance income for the year prior to the census in 1979 dollars

[a]U.S. Bureau of the Census (1981b, p. 345)

not receive more than natives, *ceteris paribus*. My work goes beyond that of Blau's by analyzing diachronic data, and by establishing patterns within four key race groups.

In this analysis, I employ the same race breakdown as used in the previous chapter. I expect that, compared to whites, total receipt will be significantly greater for black, Mexican, Puerto Rican, Other Hispanic and Other Asian families. Compared to whites, these groups are more apt to suffer long-term economic hardship resulting in more extensive periods of need.

Three additional characteristics of the family head that I consider are Education, Age and Age-Squared. Because better-educated welfare recipients are less likely to experience extended periods of economic difficulty, I hypothesize education to have a negative effect on total welfare receipt. However, this negative effect may be attenuated to the extent that better-educated individuals are more aware of programs available and are better able to apply for them.

Older Americans tend to qualify for more public assistance programs and those in which they do participate, such as SSI, provide greater benefits (Levitan 1985). This suggests a positive effect of age on total receipt. It is possible that the youngest welfare recipients, compared to their prime-aged counterparts, will have greater need for assistance because they are early in their age-earnings profiles. To capture this possible curvilinearity, I introduce Age-Squared and expect this term to have a positive effect on total receipt.

Need and eligibility for public assistance benefits are greatly affected by a family's structure and composition. Accordingly, a number of family characteristics are included in these models of welfare receipt. I have already established that spouse-absent families were more likely to be poor. In addition, they are the specific target of the largest public assistance program in terms of spending, AFDC. I hypothesize that spouse-absent families will have greater public assistance receipt than those headed by a married couple.

A family's level of benefits is determined, in part, by its degree of need. Families with a greater number of economic dependents are in more need of assistance. I expect economic dependency—the percent of family members not working—to have a positive effect on total welfare receipt.

Theoretically, extended family structure increases the flexibility of families in allocating labor (Tienda and Angel 1982; Angel and Tienda 1982; Tienda and Glass 1985). Robert Bach (1984) has shown that complex living arrangements among Indo-Chinese refugees maximized their ability to thrive on scarce resources. This suggests a negative effect of extended structure on total receipt. Unfortunately, the repeated cross-sectional data used in this study do not allow me to determine who helps whom in extended families. In chapter 6, I documented that such families were, other things being the same, more likely to participate in welfare programs. Therefore, the issue of whether extended families receive more or less public assistance income is an empirical question that I leave for the data to answer.

The final family characteristic I consider is the amount of nonearned, nontransfer income at a family's disposal. As a means-tested program, public assistance generally is not available to (or needed by) those with significant assets. Certain assets that welfare families do have offset the amount of benefits for which they qualify. While the amount of asset income among these welfare families will be slight, I expect this variable to have a negative effect on total public assistance receipt.

Finally, I consider three locational characteristics: Southern and Nonmetro Residence and State Average AFDC Payment per family. I have already touched on the latter. Clearly, other things being equal, welfare recipients living in states with greater benefits should receive larger average checks. This variable is important, because it may explain immigrant-native differentials in receipt.

Previous research has shown that the eligible poor residing in nonmetro areas do not avail themselves of public assistance benefits to the same degree as urban residents (Carlson, et al. 1981). However, results of the previous chapter contradicted this view. Only for blacks and Asians did significant effects obtain, and they were positively, not negatively, signed. I do not hypothesize about the effect of Nonmetro Residence on total receipt.

Despite the greater economic hardship faced by southern residents, the previous chapter found them to be generally less likely to receive public assistance benefits. Therefore, I expect southerners to receive less welfare income, other things being equal.

MODELS OF TOTAL PUBLIC ASSISTANCE RECEIPT: EMPIRICAL RESULTS

In this section, I present a series of models of total annual public assistance receipt. The units of analysis are welfare families, and equations are estimated via OLS regression.[3] The first set of models is pooled across categories of race (Table 7.4). I then re-estimate these equations for white, black, Hispanic and Asian families separately (Tables 7.5a–7.5d).

Before discussing the first of these models, two methodological points are in order. First, like the distribution of income in general, the distribution of annual public assistance receipt is highly skewed to the right. That is, while the bulk of families receive comparatively low amounts of welfare income, a minority receive relatively high amounts. The skewness statistic for annual public assistance income (1.67) and a histogram (not shown) confirm the presence of these outliers. The statistical technique employed to estimate total receipt, OLS regression, assumes normally distributed dependent variables. To achieve this normality, I have chosen to transform the dependent variable by taking the natural logarithm of total annual receipt. The skewness statistic for logged welfare income (-1.13) and a histrogram (not shown) reveal that, while the distribution becomes skewed somewhat to the left, the transformed distribution approximates the normal distribution much more closely than untransformed welfare receipt.

Second, using logged welfare income has an expository advantage. A simple transformation on the resulting unstandardized coefficients [e^b or $\exp(b)$] yields parameters that can be interpreted as the effect of a unit change in the independent variable on the proportionate change in public assistance receipt. This will become clear as I discuss parameter estimates below.

Table 7.4 estimates total annual public assistance receipt for all families who received some assistance in the year prior to the census. Model 1 predicts total receipt from year of observation and immigrant status. Because in real dollars there was little difference between 1969 and 1979 in average benefits, year of observation had little impact on amount received. The two immigrant status variables both have positive and significant effects on public assistance receipt. The transformed coefficients suggest that compared to native families (the reference group) recent immigrants received 11% more and all other immigrants received 15% more welfare income. These findings substantiate the conclusion drawn from the descriptive tables that, in the aggregate, receipt is higher among immigrants than natives.

Table 7.4
OLS Regression of Total Public Assistance Receipt: Pooled by Race[a]

	Model 1 b	Model 1 exp(b)	Model 2 b	Model 2 exp(b)	Model 3 b	Model 3 exp(b)	Model 4 b	Model 4 exp(b)
Intercept	7.47 (.02)		6.66 (.04)		5.88 (.13)		5.88 (.13)	
1980	.01 (.02)	1.01	.24* (.02)	1.27	.24* (.03)	1.26	.23* (.08)	1.26
Family Head Variables								
Immigrant, Not Recent	.14* (.03)	1.15	.00 (.03)	1.00	.00 (.03)	1.00	-.00 (.04)	1.00
Recent Immigrant	.11* (.05)	1.12	-.02 (.04)	.98	.01 (.05)	1.01	-.08 (.08)	.92
Black					.08* (.03)	1.09	.08* (.03)	1.08
Mexican					.07 (.04)	1.08	.08* (.04)	1.08
Puerto Rican					.19* (.05)	1.21	.19* (.06)	1.21
Other Hispanic					.14* (.04)	1.15	.15* (.04)	1.16
Japanese					-.07 (.10)	.94	-.07 (.10)	.93

Chinese	.01 (.08)	1.01	.00 (.08)	1.00
Other Asian	.02 (.06)	1.03	.00 (.06)	1.00
Education	-.00 (.00)	1.00	-.00 (.00)	1.00
Age	.01* (.00)	1.01	.01* (.00)	1.01
Age^2	-.10* (.04)	.90	-.10* (.04)	.90

Family and Contextual Variables

Dependency Rate	.75* (.05)	2.03	.74* (.05)	2.10
Spouse Absent	.12* (.02)	1.13	.12* (.02)	1.13
Extended Family	.06* (.03)	1.06	.06* (.03)	1.06
Other Income	-.00 (.00)	1.00	-.00 (.00)	1.00
Southern Residence	-.13* (.04)	.88	-.13* (.04)	.88

Table 7.4 (*continued*)

	Model 1		Model 2		Model 3		Model 4	
	b	exp(b)	b	exp(b)	b	exp(b)	b	exp(b)
Non-metro Residence					.02 (.03)	1.02	.02 (.03)	1.02
State Average AFDC Payment			.22* (.01)	1.25	.18* (.02)	1.20	.18* (.02)	1.20
Interaction Terms								
Immigrant, Not Recent, 1980							.01 (.05)	1.01
Recent Immigrant, 1980							.14 (.10)	1.15
Adjusted R^2	.004		.062		.099		.099	
F	11.6		155.2		52.4		47.7	
N	9323		9323		9323		9323	

Note: b = Unstandardized regresion coefficient (standard errors in parentheses); exp(b) = exponential of b.

*Parameter estimate significant at .05.

A possible explanation for the higher receipt among immigrants is the simple fact that they tend to live, more often than natives, in states with higher welfare benefits. The mean for average state AFDC payment per family per month was $296 for natives but $355 for recent immigrants and $377 for all other immigrants. In order to obtain an uncontaminated picture of the net effects of the other predictors of welfare receipt, it is important to control for state average AFDC payments. Model 2 adds to Model 1 this single variable. Clearly, State AFDC Payments has a strong effect on welfare receipt, as indicated by the positive and significant estimate for this variable. More importantly, by controlling for state benefits, the effects for immigrant status attenuate completely. The higher total receipt among immigrants is fully explained by the fact that they live in states with greater welfare benefits.

Some might argue that the benefits in these states (such as New York and California) is what attracts immigrants to them—that immigrants settle in places where they can take advantage of higher welfare benefits. This assertion has also been made regarding internal migration and has fostered heated debate (Cebula and Kohn 1975; Cebula 1976; Kumar 1977). A key dissenting position in this debate is that people migrate to places where economic opportunities are better, and that this economic vitality allows such places to offer higher welfare benefits. It seems unlikely that immigrants choose destinations based on welfare benefits alone, if at all. Rather, research has shown that immigrants settle in places where there exist employment opportunities and/or kin and friends. Taken in this light, the positive effect of immigrant status established in Model 1 can be regarded not as evidence of a disproportionate burden, but of their preference for places where employment opportunities are better. Moreover, their positive scale effects on the economy and the taxes they pay would increase public revenue and offset the burden imposed by welfare receipt.

In Model 3 of Table 7.4 I introduce the remaining main effects for the individual, family and locational characteristics. Contrary to my expectations, immigrants do *not* receive less public assistance income, other things being equal, than natives. Rather, they differed little from statistically similar natives in the amount of welfare received.

Many of the other variables in the model behaved as expected. For example, blacks, Mexicans, Puerto Ricans and Other Hispanics received more welfare, other things being equal, than whites. This effect was particularly strong among Puerto Rican families, who received over 20% more assistance than whites, *ceteris paribus*. As expected, Age had a positive net effect on total receipt. Families headed by older Americans received more public assistance income, other things being equal, than those headed by the young. However, the term for Age-Squared ran contrary to expectation. This term was negative and significant, suggesting that, while receipt increased with age, it diminished at old age.

On the whole, however, this model shows that much of the impact on amount received is due to characteristics of the family itself. Spouse-absent families received 12% more than those headed by a married couple. Also, economic dependency increased welfare income, other things being equal. Interestingly, extended families received *more* public assistance income than did those with no extended adults present. This complements the finding of the previous chapter that extended families were more likely to receive assistance in the first place. These results are somewhat counterintuitive in view of the economic flexibility that extended adults should provide. It is plausible that many extended adults are disabled or aged and, hence, eligible for SSI, which confers greater benefits.

State Average AFDC Payments per family remains a strong predictor of average receipt. Another contextual variable that has an effect on amount of welfare received is Southern Residence. This term says that net of other factors (including differences in state benefit levels) residents of the South accept 88% as much welfare benefits as do nonSouthern residents.

On balance, the amount of welfare income a family receives seems to be dictated mostly by the benefits available in that family's state and by characteristics of the family itself that determine need. Immigrant status has no direct effect on amount received, and thus, immigrants do not appear to represent an unusual burden on welfare coffers.

Chapters 4 and 5 documented a sharp rise in poverty among recent immigrants between 1969 and 1979. This finding supported claims that the United States experienced a surge in impoverished immigration since the 1965 immigration reforms. While this increase in poverty reinforced beliefs that the propensity of immigrant families to use public assistance would increase commensurately, chapter 6 refuted this possibility. The interaction between year of observation and immigrant status (Model 4 in Table 7.4) allows me to test whether there was an increase over time in total welfare receipt among immigrants. The interactions are statistically insignificant; neither recent immigrants nor all other immigrants received a particularly large amount of welfare income, other things being equal, in 1979 as compared to 1969.

In previous chapters, I uncovered differences between white, black, Hispanic and Asian families. To examine total welfare receipt within race categories, I re-estimate the above equations separately for each group. Table 7.5a contains models of total public assistance receipt for white families. Model 1 contains the main effects for year of observation and immigrant status. This model shows that all but recent white immigrants received more income from public assistance than white natives. Recent white immigrants received about the same amount as natives. In model 2 I control for state average AFDC benefits. As was true for the population as a whole, state benefit levels account for the greater receipt of white immigrants. That is, welfare income among all but recent white immigrant families was greater than that for natives because they resided in states where welfare benefits were greater.

Model 3, which introduces the main effects for the remaining variables, shows that for white families, total welfare receipt was shaped largely by family characteristics and state of residence. For example, broken families and families with greater economic dependence received more welfare income over the year, other things being equal. Model 4 introduces the interactions between year of observation and immigrant status. Note that the main effect for recent white immigrants (which represents recent immigrants in 1970) becomes negative and significant, while the interaction involving recent arrivals is positive and on the margin of significance (p = .08). This suggests that there was an increase, as the new immigration unfolded, in the amount of public assistance income received by recent white immigrants. This result complements previous findings that poverty among recent white immigrant families likewise increased over the period.

In preceding chapters, I established that black immigrant families were significantly less likely than their native counterparts to be impoverished and to receive welfare income. Model 1 of Table 7.5b reveals, however, that among black welfare participants, immigrants received just as much assistance as natives. Model 2, which introduces State Average AFDC Payment, increases the explained variation from virtually zero to 9%. Apparently, recent black immigrants concentrate in states with high welfare benefits. Controlling for this factor reveals that they received significantly *less* welfare income than natives. Net of state benefits and year of observation, recent black immigrants received only 66% as much assistance as black native families. The term for all other black immigrants is also negative in Model 2, but borders on statistical significance (p = .07).

Model 3 shows that several characteristics of the black family and its residence location influenced total receipt. As expected, broken black families and those with greater economic dependence received more welfare, other things being equal. Southern black families received less and rural black families received significantly more public assistance.[4]

Model 4 determines whether there have been changes over time in the mean receipt among immigrant blacks. The main effect for Immigrant, Not Recent is negative and significant, while that for the Immigrant, Not Recent 1980 term is positive and insignificant. This means that previous black immigrants in 1969 received only 72% as much public assistance income as natives. Receipt *did* increase among previous black immigrants; by 1979 it differed little from that of natives.[5]

Model 1 for Hispanic families reveals that, compared to Hispanic natives, all but recent immigrants received significantly more public assistance income. The effect for recent arrivals was similarly signed, but did not reach statistical significance. This confirms the conclusion from Table 7.2b that in the aggregate, Hispanic immigrant families received more assistance than

Table 7.5a
OLS Regression of Total Public Assistance Receipt: White Families[a]

	Model 1		Model 2		Model 3		Model 4	
	b	exp(b)	b	exp(b)	b	exp(b)	b	exp(b)
Intercept	7.28 (.04)		6.76 (.10)		5.93 (.28)		5.94 (.28)	
1980	.24* (.05)	1.27	.37* (.05)	1.45	.38* (.06)	1.46	.39* (.07)	1.48
Family Head Variables								
Immigrant, Not Recent	.14* (.06)	1.15	.08 (.06)	1.08	.06 (.06)	1.06	.10 (.09)	1.11
Recent Immigrant	-.12 (.19)	.89	-.22 (.19)	.80	-.16 (.18)	.85	-.70* (.35)	.50
Education					-.01 (.01)	.99	-.01 (.01)	.99
Age					.02* (.01)	1.02	.02* (.01)	1.02
Age^2					-.17* (.07)	.84	-.17* (.07)	.84
Family and Contextual Variables								
Dependency Rate					.62* (.09)	1.86	.62* (.09)	1.86
Spouse Absent					.17* (.05)	1.18	.17* (.05)	1.18

	Model 1		Model 2		Model 3		Model 4	
	b (SE)	exp(b)	b (SE)	exp(b)	b (SE)	exp(b)	b (SE)	exp(b)
Extended Family					-.06 (.05)	.94	-.06 (.05)	.94
Other Income					.00 (.00)	1.00	-.00 (.00)	1.00
Southern Residence					-.01 (.09)	.99	-.01 (.09)	.99
Non-metro Residence					.02 (.06)	1.02	.02 (.06)	1.02
State Average AFDC Payment			.13* (.02)	1.25	.14* (.04)	1.15	.14* (.04)	1.15
Interaction Terms								
Immigrant, Not Recent, 1980							-.06 (.11)	.94
Recent Immigrant, 1980							.74 (.41)	2.10
Adjusted R^2	.014		.031		.067		.068	
F	9.7		15.3		10.8		9.63	
N	1784		1784		1784		1784	

Note: b = Unstandardized regresion coefficient (standard errors in parentheses); exp(b) = exponential of b.

*Parameter estimate significant at .05.

Table 7.5b
OLS Regression of Total Public Assistance Receipt: Black Families[a]

	Model 1		Model 2		Model 3		Model 4	
	b	exp(b)	b	exp(b)	b	exp(b)	b	exp(b)
Intercept	7.50 (.03)		6.58 (.06)		6.00 (.22)		6.01 (.22)	
1980	-.03 (.04)	.97	.25* (.04)	1.28	.26* (.05)	1.30	.25* (.05)	1.28
Family Head Variables								
Immigrant, Not Recent	.07 (.08)	1.07	-.14 (.07)	.87	-.08 (.07)	.92	-.33* (.17)	.72
Recent Immigrant	-.18 (.17)	.84	-.41* (.17)	.66	-.31* (.16)	.73	.13 (.39)	1.14
Education					-.01 (.01)	.99	-.01 (.01)	.99
Age					.01 (.00)	1.01	.01 (.00)	1.01
Age^2					-.13* (.06)	.88	-.13* (.06)	.88
Family and Contextual Variables								
Dependency Rate					.72* (.08)	2.05	.72* (.08)	2.05
Spouse Absent					.12* (.04)	1.13	.12* (.04)	1.13

	(1)	(2)	(3)	(4)							
Extended Family			.05 (.04)	1.05	.04 (.04)	1.04
Other Income			-.01 (.01)	.99	-.01 (.01)	.99
Southern Residence			-.18* (.07)	.84	-.18* (.07)	.84
Non-metro Residence			.18* (.05)	1.20	.17* (.05)	1.19
State Average AFDC Payment		.27* (.01) 1.31	.23* (.03)	1.26	.23* (.03)	1.26
Interaction Terms						
Immigrant, Not Recent, 1980					.30 (.19)	1.35
Recent Immigrant, 1980					-.52 (.43)	.59
Adjusted R^2	.001	.091	.122		.122	
F	0.8	82.9	35.7		31.3	
N	3254	3254	3254		3254	

Note: b = Unstandardized regresion coefficient (standard errors in parentheses); exp(b) = exponential of b.

*Parameter estimate significant at .05.

Table 7.5c
OLS Regression of Total Public Assistance Receipt: Hispanic Families[a]

	Model 1		Model 2		Model 3		Model 4	
	b	exp(b)	b	exp(b)	b	exp(b)	b	exp(b)
Intercept	7.56 (.03)		6.62 (.07)		6.02 (.23)		6.01 (.23)	
1980	-.06 (.04)	.94	.22* (.04)	1.25	.17* (.05)	1.19	.14* (.06)	1.15
Family Head Variables								
Immigrant, Not Recent	.13* (.04)	1.14	.02 (.04)	1.02	-.00 (.04)	1.00	.11 (.09)	1.12
Recent Immigrant	.11 (.07)	1.11	.02 (.07)	1.02	.04 (.07)	1.04	.03 (.11)	1.03
Mexican					-.04 (.04)	.96	.04 (.06)	1.04
Puerto Rican					.07 (.06)	1.07	.10 (.13)	1.11
Education					.00 (.00)	1.00	.00 (.00)	1.00
Age					.01 (.01)	1.01	.01 (.01)	1.01
Age^2					-.06 (.06)	.94	-.06 (.06)	.94

Family and Contextual Variables

	Coef. (SE)		Coef. (SE)		Coef. (SE)	
Dependency Rate			.80* (.08)	2.23	.80* (.08)	2.23
Spouse Absent			.11* (.04)	1.12	.11* (.04)	1.12
Extended Family			.12* (.04)	1.13	.11* (.04)	1.11
Other Income			-.01 (.01)	.99	-.01 (.01)	.99
Southern Residence			-.16* (.07)	.85	-.18* (.07)	.84
Non-metro Residence			-.13 (.06)	.88	-.12 (.05)	.89
State Average AFDC Payment	.25* (.02)	1.28	.17* (.03)	1.19	.16* (.03)	1.17

Interaction Terms

Immigrant, Not Recent, 1980					-.01 (.08)	.99
Recent Immigrant, 1980					.24 (.14)	1.27

Table 7.5c (*continued*)

	Model 1		Model 2		Model 3		Model 4	
	b	exp(b)	b	exp(b)	b	exp(b)	b	exp(b)
Mexican Immigrant, Not Recent							-.17 (.09)	.84
Mexican Immigrant, Recent							-.20 (.17)	.82
Puerto Rican Immigrant, Not Recent							-.09 (.15)	.91
Puerto Rican Immigrant, Recent							-.03 (.21)	.97
Adjusted R^2	.003		.074		.107		.107	
F	5.0		71.5		29.2		21.1	
N	3544		3544		3544		3544	

Note: b = Unstandardized regresion coefficient (standard errors in parentheses); exp(b) = exponential of b.

*Parameter estimate significant at .05.

natives. To determine whether this result obtains because Hispanic immigrants were more apt to live in states with greater welfare benefits available, Model 2 includes the main effect for average state AFDC payment per family. This term is positive and significant, but more importantly, it attenuates the main effects for immigrant status. Once state benefits are controlled, Hispanic immigrants differ little from their native counterparts in amount of assistance received.

Including the main effects for the other variables that determine welfare receipt (Model 3) does not change the main effects for immigrant status. Hispanic immigrants received neither more nor less welfare income than did otherwise comparable Hispanic natives. One of the strongest predictors of amount received continues to be economic dependency. Families with a greater percent of nonworkers received more welfare, other things being equal, than those with less. Extended families received more public assistance income than those without extended adults present. Model 4 for Hispanics shows that the lack of any effect of immigrant status on total receipt was constant between 1969 and 1979.

The final series of models considered, those for Asians, are based on only 741 public assistance recipient families in 1969 and 1979. This contributes to a relative lack of significant coefficients in these models compared to those for the other three race groups.

Model 1 confirms that compared to native Asian families, immigrants did not receive significantly more welfare income. The positive and significant effect for year of observation in this model supports the conclusion from Table 7.2b that receipt was appreciably greater among all Asians in 1979 than 1969. Because immigrant status is already in the model, the increasing concentration of Asian immigrants cannot account for the secular rise in receipt among Asian families. Model 2 for Asians introduces state benefit levels. This variable had a positive effect on receipt and seemed to attenuate the (albeit insignificant) effects of immigrant status. Model 3 shows that, except for year of observation and economic dependency, none of these individual, family and contextual variables has a significant effect on total public assistance receipt.

Model 4, which includes the interactions between immigrant status and year of observation,[6] suggests that there has been an increase in the net receipt among recent Asian immigrants. The main effect (−1.05), which reflects the effect for recent immigrants in 1970, is negative and significant. These immigrants received only 35% as much as natives, other things being equal. However the offsetting positive and significant interaction term for recent immigrants in 1979 (1.22) suggests that they received no more than natives. This is consistent with the dramatically low mean receipt among Asian immigrants in 1969 (see Table 7.2b) and the sizable increase by 1979.

In this section, I have presented a series of models estimating total public

Table 7.5d
OLS Regression of Total Public Assistance Receipt: Asian Families[a]

	Model 1		Model 2		Model 3		Model 4	
	b	exp(b)	b	exp(b)	b	exp(b)	b	exp(b)
Intercept	7.23 (.11)		6.62 (.07)		5.81 (.54)		5.74 (.55)	
1980	.30* (.11)	1.35	.22* (.04)	1.25	.36* (.13)	1.43	.25 (.19)	1.28
Family Head Variables								
Immigrant, Not Recent	.09 (.10)	1.09	.02 (.04)	1.02	.10 (.11)	1.11	.05 (.20)	1.05
Recent Immigrant	.08 (.11)	1.08	.02 (.07)	1.02	.10 (.12)	1.11	-1.03* (.44)	.36
Chinese					-.01 (.14)	.99	.01 (.14)	1.01
Other Asian					-.02 (.13)	.98	-.01 (.13)	.99
Education					.01 (.01)	1.01	.01 (.01)	1.01
Age					.01 (.01)	1.01	.01 (.01)	1.01
Age^2					-.10 (.14)	.90	-.08 (.14)	.92
Family and Contextual Variables								
Dependency Rate					.79* (.17)	2.20	.75* (.17)	2.12
Spouse Absent					.13 (.09)	1.14	.13 (.09)	1.14

	b (se)	exp(b)	b (se)	exp(b)	b (se)	exp(b)	b (se)	exp(b)
Extended Family					.13 (.08)	1.14	.11 (.08)	1.12
Other Income					-.00 (.01)	1.00	-.00 (.01)	1.00
Southern Residence					-.32 (.22)	.73	-.18 (.23)	.84
Non-metro Residence					.00 (.15)	1.00	-.05 (.15)	.95
State Average AFDC Payment	.19* (.05)	1.21	.11 (.08)	1.12			.16 (.08)	1.17
Interaction Terms								
Immigrant, Not Recent, 1980							.07 (.23)	1.07
Recent Immigrant, 1980							1.20* (.45)	3.32
Adjusted R^2	.009		.030		.053		.060	
F	3.3		6.6		3.8		3.8	
N	741		741		741		741	

Note: b = Unstandardized regresion coefficient (standard errors in parentheses);
exp(b) = exponential of b.

*Parameter estimate significant at .05.

assistance income among families. The critical concern was with the effect of immigrant status on total receipt. By way of summary, I found that (1) among all race groups combined, simple models confirmed the greater aggregate receipt of welfare income first established in the descriptive tables; (2) the greater use among immigrants was fully explained by their tendency to reside, more often than natives, in states with high welfare benefits; (3) the pattern of higher aggregate benefits as a result of residence in high benefit states characterized white and Hispanic families; (4) black immigrant families differed little from natives in the simple model, but when state benefit levels were controlled, all except recent black immigrants received significantly *less* welfare income than their native counterparts; (5) Asian immigrants received neither more nor less assistance than Asian natives and (6) there was evidence of an increase over time in the amount of assistance received by all but Hispanic immigrants.

SUMMARY AND CONCLUSIONS

Chapters 6 and 7 broadly addressed the immigrant burden on public assistance coffers. Chapter 6 documented immigrant-native differentials in the propensity of families to receive public assistance income. In the present chapter, I have been concerned with another important component of the immigrant burden—the amount of assistance received by welfare families. I now synthesize the key findings of this chapter.

I opened with descriptive tables that revealed greater annual receipt of welfare income among immigrant as opposed to native families. This result obtained for all races combined and separately for white, black and Hispanic families. Regarding differences between 1969 and 1979, mean receipt among recent immigrants increased substantially over the decade. Within races, this overall increase was also observed for whites, Hispanics and Asians.

At this baseline level then, there is ample evidence that immigrants do receive more welfare benefits than natives. Also, these descriptive data give some credence to those who assert that immigrant receipt of assistance increased as the new immigration progressed. However, despite the fact that many equate the new immigrant problem with Hispanics (Cafferty, et al. 1983), the sharpest rise in receipt among recent immigrants over the decade occurred for white and Asian families.

Simple multivariate models confirmed the greater use of benefits by immigrants. However, for the population as a whole as well as within race groups (except Asians) the greater aggregate use of benefits by immigrants was explained by their tendency to live in states with higher welfare benefits. I have already discussed the possibility that immigrants prefer such places to live in part to take advantage of these greater benefits. More than likely however, the positive association between welfare benefits and immigrant concentration is spurious. Both higher benefits and immigrant residential distribution may be caused by a common endogenous factor: the strength of the local labor market and economy. Moreover, if higher benefits were a strong enough factor to attract immigrants, one would assume it would also have a positive effect on the propensity of families to receive benefits. The models in chapter 6, however, revealed no significant effect of state benefit levels on the probability of welfare receipt.

On balance, I would conclude that the immigrant families are not disproportionate users of welfare benefits, either with respect to their propensity to receive them or the amount of benefits received among welfare families. If anything, there is some evidence that immigrants pose less of a drain on public assistance resources than natives. However, this was more typical of 1969 than 1979; there is evidence of an increase in utilization over the years. While this increase resulted in use that differed little from natives by 1979, the pattern of increase should be of concern to policy analysts and bears close scrutiny in the years ahead.

NOTES

1. This small real increase runs counter to some previous findings reported by Sar Levitan (1985). He states that, in real terms, welfare benefits declined over the 1970s. While welfare benefits are rather meager in the first place—frequently inadequate in and of themselves to lift families above the absolute poverty threshold—they became even less adequate over the 1970s. That Table 7.1 shows a slight *increase* in real terms could be due to a number of factors, including greater need and destitution among the poor. That is, real benefits within eligibility categories could decline and average payment per family could increase if changes in family composition were resulting in more families being in higher benefit categories.

2. These variables are defined as they were in the previous chapter (the coding changed for some because a different statistical package was used). Therefore, I will not elaborate on variable definitions in this discussion of the conceptual framework.

3. An alternative approach to estimating models of total public assistance receipt is provided by Tobit analysis. Here one analyzes all families, including the majority with zero welfare income. The Tobit model was developed to study such truncated dependent variables. Elsewhere, this method was employed to study total receipt using 1980 Census data (Jensen and Tienda 1988). We found that, because most of the action takes place between those who received no welfare versus those who received some, the Tobit model produced results close to those reported in chapter 6. That is, other things being equal, immigrants received less welfare income than natives.

4. Again, I should point out that while a large majority of nonsouthern blacks are metropolitan and nonmetropolitan blacks are Southern, these two variables are not perfectly related ($r = .47$). Hence, I feel confident that these variables are measuring independent dimensions and not causing multicollinearity.

5. The main and interaction effects offset one another here, resulting in little net difference between all but recent black immigrants in 1979 and black natives.

6. Because of the paucity of Asian recipients, I was unable to produce estimates for all coefficients in models with additional and higher order interactions. I opted to present this simpler model.

8

Summary and Conclusions

Since the mid–1960s, the United States has experienced another of the great waves of immigration that have distinguished its history. In absolute and relative terms, the new immigration did not rival the volume of previous waves, but the absolute number of new arrivals increased sharply over the 1960s and 1970s.

Fundamentally responsible for the increased volume of immigration was the 1965 legislation, which replaced the discriminatory Quota System of immigration with a more equitable worldwide distribution of visas. This legislation also reprioritized the criteria under which immigrants were admitted, by giving preference to those wishing to rejoin kin over those entering on the merits of their occupational skills. Thus, the new immigration considered in this volume has been characterized by (1) an increase in the flow of immigration, (2) an increase (decrease) in the share of immigrants entering under the family reunification provisions (entering with needed occupational skills), (3) an increase in the percent arriving from less-developed countries (especially from Asia and Latin America) and (4) an increase in the percent of immigrants who are nonwhite.

Echoing the past, these changes engendered popular concern that the United States was admitting, to a growing extent, too many immigrants destined for the bottom of the stratification system. Both historically and currently, concern has rested less with increasing poverty among immigrants than with poverty's presumed concomitant, increasing use of social welfare institutions. In recent years these assumptions—that poverty and welfare utilization have increased with the new immigration—have been used to promote more restrictive immigration laws. However, there is a paucity of hard evidence substantiating many claims in the immigration debate. Accordingly, the aim of this study was to document and explain immigrant-native trends and differentials in poverty and public assistance utilization during the period 1960–1980.

Before summarizing my key findings, I review essential features of my statistical methodology. I analyzed data drawn from the 1960, 1970 and 1980 Public Use Samples of the U.S. Census. Special household-level files were constructed that contained information on the household head, the head's spouse (if present) and numerous characteristics of the household itself. From these household-level files I selected families, which formed the units of analysis. Variables used in the multivariate analyses were carefully computed to maximize comparability across censuses.

The analytic strategy was to first establish a baseline description of poverty and public assistance utilization. These tabular results were presented separately by year of observation to establish intertemporal differences. Using these baseline data as a reference, I moved into a multivariate treatment of poverty and public assistance utilization among families. Here, I considered individual, family and locational characteristics as predictors. These multivariate analyses were not conducted separately by year of observation. Rather, the parallel data files were concatenated and year of observation was included as a dummy variable. This technique allowed me to determine whether there were significant differences over time in the effect of immigrant status on poverty and welfare use.

SUMMARY AND INTERPRETATION OF CRITICAL FINDINGS[1]

Whereas I considered the three dependent variables—poverty, the probability of welfare receipt and total welfare receipt—in separate chapters, my present objective is to synthesize my key findings and to draw general conclusions.

During the period 1960–1980, absolute poverty among all U.S. families declined.[2] However, immigrant families showed much less decline between 1960 and 1970 and a slight increase by 1980. Much of the increase in poverty among immigrants over the 1970s was due to sizable increases among those immigrants who arrived after the 1965 immigration reform. Poverty among the most recent arrivals—those families whose head immigrated up to five years before—showed the sharpest increase between 1970 and 1980. This supports arguments that the new immigration has been characterized by an increasing flow of impoverished immigrants.[3]

My results refuted the notion, however, that this increase occurred because of the shift toward nonwhite immigrants. The sharpest rise in poverty among recent immigrants was registered for families with white heads. Recent Hispanic and Asian immigrants are the two groups most closely associated with the new immigration, and Hispanics have raised considerable concern among natives (Cafferty, et al. 1983). Nonetheless, these two groups, especially recent Hispanics, showed the smallest increase in poverty over the 1970s.

A multivariate analysis of absolute poverty allowed me to solidify these findings. Simple models estimating the probability that a family was poor confirmed the steep decline in poverty over the 1960s, the greater incidence of poverty among black and Hispanic as opposed to white and Asian families and the greater incidence of poverty among recent versus all other immigrants. More importantly, these models supported the rise in poverty among recent immigrants over time and the comparatively sharp increase for white and Asian as opposed to Hispanic families.

More complex models estimated family poverty from individual, family and contextual variables. The intent of these models was to establish the influence of immigrant status as one among several determinants of poverty. These complex models of poverty revealed that recent immigrants were more likely to be poor and all other immigrants were less likely to be poor than natives. Poverty among recent immigrants would have been even greater were they not characterized by a lower economic dependency, by a greater propensity to be in extended families and by a preference for metro areas and nonsouthern states. The lower poverty among all other immigrants, compared to natives, was also largely accounted for by these same family structure characteristics and residential preferences. These models also showed that, other things being equal, poverty among recent immigrants increased over time. However, models that were estimated within race groups continued to show that this net increase in poverty among recent immigrants obtained for white and black families only. The multivariate analyses provided no evidence of a significant increase in poverty over time among Asian or Hispanic families.

Impoverished families employ a variety of strategies to maintain income levels. One important strategy is to commit additional workers to the labor force. The ability of families to have working members in addition to the head can mean the difference between being above or below the poverty level. In both a descriptive and multivariate treatment, I examined the ameliorative impact on poverty of multiple earners—earners other than the head—on family poverty. I was able to establish that the presence of multiple earners was of greater importance for keeping immigrant families out of poverty than it was for natives. This upholds the image of the immigrant poor as an industrious group, striving to improve their lot by capitalizing on their labor force potential. However, there was ample evidence documenting a marked decline over time in the ameliorative impact of multiple earners for white, black and Hispanic immigrant families. While I was not able to determine the extent to which this decline was associated with the overall increase in poverty, clearly it was a contributing factor. I did not determine whether motivational or structural labor market factors were primarily responsible for the decline in the ameliorative impact of multiple earners.

An additional strategy of income maintenance among the poor is to seek economic assistance from the government in the form of welfare benefits. As I have stated repeatedly, immigrant use of welfare and other social services has sparked much of the controversy over the new immigration. A widespread assumption is that increasing numbers of immigrants wind up on welfare. That poverty among recent immigrants increased and that the positive impact of multiple earners for immigrant families decreased over time would lead one to expect a similar rise in the likelihood of immigrant public assistance utilization.

Two chapters studied immigrant-native differentials in public assistance utilization. Public assistance (or welfare) consists of payments made under AFDC, SSI and general assistance. First, I described the propensity of families to receive welfare and subsequently analyzed variations in the dollar amount of public assistance received among welfare families.

In regard to aggregate differences between immigrant and native families in the percent receiving welfare income, I found slightly greater use among immigrant families. However, tabular results strongly refuted the assumption, held by nearly half of all adult Americans, that most immigrants wind up on welfare. Within race categories, the greater use among immigrants characterized Hispanic and Asian families only (for Hispanics, this gap declined substantially over time). For white and especially black families it was the native-born who revealed the higher prevalence of welfare receipt. Among recent immigrants, tabular data indicated an increase in the percent receiving public assistance between 1969 and 1979. However, this rise was not in excess of the increase in public assistance receipt observed among all native families. Moreover, in relation to the rise in *poverty* among recent immigrants, the increase in welfare receipt was not nearly as great.

I then used multivariate methods to address immigrant-native differentials in the propensity of families to use public assistance. The intent was to determine the net effect of immigrant status on receipt, once other determinants of need and eligibility were controlled. This method also allowed me to establish the statistical significance of changes over time in the net propensity of immigrants to receive welfare.

I found that immigrants with over five years in the United States (who constitute a substantial majority of all immigrants) were significantly less likely than otherwise comparable natives to receive public assistance income. This statistically significant effect obtained for the population as a whole and separately for white, black and Hispanic families.

The tendency for a family to seek out and successfully apply for welfare benefits is shaped by numerous factors, which I used to model this process. Also, several actors are involved in the process of welfare receipt, including the family, welfare program officials and members of the community at large. It is possible that there are explanations for the negative effect of immigrant status on welfare utilization that could be captured by unmeasured variables. For example, perhaps immigrants, more so than natives, live in communities where welfare institutions are inadequate or where application procedures are more intractable. All this is to say that participation in welfare programs is not solely a matter of volition on the part of welfare participants themselves. However, to the extent that I have controlled for many factors determining need and eligibility, I stand by my conclusion that the negative effect for all but recent immigrants refutes the claim that they have a penchant for public assistance, and perhaps reflects an aversion to welfare. Again, this may indicate a preference for informal sources of economic assistance as well as a desire to conform to mainstream U.S. values that frown on welfare use (Feagin 1975).

Even among recent immigrants, who had higher poverty rates than either natives or other immigrants, there was no evidence of a proclivity toward welfare use compared to natives. Multivariate analyses revealed that recent immigrants were not more likely than natives to receive assistance, other things being equal. Moreover, despite the significant rise in poverty among recent immigrants over time, these data did not indicate a similar increase in the net propensity of recent immigrants to receive public assistance.

Some important differences arose between race groups that deserve mention. First, recent Asian immigrants *did* show a rise over time in their net propensity to receive welfare income. This increase was largely accounted for by the influx of Indo-Chinese refugees during the late 1970s. Many of these refugees were encouraged to use public assistance and other social programs to help them adjust to a new society and economy (Department of Health and Human Services 1983). Hispanic immigrants, on the other hand, became increasingly *reluctant* to use public assistance between 1969 and 1979. Finally, Mexican immigrants, compared to other Mexicans and Hispanics in general, were particularly disinclined to receive welfare benefits.

A key finding is that despite their appreciably higher poverty rates, immigrants—particularly recent arrivals—were not more prone to welfare receipt. Further support for this obtained when prewelfare poverty was included as a predictor of welfare receipt. Prewelfare poverty was said to exist when total family income minus total welfare income was less than the family's poverty threshold. When a flag indicating prewelfare poverty was interacted with immigrant status, destitute immigrants were found to be notably less likely to receive welfare benefits than similarly poor natives. Because immigrants were more likely to be poor but less likely to receive welfare, other things being equal, this result was expected. Still, it suggests that immigrants, to a greater degree than natives, eschew this formal source of support in times of economic hardship. Perhaps the new immigrants, particularly those from less-developed countries, felt less deprived relative to natives with similar poverty-level income: the impoverished new immigrants compared their current economic status not to that of U.S. natives, but to that which they left behind. As such, their own perceived need for state aid may be less acute, other things being equal.

The final analytic chapter explored immigrant-native differentials in the amount of public assistance received among welfare participants. Along with the absolute number of recipients, average receipt constitutes a second important component of the aggregate drain of immigrants on public assistance coffers. Descriptive tables offered much evidence for a deleterious impact of the new immigration. Mean annual welfare receipt was greater among immigrant than native families. This result obtained for white, black and Hispanic families. Moreover, tabulations showed a sizable increase over time in average annual receipt among recent immigrants.

Multivariate analysis revealed, however, that the greater annual receipt among immigrants was fully explained by their preference for states with higher welfare benefits; such states include California and New York. Finally, multivariate results did indicate some increase, between 1969 and 1979, in the amount received by recent white and Asian, and all except recent black, immigrant families.

To conclude this section, I would underscore the following findings. Central to the controversy over the new immigration is the worry that it promoted an increase in the level of poverty and welfare utilization among immigrants. My results offer only partial support for this assertion. There is ample evidence that the level of poverty among immigrants, particularly recent immigrants, increased over the 1960–1980 period. However, there was little indication of a commensurate rise in the propensity of families to receive public assistance.

Moreover, there was little evidence of a disproportionate and increasing burden of immigrants on public assistance coffers as the new immigration proceeded. On balance, at similar levels of economic deprivation, all but recent immigrants were less likely than natives to receive welfare income. Even recent immigrants were no more likely to receive welfare than otherwise comparable natives. Regarding average annual public assistance income among welfare families, my results suggest that immigrants differ little from natives in their degree of utilization. Immigrants did receive more welfare income, on average, but this was fully accounted for by their concentration in states with higher welfare benefits. To be sure, the increase over time in the level of poverty among immigrants reflects an absolute increase in the number of immigrants who are in need of public assistance income. This offsets, to some degree, their relatively lower likelihood of welfare receipt (Borjas and Tienda 1987).

Like immigrants of previous waves, the new immigrants appeared to be industrious and able to capitalize on their labor force potential to keep them out of poverty. I base this on my findings that (1) in both the tabular and multivariate context, multiple earners kept a greater percent of immigrant than native families out of poverty and (2) immigrants showed a relative dis-inclination to use welfare as an income-maintenance strategy. Still, the decline over time in ameliorative impact of multiple earners should be a source of concern. I come back to this point in the following section on the policy implications of my findings.

Also central to the concern over the new immigration is the increasing prevalence of nonwhites among immigrant cohorts. The sizable Hispanic component of the new immigration is particularly controversial.[4] Pastora Cafferty, et al., (1983, p. 76) paraphrase the worry over Hispanics in the following way.

The current invasion of large numbers of Hispanic immigrants . . . constitutes a radically different crisis because the immigrants are, for the most part, so unskilled and uneducated that they cannot find employment in adequately paid jobs. Instead, they are segregated in dead-end, low-wage jobs, and threaten to enlarge the poverty class. They are likely to become a further burden on an already-overworked welfare system.

Some feel that the decreasing flow of white immigrants and increase in Hispanic immigration could only have negative economic repercussions. However, among my most striking and consistent discoveries is the apparent deterioration in the economic status of white immigrants and the noticeable lack of any similar deterioration among Hispanic families. For example, among all the groups studied, recent white immigrants registered the most sizable increases in poverty over time. Poverty among recent Hispanic immigrants did not increase as sharply. Also, Hispanics became increasingly reluctant to use public assistance income (whereas recent white immigrants did not) and revealed an increase in mean annual welfare receipt not nearly as great as that for white and Asian families. Admittedly, rates of poverty and public assistance receipt continue to be greater among Hispanics than whites. Still, changes over time revealed a marked deterioration among whites but no such deterioration among Hispanics.

IMPLICATIONS FOR ASSIMILATION THEORY

This volume was not meant to be an empirical test of assimilation theory. However, I do draw on this literature in my approach to the research problem and in the interpretation of results. In chapter 2, I discussed the links between the history of U.S. immigration and the development of assimilation theory. The social and economic integration of groups such as the Irish and Polish served as the empirical referent for such scholars as Oscar Handlin (1941), W. Lloyd Warner and Leo Srole (1945) and William Thomas and Florian Znaniecki (1918). By documenting the upward economic mobility of second-wave immigrants, this literature gave rise to an image of poverty among immigrants as being a temporary, rather than chronic, problem (Segalman and Basu 1981).

This has clear implications for the new immigration. There are important parallels between the second and third waves of immigration to the United States. Both were characterized by a shift toward relatively less-developed countries of origin and toward immigrants who were racially distinct from the native stock. An important question is whether the newest arrivals—those who entered after the 1965 immigration reforms—are assimilating economically as fast as the second wave did. While some work has documented considerable upward economic mobility among third-wave immigrants (Chiswick 1979), there is reason to doubt the validity of this generalization on methodological grounds (Borjas 1985).

It is important to speculate on the relevance of my results for assimilation theory. I posit that the movement out of poverty is a reasonable indicator of structural assimilation.[5] The tables in chapter 4 show a clear decline in poverty rates with duration of residence in the United States. That is, within census years, poverty among recent immigrants was greater than that among previous arrivals. The decline in poverty with duration of residence also obtained when more detailed years-since-immigration categories were utilized.

These results could be due in part to a decline in the human capital background of immigrants. That is, poverty may be lower among those with longer U.S. residence not because of assimilation, but because the newer arrivals are inherently more prone to poverty. To correct for this, the descriptive tables in chapter 4 did offer one comparison of a real immigrant cohort over time. Specifically, I was able to estimate the poverty rate among those immigrants who arrived during the 1960s in both 1969 and 1979. These data confirmed a decline in poverty over time for this population as a whole, with an interesting caveat. Among blacks and Hispanics, there was little evidence of a decline in poverty between 1969 and 1979. In fact, among those black families who immigrated during the 1960s, poverty increased over time. This confirms the prediction of Milton Gordon (1964) and others about how racial differences can significantly inhibit the pace of assimilation for immigrants.

The decline in poverty with duration of U.S. residence also obtained in the multivariate models of poverty. That is, recent immigrants were shown to be more prone to poverty than other immigrants. This evidence of assimilation was more robust because I was able to control for aging effects and human capital characteristics.

IMPLICATIONS FOR IMMIGRATION POLICY

I address three questions in this section. First, what were the implications of the 1965 legislation for poverty and public assistance utilization among immigrants? Second, should existing policy regarding legal immigration be changed? Third, what are the implications of my results for recent legislative initiatives regarding undocumented immigration?

The new immigration was fostered in large measure by a change in immigration policy. The 1965 amendments to the Immigration and Nationality Act shifted the flow of immigrants toward Asian and Latin American countries and gave greater priority to family reunification over job skills as criteria for admission. As I have documented, the new immigration was also characterized by an increase, over time, in poverty among immigrants.

While I did not attempt to quantify the degree to which the 1965 legislation was directly responsible for this rise in immigrant poverty, clearly it had some effect. For one thing, it increased the percent of all immigrants who were Hispanic. Because these Hispanic immigrants had higher poverty rates than immigrants generally, this compositional change contributed to the rise in immigrant poverty. However, the shift in country of origin was by no means solely responsible. The rise in poverty characterized all groups of families and was particularly sharp among whites. This would suggest that the diminished emphasis on occupational skills may have been a contributing factor. It is also possible that compared to 1969, the generally worse macroeconomic conditions in 1979 caused some of the rise in poverty among immigrants. Some corroboration resides in evidence of increasing unemployment over this time period (Ehrenberg and Smith 1982).

While the 1965 legislation brought about at least some of the increase in poverty among immigrants in recent years, I stress that it did *not* spawn a corresponding rise in the level of welfare utilization among immigrants. Compared to poverty, utilization of public assistance is probably a more important gauge of the economic effects of the 1965 legislation, because it represents an immediate and direct draw on public coffers. It has certainly caused the greater controversy.

But does this call for immigration reform? The 1965 legislation engendered an immigration similar to the second wave of the turn of the century. The shift toward less-developed countries (then, southern and eastern Europe) brought about an increase in the prevalence of destitute immigrants. Despite protests from natives who feared economic repercussions, poverty among these groups turned out to be temporary, not chronic. Since 1965, we have experienced another new immigration, a shift toward less-developed countries from which new arrivals tend to be disadvantaged minorities in the United States. We have seen a rise in poverty among immigrants, but one without a commensurate rise in public assistance receipt. These trends illustrate how history repeats itself. As such, this new immigration is likely to be a net economic benefit to the United States in the long run. Any attempt to change legal immigration policy—to make it more restrictive—would seem to be unwarranted.[6]

The 1965 amendments to the Immigration and Nationality Act were crafted at a time when the economy was comparatively strong and when unemployment rates were low. While the resemblance to the past is a sign of hope for the newest immigrants, there are some unique characteristics of the modern era that constitute potential areas of stress. The 1960–1980 period was one of considerable change in the occupational and industrial structure of the U.S. economy. There was a gradual decline in the relative importance of agriculture and transformative industries and an increase in the service sector. The occupational distribution changed accordingly. There was a relative decline in blue collar and increase in professional and service occupations (Singelmann and Tienda 1985). There was also a considerable influx of women into the labor market. The new immigration took place at a time when the demand for unskilled and semiskilled labor declined (Cafferty, et al. 1983). Because immigrants, particularly new arrivals, frequently have or seek such jobs, these structural shifts constitute a potential source of stress that calls for close monitoring of the costs and consequences of immigration in the years ahead.

Certain findings in this volume may reflect this economic stress. These results include (1) the fact that economic assimilation (as indicated by a declining poverty rate) did not occur for a real cohort of black and Hispanic families after ten years in the United States (see discussion of Table 4.2), (2) the fact that the ameliorative impact of multiple earners seemed to decline and (3) the fact that average annual welfare receipt, in dollar terms, increased during the 1970s.

These points of stress have prompted some to call for a more direct relationship between employment and immigration policy. Specifically, Vernon Briggs (1985) would like to see primacy restored to the occupational preference categories as well as flexible ceilings that would float with extant labor market conditions. Others are less concerned. Cafferty and her associates (1983) point out that, family reunification notwithstanding, an appreciable share of immigrants are skilled or semiskilled. Even among Hispanics, the group with lowest skill levels, there are craftspersons and other skilled workers of urban origin. Also, there will always be jobs available for those untrained workers who immigrate or natives who do not. On balance, there is little evidence of a decline in the absorptive capacity of the U.S. labor market for immigrant labor (Borjas and Tienda 1987). This argues against changing existing legal immigration policy at this time.

In the fall of 1986, Congress passed the Immigration Reform and Control Act, which was intended to stem the tide of undocumented immigration. A controversial component of this bill was the amnesty program that granted legal status to a subset of all undocumented immigrants who have been in this country since 1982. While some argued against amnesty on the grounds that it would reward lawbreakers, greater concern was voiced regarding its economic impact. Many feared that amnesty would result in a dramatic increase in welfare utilization. Such concerns made their mark on the nature of the amnesty program.

The Immigration and Naturalization Service proposed that in order to *apply* for amnesty, each currently undocumented immigrant pay a fee of $185 (plus an additional $50 for each child). This application fee in no way guarantees eventual amnesty. The reason for this charge is clear—much as it was clear when head taxes were levied on ship captains in the 19th century—it is to inhibit the entrance of those likely to wind up on welfare. Paraphrasing from an interview with the INS commissioner, "If the family could not come up with the 300 or so dollars needed to apply for amnesty, we'd have to assume we were in a public charge mode." This highlights the concern that the amnesty program will spawn a rush on the welfare office. My results indicate that, to a large degree, these fears are misplaced.

In part, this discussion of the policy implications of my results suggests a number of areas where future research is needed. This is the topic of the final section of this chapter.

SUGGESTIONS FOR FUTURE RESEARCH

An important motivation for this volume was the lack of hard data surrounding many contentious immigration issues. Because of this paucity of evidence and because of the need among policy analysts to be better informed, there are a number of areas of research that could be pursued.

The data I have analyzed here could easily be used to study these same questions for nonfamily households. One could also use these data to study use of Social Security among immigrants, even though that impact will not be fully felt for a few decades. Moreover, much of the controversy regarding Social Security use among immigrants surrounds those who have their benefits remitted to them overseas (General Accounting Office 1983).

In the previous section, I pointed out the similarities between the new wave of immigration of the 1960s and 1970s and the wave of immigration of the turn of the century. In my analysis, I was unable to get a firm handle on a key dimension of this similarity, the extent to which poverty among the most recent new immigrants is temporary and not chronic. This is a critical empirical question, because it has very important implications for the likely cost to society of the new immigration. In this volume, I used repeated cross-sectional data. While these data provided an in-depth look at a number of aspects of the new immigration, it was less than adequate for assessing cross-time comparisons for specific immigrant cohorts. The need for longitudinal data on immigrants is great. While panel data would be preferable to retrospective data, either would provide a more definitive account of the trend in the economic status of the new immigrants.

A number of panel data sets are available for study. These include the Panel Study of Income Dynamics (PSID), the Survey of Income and Program Participation (SIPP) and the National Survey of Families and Households (forthcoming). By providing more detailed information on income sources and interhousehold transfers of labor and income, such data could offer stronger empirical support for questions about whether immigrants prefer family and friends to formal assistance programs in times of need. Unfor-

tunately, such data sets typically have far too few cases to study immigrants—recent arrivals in particular—who constitute a rather small portion
of the total population. Because of this, such studies lack detailed questions
on the immigration experience, such as year of arrival and nativity of
relatives and friends.

From a cost-benefit perspective, it would be imprudent to carry out a
national survey of immigrants that would contain the kind of information
that is needed. It is more realistic, however, to call for the gathering of
detailed data on immigrants within cities and communities in which they
concentrate. A number of such surveys have already been carried out and
their data very fruitfully analyzed.[7] A most promising avenue for future
research on immigration is to continue to compile such richly detailed data
sets. If enough such surveys are taken, results could begin to be generalized
to the experience of all immigrants.

Such small area studies offer another advantage. Most agree that aggregate
studies at the national level fail to capture some of the deleterious consequences of immigration in particular cities and towns (Briggs 1985). While
the economic effects of immigration in the aggregate appear to be positive,
small area studies could establish the dynamics of a considerable influx of
immigrants in a particular community. A related question that needs to be
addressed is the dislocation of native labor and consequential increase in native use of assistance programs such as unemployment insurance and public
assistance. If natives are being displaced by immigrants[8] and are turning to
public programs for support, this represents an indirect economic cost of
immigration.

Data on immigrants are elusive. This represents one of the exciting
challenges of immigration research. There are many pressing and interesting unanswered questions on this topic. They will no doubt be addressed by
bright and energetic researchers who will enter the field and collect the
necessary data. Given the state of existing data, until they do, these questions
will remain unanswered.

NOTES

1. More detailed summaries of findings can be found at the conclusion of chapters
and analytic sections. Here I synthesize the most important findings.

2. To achieve cleaner prose in this section, I do not identify specific chapters or
tables. To recapitulate, the descriptive treatment of poverty is in chapter 4, the multivariate analysis of poverty is in chapter 5, the descriptive and multivariate analyses
of the propensity of families to receive public assistance income can be found in
chapter 6 and the descriptive and multivariate analyses of total public assistance
receipt are presented in chapter 7.

3. This rise in poverty among immigrants over the period appeared more dramatic
when poverty was defined in relative terms. Loosely conceived, relative poverty monitors the extent to which families have an annual income that is less than half the me-

dian family income in the population. A rise in real income over the 1960s accounted for much of the decline in absolute poverty. Because the level of income inequality changed little over the period, a commensurate decline in relative poverty in the population as a whole was not observed. Because absolute poverty among recent immigrants actually increased steadily between 1960 and 1980, when viewed in relative terms, this increase was all the more dramatic.

4. Admittedly, an appreciable amount of the worry over Hispanics concerns cultural issues. That the United States is currently the seventh largest Spanish-speaking country and that a greater number of immigrants speak one language (Spanish) than at any other time in our history has sparked great apprehension among those who wish to maintain the primacy of the English language.

5. Following Gordon (1964), I hold that structural assimilation is characterized by increasing participation in key societal institutions. Increased participation in the labor market reflects structural assimilation and will bring lower poverty rates.

6. Influential groups such as the Federation for American Immigration Reform (FAIR) would like to see tighter restrictions on legal immigration, fewer numbers arriving and a re-emphasis on job skills as a criterion for entry (Tanton 1980).

7. These data include Doug Massey's (1986) study of Mexican immigrants living in both Mexico and California, Robert Bach's data on Indo-Chinese refugees (Goza 1987) and Alejandro Portes's recent data on Cuban and Haitian immigrants in Florida (Portes and Stepick).

8. While existing evidence suggests that very little such displacement occurs (Borjas and Tienda 1987), this remains an understudied possibility that deserves greater attention in the future (Brinkley-Carter 1980).

References

Angel, Ronald and Marta Tienda. 1982. "Headship and Household Composition among Blacks, Hispanics and Other Whites." *Social Forces,* 61: 508–531.

Atchley, Robert C. 1978. "Aging as a Social Problem: An Overview." In *Social Problems of the Aging: Readings,* edited by M. Seltzer, S. Corbett and R. Atchley. Belmont, CA: Wadsworth.

Bach, Robert L. 1983. "Emigration from the Spanish-Speaking Caribbean." In *U.S. Immigration and Refugee Policy: Global and Domestic Issues,* edited by Mary M. Kritz. Lexington, MA: Lexington Books.

_____. 1984. *Labor Force Participation and Employment Among Southeast Asian Refugees in the United States.* Report prepared for the Office of Refugee Resettlement, U.S. Department of Health and Human Services. Washington, DC: United States Government Printing Office.

Bacon, Lloyd. 1971. "Poverty among Interregional Rural-to-Urban Migrants." *Rural Sociology,* 36(2): 125–140.

_____. 1973. "Migration, Poverty, and the Rural South." *Social Forces,* 51(3): 348–355.

Baker, R. J. and J. A. Nelder. 1978. *The GLIM System, Release 3, Generalised Linear Interactive Modelling.* Oxford, UK: Numerical Algorithms Group.

Bean, F. D., A. G. King and J. F. Passel. 1986. "Estimates of the Size of the Illegal Migration Population of Mexican Origin in the United States: An Assessment, Review and Proposal." In *Mexican Immigrants and Mexican Americans: An Evolving Relation,* edited by H. Browning and R. de la Garza. Austin, TX: CMAS Publications.

Bean, F. D. and M. Tienda. 1986. *The Hispanic Population of the United States.* New York, NY: Russell Sage.

Becker, Gary S. 1975. *Human Capital: A Theoretical Analysis with Special Reference to Education.* Chicago, IL: University of Chicago Press.

Bennett, Marion T. 1963. *American Immigration Policies: A History.* Washington, DC: Public Affairs Press.

Bentley, Judith. 1981. *American Immigration Today: Pressures, Problems, Policies*. New York, NY: Julian Messner.

Blau, Francine. 1984. "The Use of Transfer Payments by Immigrants." *Industrial and Labor Relations Review*, 37(2): 222–239.

Blau, Peter M. and Otis Dudley Duncan. 1967. *The American Occupational Structure*. New York, NY: John Wiley & Sons.

Blumberg, Paul. 1980. *Inequality in an Age of Decline*. New York, NY: Oxford University Press.

Borjas, George J. 1984. "The Impact of Assimilation on the Earnings of Immigrants: A Reexamination of the Evidence." Unpublished Manuscript, October.

_____. 1985. "Assimilation, Changes in Cohort Quality, and the Earnings of Immigrants." *Journal of Labor Economics*, 3(4): 463–489.

Borjas, George J. and Marta Tienda. 1987. "The Economic Consequences of Immigration." *Science*, 235: 645–651.

Bouvier, Leon F. and Robert W. Gardner. 1986. "Immigration to the U.S.: The Unfinished Story." *Population Bulletin*, 41(4): 1–50.

Bouvier, Leon F., Henry S. Shryock and Harry W. Henderson. 1979. "International Migration: Yesterday, Today, and Tomorrow." *Population Bulletin*, 32(4): 1–44.

Briggs, John Walker. 1978. *An Italian Passage: Immigrants to Three American Cities, 1890–1930*. New Haven, CT: Yale University Press.

Briggs, Vernon M., Jr. 1985. "Employment Trends and Contemporary Immigration Policy: The Macro Implications." In *Immigration: Issues and Policies*, edited by Vernon M. Briggs, Jr. and Marta Tienda. Salt Lake City, UT: Olympus.

Briggs, Vernon M., Jr. and Marta Tienda (eds.). 1985. *Immigration: Issues and Policies*. Salt Lake City, UT: Olympus.

Brinkley-Carter, Christina. 1980. "The Economic Impact of the New Immigration on 'Native' Minorities." In *Sourcebook on the New Immigration: Inplications* [sic] *for the United States and the International Community*, edited by Roy Simon Bryce-Laporte. New Brunswick, NJ: Transaction Books.

Browning, H. L. and N. Rodriguez. 1985. "The Migration of Mexican Indocumentados as a Settlement Process: Implications for Work." In *Hispanics in the U.S. Economy*, edited by G. J. Borjas and M. Tienda. Orlando, FL: Academic.

Bryce-Laporte, Roy Simon (ed.). 1980. *Sourcebook on the New Immigration: Inplications* [sic] *for the United States and the International Community*. New Brunswick, NJ: Transaction Books.

Cafferty, P. S., B. R. Chiswick, A. M. Greeley and T. A. Sullivan. 1983. *The Dilemma of American Immigration: Beyond the Golden Door*. New Brunswick, NJ: Transaction Books.

Carlson, John E., Marie L. Lassey and William R. Lassey. 1981. *Rural Society and Environment in America*. New York, NY: McGraw-Hill.

Cebula, Richard J. 1976. "A Note on Nonwhite Migration, Welfare Levels, and the Political Process." *Public Choice*, 31: 117–119.

_____. 1977. "Migration and Welfare Benefit Levels: An Analysis of the Netherlands and United States Experiences." *Kyklos*, 30: 691–698.

Cebula, Richard J. and R. A. Kohn. 1975. "Public Policies and Migration Patterns in the United States." *Public Finance*, 30: 186–196.

Chiswick, Barry R. 1979. "The Economic Progress of Immigrants: Some Apparently

Universal Patterns." In *Contemporary Economic Problems,* edited by W. Felner. Washington, DC: American Enterprise Institute.

_____. 1980. *An Analysis of the Economic Progress and Impact of Immigrants.* Final Report to the Employment and Training Administration, U.S. Department of Labor. Washington, DC: United States Government Printing Office.

Council of Economic Advisors. 1986. "The Council of Economic Advisors on U.S. Immigration." *Population and Development Review,* 12(2): 361–374.

Crewdson, John. 1983. *The Tarnished Door: The New Immigrants and the Transformation of America.* New York, NY: Times Books.

Davis, Kingsley. 1974. "The Migrations of Human Populations." In *The Human Population, A Scientific American Book,* edited by Gerard Piel, et al. San Francisco, CA: W. H. Freeman.

Department of Health and Human Services. 1983. *Report to Congress: Refugee Resettlement Program.* Washington, DC: Social Security Administration, Office of Refugee Resettlement.

Doeringer, P. B. and M. J. Piore. 1971. *Internal Labor Markets and Manpower Analysis.* Lexington, MA: D. C. Heath.

Douglas, Paul H. 1919. "Is the New Immigration More Unskilled Than the Old?" *Publication of the American Statistical Association,* 16: 393–403.

Easterlin, Richard A., David Ward, William S. Bernard and Reed Ueda. 1980. *Immigration.* Cambridge, MA: Harvard University Press.

Ehrenberg, Ronald G. and Robert S. Smith. 1982. *Modern Labor Economics: Theory and Public Policy.* Glenview, IL: Scott, Foresman.

Ehrlich, Paul. 1968. *The Population Bomb.* New York, NY: Ballantine.

Fallows, James. 1983. "Immigration: How It's Affecting Us." *The Atlantic Monthly,* 252(5): 45–106.

Feagin, Joe R. 1975. *Subordinating the Poor: Welfare and American Beliefs.* Englewood Cliffs, NJ: Prentice-Hall.

Ferman, Louis A., Joyce L. Korbluh and Alan Haber (eds.). 1976. *Poverty in America: A Book of Readings.* Ann Arbor, MI: University of Michigan Press.

Findley, Sally E. 1977. *Planning for Internal Migration: A Review of Issues and Policies in Developing Countries.* Washington, DC: U.S. Bureau of the Census.

Fuchs, Victor R. 1967. "Redefining Poverty and Redistributing Income." *The Public Interest,* (Summer): 89–94.

Fuller, Richard C. 1939. "Social Problems." In *An Outline of the Principles of Sociology,* edited by Robert E. Park. New York, NY: Barnes & Noble.

Gans, Herbert J. 1982. *The Urban Villagers: Group and Class in the Life of Italian-Americans.* New York, NY: The Free Press.

Gardner, Robert W. 1986. "Review of *The Immigration Time Bomb: The Fragmenting of America* by Richard D. Lamm and Gary Imhoff (1986)." *Population Today,* 14(4): 11.

Gardner, Robert W., Bryant Robey and Peter C. Smith. 1985. "Asian Americans: Growth, Change and Diversit." *Population Bulletin,* 40(4): 1–44.

General Accounting Office. 1979. *The Indochinese Exodus: A Humanitarian Dilemma.* A Report to the Congress of the United States by the Comptroller General (GAO ID-79-20). Washington, DC: United States Government Printing Office.

_____. 1983. *Issues Concerning Social Security Benefits Paid to Aliens.* A Report to the

Congress by the Comptroller General (GAO/HRD-83-32). Washington, DC: United States Government Printing Office.

Ghelfi, Linda M. 1986. *Poverty among Black Families in the Nonmetro South*. Economic Research Service, USDA, Rural Development Research Report Number 62. Washington, DC: United States Government Printing Office.

Glazer, Nathan (ed.). 1985. *Clamor at the Gates: The New American Immigration*. San Francisco, CA: ICS Press.

Glazer, Nathan and Daniel P. Moynihan. 1970. *Beyond the Melting Pot: The Negroes, Puerto Ricans, Jews, Italians and Irish of New York City*. Cambridge, MA: D. C. Heath.

Gordon, Milton. 1964. *Assimilation in American Life: The Role of Race, Religion, and National Origins*. New York, NY: Oxford University Press.

Goza, Franklin William. 1987. *Adjustment and Adaptation among Southeast Asian Refugees in the United States*. Unpublished Doctoral Dissertation in Sociology. Madison, WI: The University of Wisconsin—Madison.

Handlin, Oscar. 1941. *Boston's Immigrants: A Study of Acculturation*. Cambridge, MA: Harvard University Press.

—————. 1951. *The Uprooted: The Epic Story of the Great Migrations that Made the American People*. Boston, MA: Little, Brown.

Hansen, Marcus Lee. 1940. *The Immigrant in American History*. New York, NY: Harper & Row.

Hanushek, Eric A. and John E. Jackson. 1977. *Statistical Methods for Social Scientists*. New York, NY: Academic.

Hauser, Phillip. 1981. "The U.S. Census Undercount." *Asian and Pacific Census Forum*, 8(2): 81-84.

Hunter, Robert. [1904] 1965. *Poverty: Social Conscience in the Progressive Era*. New York, NY: Harper Torchbooks.

Immigration and Naturalization Service. 1984. *Statistical Yearbook of the Immigration and Naturalization Service*. Immigration and Naturalization Service, U.S. Department of Justice. Washington, DC: United States Government Printing Office.

Immigration and Naturalization Service. Western Regional Office. 1983. "Illegal Immigration Costs to U.S. Taxpayers." News release, San Pedro, CA.

Jasso, Guillermina and Mark R. Rosenzweig. 1982. "Estimating the Emigration Rates of Legal Immigrants Using Administrative and Survey Data: The 1971 Cohort of Immigrants to the United States." *Demography*, 19(3): 279-290.

—————. 1986. "Family Reunification and the Immigration Multiplier: U.S. Immigration Law, Origin-Country Conditions, and the Reproduction of Immigrants." *Demography*, 23(3): 291-311.

Jensen, Leif. 1988. "Poverty and Immigration in the United States: 1960-1980." In *Divided Opportunities: Minorities, Poverty and Social Policy*, edited by Gary Sandefur and Marta Tienda. New York, NY: Plenum.

Jensen, Leif and Marta Tienda. 1988. "Nativity Differentials in Public Assistance Receipt: A Research Note." *Sociological Inquiry*, 58(3): 305-321.

Jones, Maldwyn Allen. 1960. *American Immigration*. Chicago, IL: University of Chicago Press.

Keely, Charles B. 1971. "Effects of the Immigration Act of 1965 on Selected Population Characteristics of Immigrants to the United States." *Demography*, 8(2): 157-169.

———. 1975. "Effects of U.S. Immigration Law on Manpower Characteristics of Immigrants." *Demography*, 12(2): 179–190.

———. 1980. "Immigration Policy and the New Immigrants." In *Sourcebook on the New Immigration: Inplications* [sic] *for the United States and the International Community*, edited by Roy Simon Bryce-Laporte. New Brunswick, NJ: Transaction Books.

Kerbo, Harold R. 1983. *Social Stratification and Inequality: Class Conflict in the United States*. New York, NY: McGraw-Hill.

Kritz, Mary M. 1983. *U.S. Immigration and Refugee Policy: Global and Domestic Issues*. Lexington, MA: Lexington Books.

Kritz, Mary M. and D. T. Gurak. 1984. "Kinship Networks and the Settlement Process: Dominican and Columbian Immigrants in New York City." Paper presented at the annual meeting of the Population Association of America, Minneapolis.

Kumar, R. 1977. "More on Nonwhite Migration, Welfare Levels, and the Political Process." *Public Choice*, 32: 151–154.

Lamm, Richard D. and Gary Imhoff. 1985. *The Immigration Time Bomb: The Fragmenting of America*. New York, NY: E. P. Dutton.

Lee, E. S. 1966. "A Theory of Migration." *Demography*, 3(1): 47–57.

———. 1969. "A Theory of Migration." In *Migration*, edited by J. A. Jackson. Cambridge, UK: Cambridge University Press.

Levitan, Sar A. 1985. *Programs in Aid of the Poor*, 5th ed. Baltimore, MD: Johns Hopkins.

Lieberson, Stanley. 1980. *A Piece of the Pie: Blacks and White Immigrants Since 1880*. Berkeley, CA: University of California Press.

Lopata, Helena Znaniecki. 1973. *Widowhood in an American City*. Cambridge, MA: Schenkman.

McLaughlin, V. Y. 1973. "Patterns of Work and Family Organization: Buffalo's Italians." In *The American Family in Social-Historical Perspective*, edited by M. Gordon. New York, NY: St. Martin's.

Massey, Douglas S. 1986. "The Settlement Process among Mexican Migrants to the United States." *American Sociological Review*, 51(5): 685–689.

Massey, Douglas S and Brooks Bitterman. 1985. "Explaining the Paradox of Puerto Rican Segregation." *Social Forces*, 64(2): 306–331.

Mayo-Smith, Richmond. 1890. *Emigration and Immigration: A Study in Social Science*. New York, NY: Charles Scribner's Sons.

Mincer, Jacob. 1974. *Schooling, Experience and Earnings*. New York, NY: Columbia University Press.

Moore, Joan W. 1971. "Mexican Americans and Cities: A Study in Migration and the Use of Formal Resources." *International Migration Review*, 5: 292–308.

Morrissey, Elizabeth S. 1985. *Characteristics of Poverty in Nonmetro Counties*. Economic Research Service, USDA, Rural Development Research Report Number 52. Washington, DC: United States Government Printing Office.

Nelson, Candace and Marta Tienda. 1985. "The Structuring of Hispanic Ethnicity: Historical and Contemporary Perspectives." *Ethnic and Racial Studies*, 8: 49–74.

O'Hare, William P. 1985. "Poverty in America: Trends and New Patterns." *Population Bulletin*, 40(3): 1–43.

Ornati, Oscar. 1966. *Poverty Amid Affluence*. New York, NY: The Twentieth Century Fund.

Orshansky, Mollie. 1965. "Counting the Poor: Another Look at the Poverty Profile." *Social Security Bulletin,* 28(1): 3–29.

Orshansky, Mollie, Harold Watts, Bradley Schiller and John Korbal. 1978. "Measuring Poverty: A Debate." *Public Welfare,* 36(2): 46–55.

Osterman, Paul. 1975. "An Empirical Study of Labor Market Segmentation." *Industrial and Labor Relations Review,* 28(4): 508–523.

Papademetriou, Demetrios G. and Mark J. Miller. 1983. *The Unavoidable Issue: U.S. Immigration Policy in the 1980s*. Philadelphia, PA: Institute for the Study of Human Issues.

Pear, Robert. 1986. "New Restrictions on Immigration Gain Public Support, Poll Shows." The *New York Times* (July 1).

Perez, Lisandro. 1986. "Immigrant Economic Adjustment and Family Organization: The Cuban Success Story Reexamined." *International Migration Review,* 20(1): 4–20.

Petersen, Trond. 1985. "A Comment of Presenting Results from Logit and Probit Models." *American Sociological Review,* 50(1): 130–131.

Piore, Michael J. 1979. *Birds of Passage: Migrant Labor and Industrial Societies*. New York, NY: Cambridge University Press.

Plotnick, Robert and Felicity Skidmore. 1975. *Progress against Poverty: A Review of the 1964–1974 Decade*. New York, NY: Academic.

Portes, Alejandro. 1978. "Migration and Underdevelopment." *Politics and Society,* 8(1): 1–48.

_____. 1981. "Modes of Structural Incorporation and Present Theories of Labor Immigration." In *Global Trends in Migration: Theory and Research on International Population Movements,* edited by Mary M. Kritz, Charles B. Keely and Silvano M. Tomasi. New York, NY: Center for Migration Studies.

Portes, Alejandro and Robert L. Bach. 1985. *Latin Journey: Cuban and Mexican Immigrants in the United States*. Berkeley, CA: University of California Press.

Portes, Alejandro and Alex Stepick. 1985. "Unwelcome Immigrants: The Labor Market Experiences of 1980 (Mariel) Cuban and Haitian Refugees in South Florida." *American Sociological Review,* 50(4): 493–514.

Premus, Robert and Robert Weinstein. 1977. "Non-White Migration, Welfare Levels, and the Political Process: Some Additional Results." *Review of Regional Studies,* 7(1): 11–19.

Presidential Commission on Immigration and Naturalization. 1953. *Whom Shall We Welcome: Report of the President's Commission on Immigration and Naturalization*. Washington, DC: United States Government Printing Office.

Ravenstein, E. G. 1885. "The Laws of Migration." *Journal of the Royal Statistical Society,* 48(2): 167–235.

_____. 1889. "The Laws of Migration." *Journal of the Royal Statistical Society,* 52(2): 241–305.

Reid, John. 1986. "Immigration and the Future U.S. Black Population." *Population Today,* 14(2): 6–8.

Reimers, David M. 1985. *Still the Golden Door: The Third World Comes to America*. New York, NY: Columbia University Press.

Rein, Martin. 1976. "Problems in the Definition and Measurement of Poverty." In

Poverty in America: A Book of Readings, edited by Louis Ferman, Joyce Kornbluh and Alan Harber. Ann Arbor, MI: University of Michigan Press.

Ross, Christine, Sheldon Danziger and Eugene Smolensky. 1987. "The Level and Trend in Poverty in the United States, 1939–1979." *Demography,* 24(4): 587–600.

Rowntree, Benjamin S. 1941. *Poverty and Progress. A Second Social Survey of York.* London, UK: Longmans, Grenn.

Samora, Julian, Jorge A. Bustamante and Gilbert Cardenas. 1971. *Los Mojados: The Wetback Story.* Notre Dame, IN: Notre Dame University Press.

Sassen-Koob, Saskia. 1979. "Formal and Informal Associations: Dominicans and Colombians in New York." *International Migration Review,* 13: 314–332.

Schiller, Bradley R. 1980. *The Economics of Poverty and Discrimination,* 3rd ed. Englewood Cliffs, NJ: Prentice-Hall.

Schmidt, Aurora. 1981. "Refugees and Immigrants: In Conflict with American Poor?" *Migration Today,* 9(4/5): 17–21.

Segalman, R. and A. Basu. 1981. *Poverty in America: The Welfare Dilemma.* Westport, CT: Greenwood.

Select Commission on Population. 1978. *Legal and Illegal Immigration to the United States.* U.S. House of Representatives, Ninety-fifth Congress, second session. Washington, DC: United States Government Printing Office.

Sewell, William H., Archibald O. Haller and George W. Ohlendorf. 1970. "The Educational and Early Occupational Status Attainment Process: Replication and Revision." *American Sociological Review,* 35: 1014–1027.

Sewell, William H. and Robert M. Hauser. 1975. *Education, Occupation and Earnings: Achievement in the Early Career.* New York, NY: Academic.

Shryock, Henry S., Jacob S. Siegal, et al. 1976. *The Methods and Materials of Demography.* New York, NY: Academic.

Simon, Julian. 1980. *What Immigrants Take from and Give to the Public Coffers.* Final Report to the Select Commission on Immigration and Refugee Policy. Washington, DC: United States Government Printing Office.

Simon, Julian. 1981. *The Ultimate Resource.* Princeton, NJ: Princeton University Press.
_____. 1984. "Immigrants, Taxes and Welfare in the United States." *Population and Development Review,* 10(1): 55–69.

Simon, Rita. 1985. *Public Opinion and the Immigrant: Print Media Coverage, 1880–1980.* Lexington, MA: Lexington Books.

Simpson, George E. and Milton J. Yinger. 1985. *Racial and Cultural Minorities: An Analysis of Prejudice and Discrimination.* New York, NY: Plenum.

Singelmann, Joachim and Marta Tienda. 1985. "The Process of Occupational Change in a Service Society: The Case of the United States, 1960–1980." In *New Approaches to Economic Life: Economic Restructuring, Unemployment and the Social Decisions of Labor,* edited by Bryan Roberts, Ruth Finnegan and Duncan Gallie. Manchester, UK: University of Manchester Press.

Smith, James P. 1988. "Poverty and the Family." In *Minorities, Poverty and Social Policy,* edited by Gary Sandefur and Marta Tienda. New York, NY: Plenum.

Stephenson, George M. 1926. *A History of American Immigration: 1820–1924.* Boston, MA: Ginn and Co.

Stouffer, Samuel A. 1940. "A Theory Relating Mobility and Distance." *American Sociological Review,* 5(6): 845–867.

Tanton, John. 1980. "Rethinking Immigration Policy." *FAIR Immigration Paper 1*. Washington, DC: Federation for American Immigration Reform.

Teitelbaum, Michael S. 1986. "Intersections: Immigration and Demographic Change and Their Impact on the United States." In *World Population and U.S. Policy: The Choices ahead,* edited by Jane Menken. New York, NY: W. W. Norton.

Thomas, W. I. and F. Znaniecki. 1918. *The Polish Peasant in Europe and America*. New York, NY: Knopf.

Tienda, Marta. 1980. "Familism and Structural Assimilation of Mexican Immigrants in the United States." *International Migration Review,* 14: 383–408.

———. 1983. "Socioeconomic and Labor Force Characteristics of U.S. Immigration: Issues and Approaches." In *U.S. Immigration and Refugee Policy: Global and Domestic Issues,* edited by Mary Kritz. Lexington, MA: D. C. Heath.

———. 1984. "The Puerto Rican Worker: Recent Evidence and Future Prospects." In *Puerto Ricans in the Mid-Eighties: An American Challenge,* edited by the National Puerto Rican Coalition. Washington, DC: National Puerto Rican Coalition.

Tienda, Marta and Ronald Angel. 1982. "Headship and Household Composition among Blacks, Hispanics and Other Whites." *Social Forces,* 61: 508–531.

Tienda, Marta and Jennifer Glass. 1985. "Household Structure and Labor Force Participation of Black, Hispanic and White Mothers." *Demography,* 22(3): 381–394.

Tienda, Marta and Leif Jensen. 1986. "Immigration and Public Assistance Participation: Dispelling the Myth of Dependency." *Social Science Research,* 15: 372–400.

———. 1988. "Poverty and Minorities: A Quarter-century Profile of Color and Socioeconomic Disadvantage." In *Divided Opportunities: Minorities, Poverty and Social Policy,* edited by Gary Sandefur and Marta Tienda. New York, NY: Plenum.

Tienda, Marta, Leif Jensen and Robert L. Bach. 1984. "Immigration, Gender and the Process of Occupational Change in the United States, 1970–1980." *International Migration Review,* 18(4): 1021–1044.

Todaro, M. 1969. "A Model of Labor Migration and Urban Unemployment in Less Developed Countries." *American Economic Review,* 59: 138–148.

U.S. Bureau of the Census. 1973. *Census of the Population: 1970. Vol. 1, Characteristics of the Population. Part 1, United States Summary—Section 2*. Washington, DC: United States Government Printing Office.

———. 1981a. *1980 Census of the Population. Vol. 1, Characteristics of the Population. Part 1, United States Summary.* PC80-1-C1. Washington, DC: United States Government Printing Office.

———. 1981b. *Statistical Abstract of the United States: 1981,* 102d ed. Washington, DC: United States Government Printing Office.

———. 1982. "Coverage of the National Population in the 1980 Census, by Age, Sex, and Race: Preliminary Estimates by Demographic Analysis." *Current Population Reports. Series P-23, No. 115*. Washington, DC: United States Government Printing Office.

———. 1983. *1980 Census of the Population. Vol. 1, Characteristics of the Population. Chapter B, General Population Characteristics*. PC80-1-B1. Washington, DC: United States Government Printing Office.

van den Berghe, Pierre L. 1978. "Ethnicity and Race." In *Sociology: The Basic Concepts,* edited by Edward Sagarin. New York, NY: Holt, Rinehart and Winston.

Wallerstein, E. 1974. *The Modern World-System: Capitalist Agriculture and the Origins of the European World-Economy in the Sixteenth Century.* New York, NY: Academic.

Warner, W. Lloyd and Leo Srole. 1945. *The Social Systems of American Ethnic Groups.* New Haven, CT: Yale University Press.

Warren, R. and J. S. Passel. 1983. "Estimates of Illegal Aliens from Mexico Counted in the 1980 United States Census." Paper presented at the annual meetings of the Population Association of America. Pittsburgh, PA.

Warren, Robert and Jennifer Marks Peck. 1980. "Foreign-born emigration from the United States: 1960 to 1970." *Demography,* 17(1): 71–84.

Wilson, Kenneth L. and W. Allen Martin. 1982. "Ethnic Enclaves: A Comparison of the Cuban and Black Economic in Miami." *American Journal of Sociology,* 88(1): 135–160.

Wilson, Kenneth L. and Alejandro Portes. 1980. "Immigrant Enclaves: An Analysis of the Labor Market Experiences of Cubans in Miami." *American Journal of Sociology,* 86(2): 295–319.

Wong, Morrison G. 1985. "Post-1985 Immigrants: Demographic and Socioeconomic Profile." In *Urban Ethnicity in the United States: New Immigrants and Old Minorities,* edited by Lionel Maldonado and Joan Moore. Beverly Hills, CA: Sage.

Index

ABOUT THE AUTHOR

LEIF JENSEN is Assistant Professor of Sociology and Anthropology at Bates College in Lewiston, Maine. He has contributed articles to *Sociological Inquiry, Policy Studies Journal,* and the *International Migration Review,* and two chapters to *Divided Opportunities: Minorities, Poverty and Social Policy.*